# Surviving Complaints Against Counsellors and Psychotherapists: towards understanding and healing

Edited by
Roger Casemore

*PCCS BOOKS*
Ross-on-Wye

First published in 2001

PCCS BOOKS
Llangarron
Ross-on-Wye
Herefordshire
HR9 6PT
United Kingdom
Tel +44 (0)1989 77 07 07
www.pccs-books.co.uk
email: contact@pccs-books.co.uk

**Surviving Complaints Against Counsellors and
Psychotherapists: Towards understanding and healing**

ISBN  1 898059 38 1

*Cover design by Old Dog Graphics*
*Printed by Bell & Bain, Glasgow.*

# Contents

Foreword by Mark Aveline    i

Introduction — *Roger Casemore*    iii

**Towards understanding the experience and enduring the procedures**

1. The Victim's Tale — *'Poppy'*    1
2. The Person Complained About Was Me — *'Chris'*    9
3. Surviving a Complaint: A practical guide — *Alan Jamieson*    19
4. Surviving Organisational Complaints as a Counsellor Trainer — *Peter Jenkins*    29

**Towards understanding the process**

5. Some Underlying Psychodynamics of Complaints — *Michael Jacobs*    41
6. Therapeutic and Adversarial Relationships — *Derek Hill*    51
7. Complaints in Organisations — *James Greer*    61
8. Complaints: A challenge to the structures and practices of counselling organisations — *Derek Hill*    71
9. Complaints, Boundary and Training Issues: Comparisons between Britain and U.S.A. An Adjudicator's View — *Rob Hooper*    87
10. Scapegoats and Sacred Cows: Towards good enough conflict resolution — *Nick Totton*    99

**Towards good practice**

11. Managing the Boundaries: It's the little things that count — *Roger Casemore*    111
12. Working Safely: Counsellor competence — *Moira Walker*    121
13. Acceptance of Uncertainty — *Caroline Jones*    131
14. Good Counsel from a Solicitor — *Tessa Roxburgh*    143
15. Supervision, Support and Surviving Complaints — *Paul Carney*    153

Contributors    161

Index    164

## Dedication

To 'Nadge' my very first client, who also taught me that to make mistakes is human and that to refuse to acknowledge them is to court disaster. To my children, Helen and Alastair, who gave up a lot of my time and attention in order that I could give it to my clients. To Ruth who was always there supporting me in my work as a therapist and allowed me to keep that part of my life and all those privileged conversations with clients, completely confidential and private. To all my clients over the past 34 years who accepted my failings and mistakes and particularly to those whose direct feedback taught me what I could do differently and how to do that.

Roger Casemore

# Foreword

Counselling and psychotherapy is a particularly human endeavour. One person, the practitioner, stands alongside another, a fellow human being who is presently in need of assistance. The relationship is both skilled and personal; it requires the professional application of passionate commitment and cool judgement. The subject matter is messy and often distressing and sad. Circumstance and entrenched relationship patterns may set limits to what can be achieved; there is no guarantee of success. When things go wrong or are seen to have gone wrong, a complaint may be made. Even when the practitioner is without fault, being complained about is stressful. This book offers practical help in coping with a difficult situation that everyone hopes will not arise. However in our 'customer' focused, ever more litigious culture, complaints are likely to be part of every therapist's working life, sometimes entirely appropriately, sometimes not, but always having to lived through.

For most practitioners, the formal process of being complained about and investigated is unfamiliar territory. Contributors to this volume write out of their experience of being involved in these processes - as authors of ethical codes, as administrators of complaint procedures and, most valuably, as the objects of complaint themselves. They extend the hand of colleagueship in a time of trial.

Defensive practice is an understandable response to the risk of being complained about but is not synonymous with good practice. Mistakes and misunderstanding inevitably occur, especially when the distortions of transference and counter-transference turn up the heat under the cauldron of emotional turmoil. They are added to by another category of error, that of malign or harmful idiosyncratic practice. All these happenings are opportunities for learning by the reflective practitioner, especially one committed to systemic understanding of the process of errors. Good training and supervision can minimise their occurrence. Saying 'sorry', a good professional attitude when mistakes have been made, may avert the escalation of complaints into the realm of formal procedures. Even so, formal complaints will occur and must be lived through. The practitioner will have to contain their anxiety, meet the requirements of the complaints procedure and, often simultaneously, try to maintain a professional therapeutic relationship with the complainant. This is not easy. I commend this book to those facing a complaint and the rest whose time will surely come.

Mark Aveline
Past-President, British Association for Counselling and Psychotherapy

# Introduction

## Roger Casemore

All the authors in this book are experienced therapists from a range of counselling modalities and the majority of them are also trainers and supervisors. Together we share a common concern about the nature and number of complaints against therapists or against the organisations and agencies which employ them. All of us have also had significant involvement in one way or another, with the processes and procedures which deal with these complaints. As a consequence we are very aware of the impact that complaints have on the complainant, the therapist complained against and their families, friends and colleagues. We are also aware that very few of the therapists complained against have given little, if any, thought to the possibility of a complaint being taken out against them, the likely consequences of that happening and what action to take should it do so.

This book is a collection of individual contributions, each with its own distinctive style, to reflect each author, and is aimed at a wide readership within the counselling and psychotherapy profession. The underlying concept of the book is based on the fact that even the most experienced and competent of therapists could have a complaint brought against them. It could be a specious or a vexatious complaint, or a complaint arising from the therapist's incompetence, their abusive unethical behaviour or it could be the result of a genuine error on the part of the therapist. There are also lots of things that either an experienced or an inexperienced therapist or a trainee therapist might do that could result in a complaint being brought against them, as a result of their lack of knowledge or their inexperience. In addition there is the whole field of organisational management issues which may result in a complaint being brought against a counselling organisation or an agency which employs therapists or against an individual therapist employed in an agency. None of us is safe from the possibility of being complained against and we all need to be better prepared to understand how we can avoid unnecessary complaints, live with and be accountable for our mistakes and cope with the impact of being complained against.

In this book, the authors are setting out to raise the consciousness, particularly of trainee therapists but also of the wider more experienced parts of the counselling and psychotherapy profession, with regard to:

• What might, can and does go wrong in therapy and what it might be possible

to do about it.
- The impacts that having a complaint against them might have on therapists and those close to them.
- What can be done to reduce, ameliorate, manage and come to terms with those impacts and to survive the process.
- What will happen if a complaint is lodged and what the therapist needs to do in responding.
- What strategies and actions need to be developed for legitimately avoiding complaints, whilst remaining accountable.

The book also seeks to explore the current position in relation to the nature of complaints against therapists, supervisors and trainers, how the complaints processes are experienced by complainant and complained against, including the effects of being complained against, even where the therapist is innocent. Different sections will look at what support and help might be needed both before, during and after a complaint, how a therapist can best represent themselves, what support and help is available, the relationship between ethics, standards of conduct and practice, complaints procedures and the law, and where else the complainant might take their complaint — including a brief look at the dangers for the unaware therapist, trainer or supervisor, in relation to breaches of trading standards or other aspects of the civil or criminal law.

At the time of writing, the British Association for Counselling and Psychotherapy (BACP) is developing a new and simplified Statement of Fundamental Ethical Principles, supported by Guidelines for Practice in Counselling, Supervision and Training, and a new revised Complaints Procedure. This provides a significant context for the content of this book, along with the rapidly increasing move towards statutory registration of therapists, which is forecast to occur as soon as 2003.

As practising therapists in a range of modalities, all of the authors carry a significant concern for the safety of clients and for ensuring that the good name of the counselling and psychotherapy profession is not brought into disrepute. We are also concerned about the importance of supporting and protecting therapists from the vicissitudes of practising their art. We do not wish to provide any means for those who practice unethically, abusively or incompetently, to avoid being dealt with appropriately. Rather we wish to encourage the readers to continue to develop their internal supervisor in ways that will appropriately raise and maintain the standards of their therapeutic practice, by raising awareness of the issues and dangers and encouraging the asking of those important 'What if?' questions.

We see complaints processes, at times, as having the possibility of being therapeutic in themselves and offering the possibility of change for both client and therapist. We also recognise that so often the complaint is evidence of a serious hurt which has occurred between therapist and client and that as therapists, supervisors and trainers, we want to try to reduce the number of hurts that occur and to enable those who are hurting or being hurt, to work towards healing the wounds and easing the pain.

# Chapter 1

# The Victim's Tale

## 'Poppy'

My real name is not Poppy. I have changed it to protect my family and myself. At the time of my story I was a teacher and enjoying my career, which I then gave up partly as a consequence of my experience. I have now returned to teaching and am also training to qualify as a counsellor.

Several years ago, at my request, I was referred by my GP for counselling. I opted to see a counsellor privately because the NHS counsellors could offer daytime appointments only, and I didn't feel able to be absent from my job on any regular basis. After about two weeks the counsellor telephoned me to arrange a first appointment. Even this seemed slightly odd to me at the time, because he left a very detailed message on the answer machine at home. He explained that he was a psychotherapist who had been given my telephone number by Dr. X, and requested that I call him to arrange an appointment. I remember being a little disconcerted at the amount of unnecessary information in the message that could have been accessed by other members of the household. As it happened, my husband was aware of the situation and my children were really too young at the time to have understood, but nonetheless it was potentially embarrassing.

The first appointment was a Saturday morning, at a different GP practice from my own. He worked for several practices and this was the one where he had use of an attic room for his private work. The surgery itself was open and busy and I remember feeling scared and very, very vulnerable. The counsellor seemed rather aloof and, at the same time, was very familiar — a difficult experience for me to describe. I did feel a sense of being looked after though. Here was the answer to all my problems: he was going to sort it for me. I immediately felt that he was absolutely wonderful.

At the beginning he quoted a price of £30 an hour and told me that a session would be one hour. On this first occasion I was there for more than two hours and when he finally drew the session to a close, I found myself offering to pay more. This he accepted grudgingly, and asked for £50. He expressed gratitude, telling me how 'lovely' it was for me to make the offer and that he appreciated it.

During this session he revealed quite a bit about himself to me, in terms of his lifestyle and attitudes. He drew attention to the fact that we were the same age, give or take a couple of months, and as he helped me on with my coat at the end, he commented on what a nice colour it was. All these subtle factors registered with me straight away, although I had no reason to believe that there was anything untoward at all. A part of me felt sure that he liked me and yet another part rationalised that it was probably just all part of the therapy. Looking back on it though, I think I felt that I was a 'special' client to him from the very beginning. However this was not a conscious thought to me at the time.

The next appointment was during the following week on a Wednesday evening, when the surgery itself was closed. This became a regular appointment time, and each session would begin with a lot of informal chatter whilst he made coffee for us both. He would occasionally make positive comments about the clothes that I was wearing, but other than that, there was no undue flattery or anything to lead me to wonder about his authenticity as a counsellor. It really did feel as though we were close friends more than anything else because of the informality and the fact that he did a lot of talking about himself.

Initially during the actual 'counselling' sessions, he would listen to me and challenge me a lot, which I found very exciting and helpful. As time went on though, I experienced a sense of frustration and irritation at the amount of space he took up talking about himself. The focus was not always on me by any means, and I found myself increasingly put in the role of listener. Even in my naivety this didn't feel right. He talked about his childhood and adolescence, his sense of loss when his father died, his disastrous first marriage, his relationship with his partner and his current lifestyle. In fact he shared with me an enormous amount of information concerning his beliefs and attitudes to a wide range of issues. However, as well as feeling irritated I felt extremely privileged. Although I knew little at this stage about counselling and the boundaries that surround the counsellor/client relationship, I felt sure that this must be different. I thought he needed me in some way, like I thought I needed him. I felt thrilled and kind of heady with excitement. The initial problem that led me to seek help seemed to be getting better, in the excitement of this bizarre relationship. I told myself that it was because he was such a brilliant counsellor, but even then I knew that I was deluding myself. The time spent in each session with the focus on me was becoming minimal.

Our sessions frequently went into two or even three hours, although he refused to take extra money after that first appointment. Instead he told me that he loved 'chatting' to me. He was sometimes cold and aloof, yet at other times he was warm and welcoming. He was so unpredictable that I used to find myself wondering how he would be on my way to each appointment. I got the sense that he was playing games with me and that I was a source of consternation to him.

Over the weeks there were many signs, both in his comments and his behaviour, which suggested something else was happening in the relationship. On one occasion we had an afternoon appointment during the school holidays. Again the surgery was closed and he invited me to stay on and have another coffee. Of course I agreed and was there for about three hours. During this time he brought up the subject of sex. He spoke at length on the subject, in a kind of caressing and gentle tone. The atmosphere in the room seemed to me to be electric, and yet as always, I told myself that it was probably part of the therapy, and any other interpretation was possibly just my imagination.

On another occasion he pointed out that as we were born in the same year and had particular star signs, it was meant to mean that we were very compatible, especially as we were opposite sexes. Never having believed in any such nonsense myself I found I was feeling delighted by this revelation and sure now that he was trying to tell me something. Another time I asked him if he ever had clients who scared him when working alone in the building. He looked at me hard, paused for several seconds and then pointed his finger at me almost accusingly and said, 'you are the client who scares me'. I knew then what he meant and yet I felt powerless to do or say anything very much in response. I just kind of laughed it off, but I felt secretly ecstatic. I really don't know why I was such a wimp.

On one occasion we got onto the subject of the Universe and the meaning of life. We did, in fact spend the whole session discussing this. Perhaps this marked a turning point because I vividly remember how he switched off the lights in the room and then put his arm round me, as he pointed out some of the stars in the night sky. That is all that happened at this stage and yet it seemed like such a romantic gesture on his part. I felt it was dangerously exciting and knew then for certain that this could not be part of any conventional therapy that my GP would approve of! Nevertheless, I had no intention of terminating the relationship — it was far too thrilling for that.

Another time he reached forward and touched my knee and lower leg to explain why I had developed 'shin-splints' after doing a lot of running. It was a gentle and lingering caress, rather than a matter-of-fact, innocent touch. He produced a bandage, for my leg, from the surgery. The delight that I felt at his concern and care was such that I couldn't have been more thrilled had he given me a diamond necklace! I was pleased on a childlike sort of level, and was left in no doubt now that I must be special to him in some way. I knew what was happening and it all felt very safe and yet very dangerous. I felt that we were special to each other, and I acknowledged to myself that I was very much in love with him from this point onwards.

Over the next few weeks the little signs built up one upon the other until he asked me one evening if I would like a hug. I don't know why I didn't immediately say that I did, but I just sort of mumbled 'probably'. He repeated the question and I said that I would. We stood up and hugged for ages and he asked me what I was thinking. I didn't mention love, but told him I had strong feelings for him. He said that he knew already and I felt a bit of a fool. The following week no reference was made to the hugging and I thought that I had been totally mistaken in thinking that he had any feelings for me. All that had happened had been part of the therapy or had been wishful thinking on my part. Either way, I felt disappointed and yet relieved in some sense. It had been driving me mad and I had felt powerless to take control. The situation had resolved itself, it seemed. I felt flat but more level headed than I had felt for months. It was the week after, that it all became more concrete.

Things finally came to the crunch the following week when he instigated a discussion about his feelings about our relationship. He said he felt that something very 'powerful' was going on 'between us sexually'. We needed to address it he told me, in order to carry on working together. He told me he was very attracted to me and that he could no longer fool himself into thinking that I was simply 'projecting' it all onto him. He realised that he had got feelings for me, which he had got to acknowledge as his own. He then asked me for a hug saying that he needed this from me, comparing it to the first hug when he felt that I needed that from him! We hugged again for a long time breaking off every so often to make a lot of eye contact. Finally it developed into a lot of passionate kissing, and yet it was all very loving and tender.

I remember sitting back down in the chair, in a daze that I believed to be mutual at the time, and he crouched down on the floor beside me holding both my hands. He became emotional as he told me of his inner struggles with himself over his feelings for me. He felt that he had constantly been 'building barriers' against me, and then 'knocking them all down again'. I remember his exact words because they had such an impact on me. He said, 'I think you are a lovely, lovely person'. I replied 'and I think you are absolutely wonderful'. He looked sad and followed with 'ah, but you don't know me'. At this moment, and in the future, I found his tendency to think badly of himself both endearing and proof of his genuineness. I also saw it as a challenge to me to help him believe in himself.

I told him how confusing I had found the whole situation, and he apologised for his moodiness, explaining that now I knew the reason why. He said that whilst it was quite usual to fall in love with your therapist it was not so usual the other way round. There, I had confirmation from him at last! In an indirect way he was telling me that he loved me. It was what I had been waiting for and hoping for, for so long, it seemed. We arranged to meet outside the 'counselling' environment to have coffee.

We met two days later, and no reference was made of our last meeting. We both seemed to want to avoid the subject, and yet I would have welcomed talking about it had he initiated the conversation. Again, I had that sense of powerlessness. I was left feeling disconcerted and puzzled, but in a sense more smitten than ever. His reticence and lack of urgency (to get me into bed) just seemed to prove to me further that this was something he didn't make a habit of.

Halfway through our next counselling session, he commented on how odd he thought it was that neither of us had mentioned the physical contact between us, or the meeting for coffee. It began to occur to me that he was looking for me now to develop things further. However, I didn't actually respond to this much at all. Again I had this feeling of powerlessness. He then said that what had happened was wrong and shouldn't have happened. It had got to stop before it went any further, because he still wanted to carry on working with me as a counsellor. I felt very rejected and confused, said at first that I could carry on as his client, next said I couldn't, and then went out of the room to cool off. He followed me, and we ended up hugging, kissing and caressing. Although the sexual chemistry between us was intense and urgent at this point, we didn't actually have sex because I remember saying, 'we can't do it here!' but it would have been a normal progression otherwise. He told me that I made him feel eighteen years old again, and the really wonderful thing was that I felt exactly the same way.

A natural break occurred at this point whilst I went on holiday for a couple of weeks. I had great difficulty in enjoying the holiday or concentrating on the family. I was fearful that he would have changed his mind by the time I got back, and I felt terribly alone and insecure, at the thought of this possibility. Upon my return, he made what seemed like another U-turn, telling me that he wanted to carry on seeing me, but not as a client. He wanted to see me as a friend and lover. He explained that he was marrying his partner shortly, but that the sex between them was infrequent because she wasn't interested. However he knew that he loved her, and could morally justify an affair with me to himself, on the grounds that he didn't believe that one single person could give another all that was needed from a relationship. He then revealed that he thought about me a great deal and had been having fantasies about me for a long time. I felt deliriously happy, believing him to have been very honest with me and yet obviously as crazy about me as I was about him. I remember him saying 'I don't believe this — we are actually planning to have an affair'. He expressed relief that we were no longer in a client/counsellor relationship (were we ever?) and we once again arranged to meet.

I was now in total turmoil. I couldn't sleep or eat and felt like an excited wreck. I had been in love before and had experienced powerful feelings but nothing had ever come close to this. I was convinced that this must be something extremely special. We met as arranged and he was rather distant. However I had experienced this with him before so I was not unduly surprised. He told me that he had been unable to concentrate on anything and couldn't sleep. I took this as a positive sign until he finally told me that he wasn't into this 'cloak and dagger stuff' and couldn't do it. He became tearful and, when I asked if it meant that we wouldn't see each other again, he hinted that he would always be pleased to hear from me. I became angry and told him that there was no way that I would ever contact him. He seemed both annoyed and surprised at this. We parted and I was overwhelmed by feelings of anger and amazement. I drove off leaving him sitting in his own car, and when I passed by the same spot about half an hour later, he was still sitting there. I felt sure that my pride would never allow me to contact him again and yet I still felt certain that he did have feelings for me, which, he was either denying or suppressing.

Over the next few weeks I found that I was unable to let the thought of him go. I really tried to pick up the pieces of my life and become involved with my family and my work. I felt that I was losing a battle because the more I tried to rid my mind of what had happened, the memory of him and how I felt about him, the less able I was to find any sense of peace or comfort. I began drinking heavily every evening as soon as I got home from work. I confided in a couple of close friends who listened with anger and indignation at what I was telling them. I was certainly well rid of him they said, and yet that was not what I wanted to hear. I needed someone to hear my pain and understand the depth of my feelings. I also wanted to have my hopes confirmed by them that he was not simply an evil bastard who had abused his power and my trust, but was genuinely confused by the depth of his feelings for me. This thought took root and began to grow and flourish, until I reached a decision to contact him. He had after all indicated that this would be acceptable. Nevertheless it took a lot of swallowing of pride and plucking up of courage to make that contact. I wrote a brief note to him, simply stating that I needed to talk to him and indicating several times when he could phone me. He phoned very promptly and we arranged to meet in the old counselling venue.

My expectation was that the meeting would at least bring things to a proper close; it had very much felt to me that there was unfinished business between us. In fact it turned out not to be as simple as this. He said that he had missed me and thought about me every day. He spoke of the regret and guilt that he felt, in that he was supposed to have helped me and yet must have made things worse. I made no comment on this. It was a very strange fact that I never felt able to speak much of my feelings to him. This would have been a good opportunity to do so and yet I found myself simply listening to him and his feelings. I think I felt the need to protect him in some way. I also felt that I would scare him right off if I really let him know the extent of my suffering. He said he would like us to meet as friends, because talking to me really 'cleared' his head. This meeting resulted in our going for a drink, and ended with a passionate embrace and a decision to begin seeing each other as lovers.

I felt swept up by events, and once again deliriously happy and excited. This time he seemed more certain that this was what he really wanted, and I remember deciding that this was because he was now actually married and maybe, in some perverse way, he didn't feel as guilty now about it all. The relationship at last moved into a deeper level and we met on a fairly regular basis. Sex featured in the relationship, in a variety of places, including the counselling venue, and yet we often only met to talk. This seemed proof to me at the time that there was more to the relationship than physical attraction. I was almost always on the listening end, and found that I was usually happy to do this. He often said that talking to me cleared his head. I took this as a huge compliment, and a sign that he needed me and that I was special to him in some way.

A break came in the relationship when I went into hospital for minor surgery. It was always me who did the phoning to arrange meetings because it felt safer that way. I thought, though, that this time I would wait for him to contact me. He didn't phone and I felt quite strong and certain that I could get along without him probably better than he could without me. I really thought it would be simply a question of time before he would contact me. I was wrong and when this became obvious I began to make all sorts of excuses for him to myself. I also began to experience the same sense of desolation that I had felt a few months back.

I finally gave in to my urge to phone him. We met, and he said it was good to see me again. Tentatively we started to meet for friendship but soon the relationship developed again into more, and we continued from where we left off. It lasted for the next fifteen months and, in addition to having sex, took the form of walking, talking and meeting in cafes. During this time he would occasionally fail to keep the arrangements, and was unpredictable in his behaviour. He could be aloof and yet at other times he was affectionate and loving. I told him on several occasions that if he ever wanted to stop seeing me, I would like him to be honest and say so. He always replied with certainty that he didn't want to end the relationship.

The last time we met he was cool and rather irritable. I was about to go on holiday and he was sarcastic about the amount of holidays I seemed to have. In fact he seemed really quite pissed off about it. He was also annoyed when, for fear of being seen by my husband, I refused to go on to a more public place with him. We parted not on the best of terms, with him instructing me to contact him when I got back from holiday. By this time I had been having counselling with a female counsellor for quite a few months and was working through some of the conflicting feelings I was experiencing. Something in me kind of clicked into place, as he issued his command, and I drove off in the absolute certainty that I would never contact him again and wanted nothing more to do with him. The finality of my decision, and the extent of my anger towards him, amazed me. I suddenly seemed to wake up to the fact that I was worth much more than this.

In that next fortnight I found that I was able to enjoy the holiday and, to some extent, put a lot of it behind me. Over the weeks that followed, I spotted him a few times in several different places near where I live. I had the impression that it was not by accident, although I can't know that for sure. It took me a long time to work through the feelings of sadness and loss that I experienced in not seeing him, but I always felt sure that I had done the right thing. However, a needle of doubt persisted to dominate my thoughts, where he was concerned: was he simply bad, or was he weak, confused and unable to deal with his feelings? Whichever it was, I accepted that I would never know the answer to that question, and I was most definitely much better off without him.

Three years later I read something in the local paper that enabled me to find an answer to my question. What I read filled me with a sense of absolute horror and disbelief. At the same time I felt released from the sense of doubt and confusion that had persisted in dogging me for the last few years. The headline read ' Counsellor Admits Indecent Assault'. Interested, I read on, only to discover that the counsellor in the article was actually him. A female client had reported him to her GP, but when questioned by the Police, he had denied that any physical contact ever took place between him and a client. It was only when another woman made a similar complaint against him, according to the article, that he admitted the assault charge. A couple of months later I read that he had been convicted and sentenced to a term of imprisonment, and was to register as a sex offender upon his release. I actually felt a whole mixture of emotion. I was filled with a sense of revulsion that he had degenerated into a sex offender. Had he always been one, I wondered? It seemed such a far cry from the man I thought I had known. I was horrified to think that I had been conned in such an enormous way. I also felt tremendous relief in knowing, at last, the true nature of the man that I had fallen so hopelessly in love with, and certain beyond a shadow of a doubt, that I had definitely done the right thing when I had walked away from it. At the same time I felt a sense of great emptiness and sorrow.

Some time later I decided to reveal my story to the GP, who had originally referred me for the counselling. She did not seem at all surprised, and told me that I was probably just the 'tip of the iceberg.' She personally knew of at least two other female clients of his, in our practice, with whom he had had affairs. This, we established, had probably taken place after I had stopped seeing him. One of the other women had described him as 'beguiling', and I could certainly agree with that. I finally felt, for the first time in all of this, a complete and utter fool. How could I have been so gullible? It took me a long time to begin to come to terms with it all and to stop blaming myself for my stupidity. He had not ever physically assaulted me, but he had certainly abused me emotionally. My GP's disclosure was actually the final nail in the coffin, and it was only after this that

I was finally able to lay it to rest.

As a final word it is perhaps useful to notice that my experience all began with such tiny breaches of the counselling codes of ethics, that gently and gradually escalated to a point of no return.

# Chapter 2

# The Person Complained About Was Me

## 'Chris'

### Introduction

I have tried to start this writing a dozen times and I realise that a big part of my difficulty is that a portion of the feelings of shame, fear, persecution, betrayal and anger that overwhelmed me when I had a complaint made against me, are still there. Of course I knew this anyway, but I don't like being reminded. This chapter is about my personal psychology and how I individually reacted to having a complaint made against me. I want to tell you, the reader, that certain things are not important — the content of the complaint; whether I was found 'guilty' or not, whether justice was done or not, my version of what really happened, whether I am a man or a woman, and my real name. In writing that simple sentence all of the contradictions and paradoxes in the complaints process come leaping out at me. I hope I will be able to describe my experience of some of these as I go along. However, I fear that for some readers it may look like me dodging the issue, whingeing, making out that I am the victim, trying to get sympathy, or whatever. This is as straightforward an account of my experience as I can write — the idea, like Poppy's chapter, is to put some flesh on the bones of the complaints process. It involves real people like you. I have deliberately chosen a *nom de plume* for myself and pseudonyms for other characters that are not gender-specific.

Also, by way of introduction, I would add, that shortly after the complaint against me was adjudicated and a judgement made, a close friend of mine also had a complaint made against them. I will describe my experiences during that time as well.

Finally, I also want you to know that after my experiences, I understand certain things to be true.

- An increasing number of counsellors, trainers and supervisors are having complaints made against them.
- It doesn't matter how defensively you practice (if that is your wont), you will not be able to prevent a complaint being made if someone has a mind to make one.
- Approved training, accredited status, number of years experience are also

ultimately no protection for your clients (against malpractice or mistakes) or you (against complaints being made about you), but they are obviously to be recommended.

- Some complaints are well-founded (a therapist has breached a code), some are because a mistake has been made (either by the complainant or the person complained about), some are false. Often it is one person's word against the other and the adjudicators are then in a near-impossible position.

- There is no agreed set of standards for practice in counselling, supervision and training of counsellors, regardless of the existence of codes of ethics. It is all a matter of interpretation. Take a look at the range of disagreements in the BACP Journal column 'Ethical Dilemmas' and imagine an adjudication panel consisting of the contributors to that column, when someone's professional reputation is at stake.

- It doesn't matter whether the complaint is founded in fact or not, there is no *guarantee* that 'justice' will be done — for the complainant or the person complained about.

- However impartially the professional body behaves, it is practically impossible for the adjudicators to weigh the evidence fairly, and one or the other party in the process will feel aggrieved by the outcome.

- There are no 'winners' in this process, regardless of outcome. The person who the adjudicators find in favour of, will also probably not feel 'happy'. If they are the person bringing the complaint, they will already be feeling hurt or they would not have brought the complaint, and a 'positive' result for them will probably not take the hurt away. If they are the person being complained about, a 'positive' result for them will not take away the hurt of being dragged through a distressing process.

- The only thing that will help you understand the complaints process is first-hand experience. Prepare now for the time that it may happen to you: use supervision, personal therapy and whatever workshops or training opportunities are available.

- Your life will be directly affected by the complaint for about one year, and responding to the complaint and preparing for the adjudication hearing will consume your attention twenty-four hours a day for days on end.

- Your personal psychology will be fully engaged by the complaints process (more of this later). Be prepared for a rough time when confronting issues that you probably thought were resolved years ago. Complaints procedures reach the parts that other life events cannot reach.

- It will hurt.

## Black Saturday

There is never a 'right time' to receive bad news. If the telephone rings at 2.30 am it sets my pulse racing because it can only mean one thing — bad news. The last thing I expected on my return from holiday, however, was a letter saying that someone had taken out a complaint against me. There are several things about receiving such a letter that had never occurred to me until it happened. The first (and I feel foolish just thinking this, let alone writing it) is that it was so *unexpected*. A bolt out of the blue — and it just about knocked me over. I was in shock as I read the letter and then read the complaint itself. As I read through it my eyes skipped about trying to take it all in. In the midst of the family returning from holiday I slipped into a quiet room and tried to read it carefully, but couldn't.

I desperately wanted to talk to someone, to show them the letter, to get them to confirm that it was really happening. But who? My partner? My best friend? Would that be breaking confidentiality? My supervisor? (It was Saturday at the end of the school half-term holidays, was this enough of an emergency to call my supervisor?) As I ran through the possibilities in my mind, I began to realise that I had started to pace up and down. I needed a cigarette for the first time in years. I also knew in that moment that there was no way I could sit on this till Monday. I would be a wreck, and after such a nice holiday with the kids!

When my absence was noticed, Les, my partner, popped into the room to find out why I had disappeared, so I spilled it all out in a jumble. I was obviously upset yet remembered to keep the name of the person and details out of the story secret. Nothing is ever simple, of course, and you will understand why if I say that Les was never really all that keen on me being a counsellor. I got support and sympathy at the height of my upset, but realised that Les would not want to, and therefore not be able to, understand the details and give me the kind of support I really wanted. I would have to wait until Monday.

## What to tell, and how to tell

### What

Ordinarily it can be fun teasing people. Not so in this case. The ethics, in terms of 'confidentiality', of the situation mean that just about the only thing the person complained against can say to anyone is something like: 'Someone has made a complaint against me through (name of professional body). It is in the process of being dealt with by the formal complaints procedure. I will let you know of the outcome of adjudication when it is made'. For the recipient of this news it is wholly unsatisfactory. Immediate commiserations are forced out of them followed by an awkward silence and offers to help in any way, despite the mass of questions which seethes inside. In that moment, they and you know that they want to know everything but dare not ask, whilst you want to tell everything but dare not say. Such details are confined to the consulting rooms of your therapist and supervisor.

Although, with hindsight, I now see that it would have been helpful to talk more about the effects of the process on me as a person, at the time, I conflated professional confidentiality concerning the content, and personal confidentiality concerning the process. Together with my feeling of shame, this effectively shut me up.

### How

As each decision and its enactment came and went, it dawned on me that I would never be satisfied that I had done something 'right', according to the book, so to speak. There was no book. Deciding *how* to say 'Someone has complained about my professional behaviour . . .' was proving to be just as difficult as deciding *what* to say. I wanted to come across as professional and competent to supervisees and clients. I wanted colleagues to understand my shock and to appreciate the very real new difficulties that this presented in an already difficult job. To friends I wanted to show my confusion and hurt. To my supervisor and therapist I wanted to reveal and explore my shame and fear. The problem was that all of my feelings were jumbled up and visited me to the point of distraction at some time or another every day.

I now lived in fear of getting it wrong. Would shame and confusion come out when I was trying to be confident, competent and professional? Would I be confused and frightened in front of my colleagues?

And another thing, how angry should I be? Inside I did occasionally feel anger toward the complainant, but I also felt what seemed to me to be genuine compassion: after all, I had developed a close relationship with this person and had been (I thought) really empathic with them — I couldn't simply turn it off, or 'un-know' those things. My feelings were a hellish mix of anger, hurt, compassion, understanding and betrayal.

Some colleagues and friends clearly (they told me so) thought that I wasn't angry enough. They thought that not only would it be good for me to be angry, but also that if I showed 'too much' compassion or empathy for the complainant, then I was either psychologically flawed, guilty, or both. Now I felt naïve as well, especially as, deep down inside, I refused to judge the complainant for being hurt and taking it out on me — I *did* understand why they had complained, but I also knew that it wasn't my fault. The complaint was worded in simple, but in my view, loaded language. As the complainant listed events it seemed so straightforward, but I wanted to scream at the top of my voice 'It wasn't like that — if you had been there you'd know what I mean!!' and, 'It's not as simple as that!!'

## Who to tell

A couple of people advised a 'Tell no-one, admit nothing' policy. My natural leaning was to tell everyone and admit everything, after all, in my view I had nothing to be ashamed about. However, as readers will have gathered, for me nothing turned out to be simple as I considered my options in this complaints process. As with many facets of this process, the right path for me was carefully chosen between the two poles of 'all' or 'nothing', and the devil was in the detail.

## Colleagues

What soon became very clear to me was that everyone I knew had a vested interest in the complaint made against me. For colleagues that I worked with it was obvious that they could only take one line. In the first place it would be much too awkward if I was guilty, since they, and the organisation we worked for would suffer by association. Second, we had to continue to work together. Third, I felt further constrained by the ethics of what I may and must not disclose, since they would probably have been able to identify the complainant, and complainants must, quite rightly, be protected. So the issue was very simple for them: I was innocent in their eyes and they would fight my corner.

Comrades at arms have their place, but what I really wanted was the very thing I could not have: sharing and critical debate. On this occasion, the names could not be changed to protect the innocent — I couldn't disclose sufficient detail in order for them to enter into critical debate. I felt very alone in the middle of this supportive crowd.

## Supervisees

In my first 'post notification of the complaint' supervision session, I realised that I would have to tell my supervisees. As professional counsellors or counsellors-in-training, they must be told that my professional behaviour was being called into question. One doesn't have to be psychodynamic in order to realise the technical, ethical, and professional difficulties that such disclosure raises for supervisees. Try putting yourself in the shoes of the supervisor (me) and the supervisees in turn.

What options did they have? Cut and run — i.e. protect themselves from guilt by association or being prey to possible bad ethical judgement at my hands, whilst appearing to be unsympathetic and unsupportive? Or stay, supervisees through thick and thin — like children, forced to support their parents by the pressure of the dynamics of the situation? What a mess.

I told them all, quietly and calmly, each at the start of their next supervision session. I offered them a little extra time to consider their position or ask me what questions I could ethically answer. I told them that I would, of course, understand completely if they decided to seek supervision elsewhere, either now or if the adjudication found me in breach of any codes. If they stayed how could I trust their reasons, and if they left how would I relate to them professionally in our small town?

This was a lose-lose situation — I will leave the reader to imagine what happened.

## Clients

The decision to inform my supervisees was easy. But where were the handbooks and notes for guidance through this damned process to help me now? Should I tell my clients? (And if so what? — 'Just before we start this session I must warn you that your counsellor is suspected of being crap or dangerous or both'.) Should I have a blanket policy — tell all or tell none? Some were trainees on counselling courses, so maybe the local 'grapevine' might get to them if I didn't tell them (the 'real' story — we all know what gossip is) first. Some were very vulnerable indeed, and would be very badly affected (I worried that one might contemplate suicide) if they knew that the practice of the person they had struggled so hard to trust, was dubious.

No the least of my problems was that I was plagued by the worry that I *actually might be* a useless and/or possibly dangerous counsellor. Thank heaven for my supervisor. I regained sufficient confidence to do the job safely, at least.

After agonising supervision, I told some but not others. The best of a bad lot. Would this be seen as unethical too? Lose-lose again. I held my breath.

## Friends

It would be comforting to think that you could count on your friends, and since I had been a counsellor for a few years, most of my friends were involved in counselling one way or another. The responses I actually got from my friends surprised me.

A couple of them made supportive noises yet were obviously signed up to the 'there's no smoke without fire' school of thought. I felt that if they were not my friend, they would have assumed that the counsellor was guilty simply because a complaint had been made. Another enduring feeling I had with them was that whenever the topic came up, they would ask questions with a very slight edge to them, as though they thought that they might be able to discern the 'truth', and then settle the issue of my guilt or innocence once and for all. These friends felt on edge with me and I became on edge with them — what trust there was in our relationship had gone. We don't see each other much now.

Other friends seemed to believe that in order to support me they must demonstrate their hatred for the person making the complaint against me. They never missed an opportunity to call the complainant names, diagnose them, and generally destroy their character. I am no saint, but my memory of the complainant (and I wanted to hold on to it) was of a caring, vulnerable, if damaged, person, struggling to live a good life.

A few friends suddenly became very distant, very peripheral in my life. It seemed to me that they thought that a complaint was an infectious disease that they might catch. Maybe they thought that they would be tarred with the same brush and ostracised by the counselling community in the town where we lived if I were to be found guilty. As the complaint progressed, I began to realise how real a possibility this was. I felt like a pariah even before the adjudication hearing. What would it be like after the adjudication had been held?

## Guilt and innocence

Throughout this chapter I have used the terms 'guilt' and 'innocence', because that's how it felt, and still feels to this day. No amount of supervision or therapy or resolution seem to shift my feelings. I felt as though I was being put on trial and the outcome would be . . . . 'Do you find the accused guilty or innocent?'

Judgement day. Some complaints procedures give a judgement on the day of the hearing, some (like BACP) let the panel consider its verdict, write a report, and consider it at a committee before they let you know. By the time it all ground through the machine, I just wanted it over with. I almost couldn't care if I was found guilty or not. On the one hand I thought I had defended my position well and, frankly, if I was found guilty, then I would lose faith in the system. On the other, I believed that the system was essential, if fallible and, that I had no right to expect justice any more than the complainant or anyone else in this imperfect world.

It still mattered though, when it came down to it.

## You should be over it by now

I'm not sure what the equivalent of a 'period of mourning' is in relation to a complaint. When, exactly, should I have felt better, should I have been able to feel free from the taint, to put it down as a learning experience? I was beginning to feel a little oppressed by my colleagues and friends who seemed to expect me to have put it all behind me within a couple of months and got on with the job. I might have succeeded, had not a close friend and colleague received a letter with 'Strictly Private' and 'To be opened by addressee only' stamped all over it, postmarked 'Coventry'. If I had been there I could have told her what it was. I had come to know those envelopes only too well.

One of her ex-clients had made a complaint to one of the professional bodies to which she belonged. I wanted to be genuinely supportive. I remembered all of the pitfalls that my friends and colleagues had fallen into, and sought to avoid them I was on hand and ready to share the benefit of my own experience of this whole terrible complaint business.

What I had overlooked was that I was not yet in any state to give support let alone advice, to anyone so soon after my own case. All of my feelings were brought back with a disturbing and vivid rawness, and completely scrambled my efforts to help my friend. I was, I am sure, better than no help at all, but I was not the cool, calm, experienced friend and colleague I wanted to be. I was most useful when dispensing advice like:

- Don't write your defence in the first couple of days. You will still be in shock.
- Get someone else (supervisor?) to read the complaint fully and explain the procedure to you. The last thing you will be able to do in your state of shock will be to understand what is being said accurately or what to do next.
- Don't overestimate your ability to cope. You will be badly shaken by this and may well have to take a day or two off seeing clients. It would not be ethical to plough on regardless.
- Find a friend — professional or personal to whom you can go at any time of the day for support, no questions asked.
- Ask for, and get, professional help:
  - Talk about it to your supervisor. Don't spare the details. Book plenty of time. If your supervisor isn't 100% behind you, change now.
  - If you are insured (and I know some prefer not to be according to their own professional value base) call the insurer's help line and get all the help they can offer.
  - BACP staff are as helpful as they can be, given that their brief is to facilitate the process. Ask for their advice on procedural matters.

I was less useful (you could read that as 'worse than useless') when it came to matters emotional (I veered between numb and over excitable), and was a complete disaster on the day of my friend's adjudication hearing (I was supposed to be there to support them) because it brought my own case back all too vividly. It is best to be very cautious about your personal limits if you find yourself in a similar situation.

## Conclusion — professional

One outcome for me has been a realisation that I am not alone. I have started to identify myself in professional meetings as someone who has been complained about and have discovered that there is a growing number of therapists who will similarly identify themselves. Generally, we are not terrible people, some of us may have made mistakes, hurting someone in the course of our work. A very small number may be guilty of malpractice and are sanctioned as heavily as professional bodies will allow. Most therapists complained about continue to work, initially with increased supervision, and although it may sound cliched to say so, I think I have learned from my experience.

I believe that those who receive services from counsellors, trainers and supervisors should be enabled to complain if they have been treated badly, and that this process should be made easy for them. However, I also believe that there should be better support for the counsellors themselves who have to endure a complaint. Guilty or innocent, our profession should not be a party to the traumatisation of anyone, least of all the paid-up members of our professional bodies.

That is one of my two bones of contention. I do believe that professional bodies must decide whether they are regulatory (policing the profession) or supportive (like a trade union). I found it confusing and distressing to be subjected to a complaint and disciplinary procedure whilst paying many tens of pounds yearly subscription for the privilege. I found the professional bodies as institutions, judgemental, impenetrable, unyielding and unsupportive. Individual staff, however, (particularly the complaints officers) did make the experience slightly more tolerable by their generosity and humanness. My recommendation to BACP, UKCP, BPS and the rest is to decide whether they are out to represent and support therapists or prosecute them — they cannot do both. My recommendation to therapists is that if professional organisations continue to be unsupportive of therapists in complaints procedures, we should organise a trade union or join one and start a therapists' division.

My second bone of contention is with the growing series of columns in professional magazines and journals giving advice and opinion on 'ethical dilemmas'. The problem is that the columnists give the impression that such issues are debatable, and invite wise sages to debate possible good practice and the implication is that it's a matter of opinion, of interpretation, of mature consideration by the practitioner and their supervisor — flexibility and pluralism being the ethos. However, try this at your adjudication/complaints hearing and they'll wipe the floor with you. No such civilised debate between peer-professionals there. The culture is 'right/wrong', 'guilty/innocent' and sanctions are not very flexible either, not much room for 'interpretation' there it would appear.

This is a strange and confusing double-message. What are practitioners to make of it? Can the clauses in a code of ethics be viewed as clear right/wrong boundaries or are they matters of interpretation? If the latter really is true (the magazine columnists version of reality) then this should be better reflected in the adjudication process, which currently behaves (as does the sanctions-setting process) as though things are much more clear-cut. If things really are so clear-cut (as the adjudication and sanctions process implies) then the magazine articles should reflect *this* and be presented more as mock courtrooms where an adjudication is given and sanctions imposed. I don't believe we can have it both ways.

Another problem as I reflect upon the experience is the role of the supervisor. Your supervisor, who supported your actions throughout, is effectively in the dock too — no consideration for the hours and pounds spent in supervision, just a panel making a decision based on a couple of hours presentation of evidence. So, in the light of a complaint what value should we put on supervision if decisions arrived at there can so easily be called into question, overturned or discredited? Should the practitioner ditch their supervisor? Perhaps the supervisor should also be cautioned and their practice reviewed as a matter of course in every case where a counsellor's practice is found wanting?

## Conclusion — personal

It is a few years since these events took place. I have learned a great deal about myself through it all. Me as an ordinary human being and how I react to stress and accusations; me as a counsellor and how I practise; and me as a person — my values and principles and my views on healing relationships, trust and human nature. I think that I suffered several of the symptoms of trauma for about a year, and having spoken to a few counsellors who have gone through this, I believe this is a common experience.

My supervisor did explain to me that no-one said that being a counsellor would be easy. I always thought that I was a confident, optimistic sort of person. I was successful in my job, had brought up children, and generally felt good about myself. I don't see myself as a pessimist or a moaner or unduly cynical about life. There were times during these events when I felt genuinely on the edge of depression. And all of this brought about by my best efforts to help someone, which may or may not have contributed to them actually feeling worse. No-one said that it would be this difficult either.

It took me a year or so to enjoy reading the monthly magazines published by our professional bodies.

I still feel very uncomfortable when reading sanctions notices.

I can easily get agitated when an unfamiliar official-looking letter arrives.

I still dread the arrival of any letter with 'Strictly private' and 'To be opened by addressee only' stamped on it.

## Postscript

I wonder if you, the reader, have had the experience of having a complaint made about your practice, and how that has affected your reading of my experiences?

I also wonder whether you, the reader, wanted to know, or thought it was important to know, the details of my complaint — whether I am a man or a woman, (and the gender of the complainant) and what the outcome was?

This chapter is dedicated to my supervisor and my friend who stood by me throughout. They transformed the experience into important learning for me.

Chapter 3

# Surviving a Complaint — A practical guide

## Alan Jamieson

The experience of being the subject of a professional practice complaint is without question one of the most personally traumatic events a therapist may face during their career. It is difficult to overstate the impact of receiving, through the post, and without prior warning, notice of a formal complaint from the practitioner's own professional body.

Reactions are invariably driven by emotion. Whether the dominant desire is for flight or fight, it is important that active attempts are made to think, to think clearly, and to consider carefully what to do. This is, of course, not easy when trying to contain a rush of powerful and often confused feelings that can include rage, horror, impotence, hurt, outrage, despair and a desire for revenge or rescue.

In this chapter I have tried to identify key action points for those who find themselves in the position of being complained against. They represent points at which you are encouraged to stop and think. They are based on experience, and in particular experience consistent over time, which suggests that a period of reflection at the earliest stage can save a lot of wasted energy and emotion. The hope is that these points will amount to a number of things you can do if someone brings a professional complaint against you, along with some tips on how to survive a complaint.

## Whom do you inform or whom can you consult?

If you receive a letter notifying you that a complaint has been lodged against you, one of the first things to think about is who to inform. I suggest you think about the following.

### Counselling supervisor

It is your counselling supervisor with whom you will usually have the closest professional relationship in respect of the work you do with clients. It is also your counselling supervisor with whom you are most likely to have discussed your work with the particular client who has lodged the complaint.

It will be a good move to arrange to see your counselling supervisor as soon as can be arranged in order to discuss events and any steps to be taken or preparations to be made. Likewise you would be wise to consider increasing the frequency of your counselling supervision sessions for the duration of the complaint and the weeks following its conclusion.

Overall consultation with your counselling supervisor should afford you a safe place in which to reflect on the nature, type and progress of your work with the client who has complained. Such actions can be very affirming when in this situation. You can also use the opportunity to reflect on the experience and its likely impact on your current therapy practice and caseload.

## Employer

If you are employed, and you saw the client who has lodged the complaint in that setting, you should inform your employer of the fact that a client has lodged a complaint against you via your professional body. How much further you can go in terms of disclosure will be very much determined by the particular circumstances of each case.

So, if a client presents to Agency A which then allocates the client to you as one of their therapists, then I think you are duty bound to inform the Agency as your employer. It is they, the service provider, to whom the client presented rather than you as an individual.

The client with whom you work is not 'yours'. If indeed the client 'belongs' to anyone it is to the agency and not to you as their employee or agent. This principle applies whether that 'employment' is on a paid or voluntary basis. I make this point because I have seen too many cases of therapists tying themselves in knots trying to conceal the fact that one of 'their' clients has brought a complaint against them. The fiction of possession is misplaced and ultimately unhelpful.

It is a moot point, in such circumstances, whether the complaint should have been made against the Agency/Service Provider or the therapist. This will in some cases be determined by the nature of the professional body and the scope of its jurisdiction. However, the fact is that the client has the right to bring a complaint against you as an individual and your professional body has a right to accept it.

If you work as an individual practitioner on a self-employed or freelance basis then the above will not necessarily apply. You would, nonetheless, be well advised to consider carefully about whether or not to tell anyone who employs you as a therapist, that you have had a professional complaint taken out against you.

## Insurer

It is a standard expectation that professional therapists will be covered by Professional Indemnity Insurance. In Agency settings this will usually have been arranged by the Agency itself. In such circumstances you need to check the facts of your insured position with the Agency itself. In self-employed/freelance settings the obligation for insurance lies with the therapist. Whether or not your Insurance Policy provides cover for legal representation in cases of complaint, and many do not, it is wise to inform your insurer that you have had a complaint brought against you, and to do so pretty quickly. Whether the insurance cover extends to complaints or not, you may well benefit from the experience your insurer will have of such situations. It will be helpful for you to bear in mind that whilst the situation of being complained against is unique to you, it will not be to them and you may have much to gain from taking advantage of their professional experience.

## Lawyers

It may be that you wish to engage the services of a solicitor, which you have the right to do. The question is whether doing so is necessary or sensible. The following comments may help you in making an informed choice on this question.

Without trying to dissuade you, lawyers do tend to be expensive, and from experience are not always necessarily the best placed to assist you if you have a complaint brought against you under the complaints or professional conduct procedures of a professional body of which you are a member.

If you are thinking of engaging a lawyer then probably the optimum time is at the time of receiving the complaint when they can assist you in drawing up your formal response to the complaint. All too often therapists who do decide to engage a lawyer do so too late in the complaints proceedings. Under most reputable complaints or professional conduct procedures notice will be given of the time frame within which you may or must lodge your response to the client complaint.

Solicitors can be helpful in formulating such responses and ensuring that they contain evidence and material relevant to the case and the procedure. It is equally the case that therapists themselves can carry out this task effectively without legal assistance. Again your particular circumstances will have a bearing on the decision you make.

A word of warning and advice here about what I would term jurisdiction. A common response, particularly in lawyer assisted cases, is to challenge the right of the professional body to conduct the proceedings at all. This often extends to challenging the way in which the proceedings are conducted. Such challenges to jurisdiction, whilst understandable, do need to be undertaken with caution as they can rapidly lead you into wasting a great deal of time and a great deal of your money too! The right to hear complaints is usually part and parcel of the package you undertake to be bound by when you contract to join the professional body e.g. BACP or BPS. In joining, you contract to be bound by the rules and regulations of the professional body in question. Challenging the right of that body when you have already agreed to be bound by its rules is essentially a pointless activity. It can also be expensive in terms of cost, time and delay.

This obviously does not apply in the case of the body that does not have tried and tested and properly thought through measures and procedures for public protection, that are binding on its members. These points are quite different from any challenge, legal or otherwise, made when the laid down procedures for handling and hearing complaints are not followed by the professional body hearing the complaint.

## Legal helplines

These often come as part of an insurance or membership package. In general they are of limited value, and in some cases downright unhelpful, in the particular circumstances of a complaint brought against a therapist via their professional body or membership association.

The staff of such helplines are usually well versed in matters of general law. This does not necessarily extend to matters concerned with general or membership regulations within particular professions. It is at this point that therapists have found them singularly unhelpful in terms of the unique circumstances of their case. They should therefore be used with caution.

## Friend(s)

There is much to be said for securing the services of a tried and trusted friend, and ideally one who is not a member of the profession. They can bring a degree of objectivity to the situation that can be helpful. They can also afford you a degree of personal support. By being outside the profession they can often see things from a lay perspective, as it were, free from jargon, interpretation in the therapy sense, and pathologisation. They can also often more readily see and respond to you as a human being rather than as a professional practitioner whose actions whilst in that professional role have become the subject of challenge through a formal complaint or professional conduct procedure.

Many therapists get hung up on the question of confidentiality which they see as prohibiting them from discussing any aspect of their work outside the formal therapeutic setting, such as the counselling supervisory relationship. It may be useful to remember that there is a difference between disclosing the content of the work done in therapy with the client and in sharing, with a trusted friend, your experience of being the subject of a complaint and its impact upon you as a person, the person they know. It would be usual and only to be expected that any discussions between you about the experience would be on an 'in confidence' basis. This can and ought to be made explicit from the outset. What you need to consider is whether you would benefit and draw comfort from the support and succour that a trusted friend, who is independent of the work and its associations, can afford you as a human being.

## Colleague(s)

Trusted colleagues can be a great source of comfort and advice. They will be more likely to understand the complexities of what can happen in a therapeutic relationship and also to understand the many layers at which that relationship will have been operating. They may also be able to see where misunderstandings and misconceptions may have occurred. They may of course judge both you and your actions along with the clients too. That is a risk you take in making any disclosure, but when it comes to the crunch many therapists feel especially vulnerable when disclosing to colleagues in these circumstances. The pros and cons need to be considered carefully and with a good degree of common sense.

Another risk, both in oneself and in conversation with colleagues is that of over-interpreting a client's behaviour. Whilst some or all of your interpretation may be true it does not always follow that it will be helpful to you. It can take your eye off the main tasks of focusing on facts and the professional actions complained about. You will be better employed in addressing relevant factual matters and actions than confusing your arguments by loading or overloading them with opinion.

## Advocacy services

It is not uncommon for a therapist who is complained against to lose the ability to articulate or express their thoughts or present their view of events and the facts that surround them. If this is the case, and if you do not have or wish to use friends or colleagues, then an Advocacy Service may be able to help you. Likewise if you do not wish to use or cannot afford to use a lawyer then you could usefully consider looking into the business of using an advocate. Advocates in this non-legal sense are individuals trained for and skilled in assisting individuals to articulate their case or position. They can assist an individual by verifying with them that they are expressing what they want to express and in the way they wish to. In this way their task is to facilitate an individual's ability to express themselves rather than to act on their behalf in the way a representative would. The availability of advocacy services varies across the U.K. Details can usually be found within or via the local Citizens Advice Bureau, via your local library or via the internet. Thus if you think you would benefit from the services of an independent skilled advocate to help you express your case, then you would be well advised to research this option. The function could of course be undertaken by a friend or colleague as part of their overall support function, but there might just be an occasion when a trained independent person would be what you would prefer.

## Professional support networks

Some professions and professional bodies have networks of individuals whose task it is to lend support to a fellow member who is the subject of a professional complaint. This is not necessarily a self-help group of people who have previously been complained against. The 'support persons' in such schemes will have a knowledge and understanding of the complaints or professional conduct procedure under which the complaint is to be heard and how it operates. Whilst 'support persons' may not represent the therapist complained against they can provide fairly informal support and guidance. Whilst usually in the same geographical region it does not follow that the two have to meet. For many therapists complained against the knowledge that they can have appointed to them a colleague experienced in the operational and emotional aspects of complaints procedures, and to whom they can talk freely or to whom they can write, is in itself enabling enough. Such a scheme also helps lessen the sense of isolation that therapists in these circumstances can feel. It can also help therapists handle their often ambivalent or angry feelings towards their professional body for accepting a complaint against them.

Although relatively novel in the U.K., at least in any formal sense, in this sector the model has worked successfully for many years in New Zealand. Similar schemes have been introduced in the U.K., e.g. by BACP.

## Therapy

Given all the above, the time a complaint is brought against you is a time to give very serious consideration to increasing the frequency of the therapy you are currently in, or to re-entering therapy. The strong and often uncomfortable emotions aroused may reactivate past experience for you or simply prove too difficult to handle. Whilst the object of the therapy will primarily be to help you to explore those issues and to deepen your understanding of yourself, the therapy can also help you manage yourself during the complaint and help you keep useful internal and professional boundaries intact.

## Complaints officers

Most organisations or at least those with reputable complaints and professional conduct procedures, will have staff dedicated to the administration of the procedures. At the very least there will be voluntary officers dedicated to the task. Consultation with those officers can often be extremely helpful. They can advise and guide you through the procedures and help you avoid pitfalls and unnecessary activity. Remember though that they are equally responsible for advising the complainant through the same procedures, and by virtue of their position, they are obliged to be impartial. It is worth trying always to bear in mind that they are in effect the impartial messengers within the process. It is not they who have devised the complaint process nor they who will have made the decision to accept the compliant against you.

You would not be the first person to find the impartiality and role of such officers difficult to take at times. It is a common misconception that because your professional body employs staff to handle complaints, those staff should favour the member against whom the complaint is made rather than the clients who bring complaints. The critical issue here is that the professional body is precisely that and not a Trades Union that exists to promote and protect your rights. On public protection grounds alone, and those are the chief grounds for having complaints procedures, this cannot be so. It certainly is not the case in those professional bodies such as BPS that undertake to bring the complaint themselves against their own member.

Any actual or proven bias or favour to one party in a complaint, irrespective of which party, would compromise the whole proceedings and then be to the ultimate benefit of neither. Such behaviour would also lay the management of a case by the professional body open to challenge, and quite properly so. The adherence of complaints officers to the strict observance of impartiality is therefore ultimately in the best interests of both parties in a complaint. It also contributes to the more efficient and timely management of the whole process of a complaint from beginning to end.

## Administration

Besides the human contact mentioned above there are a number of practical administrative actions that you are strongly recommended to take, as they will assist you during the process of the complaint.

### Diary/Logbook

From the outset you would be well advised to keep a daily diary or logbook in which you record every action relative to the complaint: every letter received, written and sent; all telephone calls with a note of their content; conversations with key advisors; action taken etc. You should also date and time every occurrence. Most people find it best to keep this as a factual record. Process recording is usually best kept separate, but you will need to weigh up what is most suited to you.

### Process recording

One way of handling the emotional as opposed to the factual side of events can be by keeping a process record in which you record the passage and development of your emotions and emotional responses during the proceedings. This can obviously be cathartic but it can again assist in keeping a clear head when it comes to the procedural matters and processes you will inevitably have to face.

### Chronology

One of the first and most useful tasks you can undertake is to create a comprehensive and accurate chronological record of events. This should begin with the first ever contact made between the client and yourself. This may mean gathering materials to hand, and recalling past events. It may also involve researching case notes and supervision notes, correspondence etc.

The record should be in date order and should include every significant event in the progress of the relationship from that first contact: dates of sessions; contact between sessions (when, how and whether with or without previous agreement); missed or cancelled sessions; late arrivals; correspondence e.g. cards or letters sent by either of you between sessions; details of gifts e.g. what and when and how they were given and received, Also, whether they were given in person or left on the doorstep etc.; gifts and offers of business services e.g. building and repair work; car maintenance; loans of money etc.; offers of personal services or sexual favours; expressions of concern about whether the client was or was not finding the therapy helpful or difficult; referrals etc. In other words any fact or incident that may be relevant to the matter under complaint.

Having such a date ordered record to hand could indeed prove very useful to you, when it comes to keeping a cool head and answering questions or preparing your own submissions as part of a complaints procedure.

## Case notes

Get your case notes in order. This is critical. If they are not up to date you are advised to do so quickly. When you are updating or writing case notes, after the formal complaint has been served on you, you must be sure to try and be as objective as possible so that the fact a complaint has been received does not contaminate the objectivity of the notes.

Obviously, reasons of confidentiality will preclude the use of case notes in proceedings but you will be able to consult and précis the work you were doing and your intentionality in that work. Case notes are essentially confidential. However, in order to assist you in the matter of receiving a fair hearing, you are entitled to use extracts from those notes, if necessary, in order to defend yourself. Extracts from those notes must be relevant and pertinent to the point at issue; any use of those notes that are not so, may be considered by a panel, and indeed the client, to be a breach of confidentiality.

These actions and preparations will help you in terms of accountability e.g. why, when or indeed whether, you took, or encouraged the client toward, a particular course of action. Naturally this will be easier if your case notes are up to date and can therefore serve as a point of reference for you. Such action can also be affirming in terms of your sense of professional self, your actions and your professional competence.

## Evidence

Gather and tabulate any evidence that you consider may be relevant for submission to those appointed to hear the complaint. This could include post cards, letters, cards, greetings cards, gifts etc. Likewise details and corroboration of any meetings outside the therapy room be they pre-arranged or chance encounters. Also relevant to have may be referrals: to whom, why, when, and whether with or without the client's informed consent, and copies of relevant correspondence.

## References/testimonials

It is not uncommon for a practitioner to put an enormous amount of time and effort into amassing a portfolio of references and testimonials from friends, family, colleagues, supervisors, trainers, personal therapists, employers etc., and indeed current and former clients.

Whilst these statements, and the act of acquiring them, may bring solace and indeed be therapeutic for the practitioner, they are very often of little or no relevance to the matter that forms the substance of the complaint or to the complaints proceedings. This may seem harsh but what actually matters is evidence that relates to the allegations raised by the complainant, i.e. your current or ex-client, that you breached professional practice and ethical standards by doing 'x' on occasion 'y'.

The panel appointed to hear the complaint will be responsible for assessing, on the evidence presented, whether you did in fact do 'x' on occasion 'y'. The panel members will be assessing evidence and professional competence and actions in particular circumstances. Their task is not to assess whether you are a nice, good or well intentioned person. Nor is their task necessarily to assess whether you are well-trained or not. Your training will be relevant only insofar as it can provide evidence of your competence to practice the type of work done with the client who has complained.

So, it is not volume but relevance that matters. There is nothing wrong in amassing lots of supportive data and character references. They, and the act of collecting them, can indeed be very supportive and affirming. In this way they can serve a purpose, and an important one, but what is helpful to you may nonetheless not be relevant material for presentation to the panel appointed to hear your case and the allegations made against you.

What is more, being, as it were, in the thick of it, you will not always find it easy to decide what is the best thing to include or submit. Thus, the general advice is to reflect and think carefully how relevant each piece of information may be in terms of the allegations lodged against you.

## Deadlines

It is important that deadlines set by a complaints procedure be adhered to, and by both parties. Bureaucratic and unfeeling as this may seem, reputable complaints procedures are geared to a principle of equality in that both parties are granted the same time period and deadlines in which to make responses and submissions. Thus to favour one party would be unfair to the other. Exceptions can, of course, usually be made in exceptional and justifiable circumstances e.g. if you were and can prove you were out of the country when the notice of complaint was first served or if you were, for example, in hospital or recovering from surgery at a critical time. Such facts need to be laid before the appropriate official of the professional body responsible for handling the complaint and will be handled according to the provisions of the complaints or professional conduct procedure.

## Complaints hearings

These vary in conduct and format according to the professional body that hears them. Some are conducted in private, some in public. You will have been informed in advance how proceedings are to be conducted. If you have not, then you ought to be, as you have a right to know how the meeting is to be conducted. You will, by the time the Hearing arrives, have made your personal choice about whether you wish to attend alone, or be accompanied by a friend, colleague or advocate, or represented by a lawyer.

As a general rule, professional bodies have and exercise the right to speak directly to their members. So, even if you are represented by a colleague, friend or lawyer, you will need to be prepared to answer questions directly and so account for your actions to your professional colleagues and any other panel members. Remember, if you are not sure on this part do check before the Hearing.

Complaints Hearings are usually formal proceedings so quality of presentation is important. You will have already submitted responses and evidence and any other material you have considered relevant. What is crucial is to listen carefully and to answer as factually as you can. You must check beforehand whether you will be able to ask questions of the complainant. If so, then have those questions ready and written out so you don't forget them. Likewise on the matter of supplementary questions. If they are allowed, then the key is again to write them down so that in the tensions of the moment you do not lose or forget them. In these ways you ought to be able to maximise the opportunities made available to you to put and clarify your case.

## Conclusion

Although it invariably does not seem or feel so, a formal complaint is not in fact calling your whole career and all your actions as a therapist into account. Nor is it the same in respect of you as a person. The reality is, of course, that it feels as if both ones' private and professional personae are being called into account.

As I have indicated earlier, a common response for a therapist who is the subject of a complaint is to enter into explanation and justification of their whole career and even their life. What in fact matters is to keep the focus on the allegation, by the client bringing the complaint, that you did 'x' on occasion 'y'.

Task focus and concentration on the precise allegations, and accounting for whatever actions you did or did not take, will help make the situation more manageable for you. It will not necessarily make it less unpleasant but it will focus your concentration and energies and thus help avoid, or at least minimise, the dangers of falling into the impotent victim position.

These notes are intended to help in a practical way. They cannot take away or alter the fact that being the subject of a professional complaint is horrible, nor do they seek to. The hope is that the points raised will help you function better and feel a little less impotent in a situation you would prefer not to be in.

# Chapter 4

# Surviving Organisational Complaints as a Counsellor Trainer

## Peter Jenkins

Any agreement to write a chapter or article is always a hostage to fortune, and this one more strongly so than most! The sense of hubris, or pride coming before a fall, is writ especially large in the title of this piece. It reads rather like an invitation to fate to send more organisational complaints my way, which is very far from being my intention. However my professional experience of working as a counsellor trainer over the last 15 years suggests that this activity runs a high occupational risk of incurring complaints, justified or not. It might be useful, therefore, to share some of my experiences with others in the same position. I intend to cover in this chapter some of the background to organisational complaints. I will then explore some of the processes involved in undergoing complaints, and finally, conclude with some strategies for survival and growth.

## Background to organisational complaints

My starting point is to spell out the differences between different types of complaint against counselling course providers. Complaints about a counselling course can be made to a professional association, such as British Association for Counselling and Psychotherapy (BACP), or United Kingdom Council for Psychotherapy (UKCP), for breaches of the relevant Codes of Ethics and Practice. Training issues are the source of roughly one third of complaints made to professional associations, according to Fiona Palmer Barnes (1998: 26). Secondly, complaints may take the form of legal action against a counselling training provider. This may be for breach of contract, where an organisation perhaps fails to provide agreed training services to a company purchasing its services. It may also be for breach of duty under legislation dealing with discrimination on grounds of race, sex or disability. Legal action will be directed here against the employing organisation rather than the individual counselling trainer, under the principle of vicarious liability. Taking legal action may, in fact, preclude making a professional complaint, under some complaints procedures. The third form of action is that of making an organisational complaint concerning counselling training. This may apply to a college, university or privately owned company. The complaint, concerning staff, course procedures or the actual quality of training provision, will be heard within whatever complaints systems are operated by the organisation itself.

My own experience has been in terms of responding to complaints within either a college or university setting, rather than in the context of working for commercial companies. One of the immediate problems is that counselling training sits very uneasily within an academic framework, precisely because of the almost unique way it focuses on aspects of the students' knowledge, behaviour and emotional development. Educational institutions are more than content with the vastly increased numbers of students applying to undergo the different levels of counselling training, as, no doubt, are commercial training organisations. However, an academic focus on mainly cognitive skills, such as research, and writing assignments, is not easy to mesh with the wider task of enabling students to develop subtle interpersonal skills, and even less with the process of facilitating personal development. The academic and counselling cultures do overlap, but they co-exist with a marked degree of tension in their relationship (Berry and Woolfe, 1997).

The problems of learning and assessment are not necessarily resolved by using the more behaviourally based methods associated with a college setting. The shift towards competency based assessment and NVQs/SVQs may be a useful step in forging closer links between training and employment or practice. However, the issue of assessment and self-assessment still remains problematic where personal development is concerned. A student may be 'competent' in some skills, but remain unfit to practice, because of the perceived impact of a recent major bereavement, for example. The more holistic models of assessment associated with counselling training may be hard to calibrate with the somewhat narrower focus of these behavioural or competency approaches.

In addition, the context in which complaints systems operate has undergone a major change in the last decade. In the consumer-led culture of the marketplace for training, organisations are rightly meant to be responsive to student feedback, and are increasingly accountable to external audit. This is linked to funding resources, and ultimately, to market placing and even to organisational survival. Charters emphasise the rights of students as consumers of education. Training organisations are highly sensitive to adverse media coverage, particularly around issues of discrimination, at a time when competition for student numbers is increasing. The shift to greater inclusion of previously marginalised student groups is a national policy measure. University counselling services, for example, have raised concerns about the numbers of students being seen with major mental health needs, but without any corresponding increase in resources geared to meeting these specific needs appropriately (Rana et al., 1999). At worst, the situation can arise where counselling courses are increasingly performance driven, but are under-resourced for largely financial reasons. Furthermore, they are required to operate according to assessment and personal development models, which fit rather uneasily with the overall bureaucratic ethos of the employing organisation. The inevitably arising tensions and complaints may then be evaluated by systems, which are not overly sensitive to the particular professional and ethical concerns of counselling training.

A further factor is that the support systems available for staff undergoing complaint may have also been undermined over the past few years. Morale amongst teaching staff, particularly in Further Education, is widely known to be low. The trades unions in Further Education and Higher Education have retreated from their previous position of being able to resist adverse changes to contracts and conditions of service. Calling upon the support of professional associations such as BACP in disputes over resource and teaching levels for courses wins few arguments with senior management, given that there are usually no immediate funding implications involved. As a result, it becomes even more vital that counsellor trainers operate within a strong community of peer support, both within and outside the institution. This support can play a crucial role in enabling counsellor trainers to survive and continue to work effectively when subject to organisational complaints.

## Process of undergoing complaints

It is important, first of all, to make a necessary distinction between different types of complaints about counsellor training. Obviously, there are bad, incompetent and even abusive counsellor trainers, and this chapter is not designed to shelter or protect them from the trainee or student's right to make a complaint against them. I own that I have made mistakes as a counsellor trainer, but this is distinct from any admission that I have actually *damaged* students by act or omission. Fiona Palmer Barnes makes a useful distinction between four categories of behaviour potentially giving rise to complaint (1998: 47–51)

- *mistakes*, e.g. giving assessment results for an assignment to the wrong student;
- *poor practice*, e.g. lengthy delays in returning assignment grades;
- *negligence*, e.g. permitting students to practise in unsafe placement settings;
- *malpractice*, e.g. trainer behaviour that is 'knowingly wrong', for example having a sexual relationship with a student currently on the trainer's counselling course.

The first three categories above are all examples of legitimate areas for dissatisfaction, which need to be addressed and resolved via negotiation and prompt action, without necessarily leading to a formal complaint. The fourth is clearly material either for an organisational complaint, a complaint to a professional association such as BACP, or in certain circumstances, legal action. In a sense, these examples could be described as *'substantive' complaints*, in that they depend ultimately on external evidence for their being decided one way or another. Either a letter was sent, an assignment was lost, a supervisor selected, or not. My main focus is not the area of substantive complaints such as the above, but what I would best describe as *'non-substantive' complaints*. This is not meant to imply in any way that these complaints are insubstantial. Rather, this is where the crucial, defining feature of the complaint is the student's perception of a trainer's behaviour as being unacceptable. This may be the case even though the behaviour in question is nevertheless fully accountable and justifiable within the particular ethos of counsellor training. Non-substantive complaints turn almost entirely on perception, interpretation, and attribution of meaning, rather than on actual hard evidence. Clearly, life, not to mention counsellor training, rests on a continuous process of interaction between objective reality and subjective experiencing. What is at issue with non-substantive complaints is that the shared experience of a specific incident, such as a tutorial, a written comment, or a conversation, cannot be given an agreed, common meaning by its participants. From this fundamental conflict of meaning, non-substantive complaints derive their key feature — their somewhat surreal experiential quality, where no communication, however innocent, is ever perceived as intended.

This is clearly a fine line of argument to tread. What I have in mind here is a situation where the counsellor trainer offers a challenge to a student about some aspect of their behaviour or experience. This may be, for example, where a student is expressing views, which are potentially open to being perceived as racially abusive, or where the student's insensitivity to another student is raised within group or individual feedback. Offering challenge and feedback is an essential aspect of the student's personal and professional development within the counselling training on offer. However, it may be adversely experienced as being aggressive, destructive, intimidating or even annihilating according to the student's personality and mind-set. Non-substantive complaints essentially depend upon the complainant challenging a socially agreed construction of the situation. By this, I mean a consensus that is substantially agreed as appropriate by other counselling students, tutors and participants such as supervisors. A non-substantive complaint is based on the student's individual perception of the trainer's behaviour as being unacceptable, even though the trainer's behaviour can be justified with reference to the specific context (a counselling skills session, for example) and with reference to wider norms of appropriate professional practice and ethics.

This is parallel, in some ways to the idea of the *Bolam* test applied to allegedly negligent cases of counselling and psychotherapy in court proceedings. Under this approach, the crucial test is whether the counsellor in question has failed to act 'in accordance with a practice of competent respected professional opinion'. By extension, the test for deciding a non-substantive complaint would be via appeal to peer professional opinion regarding the appropriateness or otherwise of adopting a particular training technique. This is tricky territory, to say the least, perhaps best illustrated with a case example.

> *Jackie was an adult survivor of childhood sexual abuse, which had left her with a heightened sensitivity to others' emotional pain, but also prone to outbursts of rage in therapeutically inappropriate situations. On being offered feedback to this effect, in both individual and small-group skills practice situations, she felt she was being verbally attacked in a brutal manner by the tutors. It seemed to her that she was being forced to leave the counselling work upon which her newly reconstructed self-esteem now depended. She charged the tutors with discrimination against mental health system survivors such as herself, and made a complaint to this effect to the university authorities.*

The issues at stake here need separating out. The tutors may be prejudiced against students with a history of mental health problems in ways that cannot be justified.

However, the tutors may also be acting entirely appropriately to protect the student from further distress, and to protect potentially vulnerable clients. It could be argued that the trainee in this situation has major, unresolved emotional issues, which may directly affect their capacity to work competently and ethically. These are matters of degree, but also, in the end, matters of professional judgement. This aspect of professional judgement does not sit at all comfortably with complaints procedures which rely primarily on clear breaches of academic regulations, or of disciplinary procedure, in order to take proper effect.

## Group dynamics

A further complicating factor can be the response of the counselling student group to the complaint, to the personal material which it represents. Depending upon the maturity of the group and its group dynamics, it will often be the case that at least a section of the student group moves in quickly to 'rescue' the complainant as 'victim'. The resulting split in the group, expressed in terms of hostility and anger towards the tutors, further complicates any attempt to reach some kind of resolution of the problem. The course members then engage in an all-enveloping version of group experience aptly described as 'Uproar', using a perspective drawn from Transactional Analysis.

This situation presents a real dilemma for counsellor trainers, in my experience. Where the entire student group is convinced that the student concerned is acting in inappropriate ways, and even needs to leave the course, then the views of the course members may offer some supporting evidence for the correctness of the tutors' stance. Where the group is manifestly split, then the tutors are often unable to act, despite their misgivings. This difficult situation may need to be somehow held and contained, until there is a wider plurality of views within the group. This may then offer at least a minimal degree of support for the tutors' stated concerns.

When a situation arises where the trainer can perceive inappropriate student behaviour or attitudes at an early stage, there is often a period of professional isolation, waiting for others, students or fellow trainers, to come to share these views. This is almost the price the trainer has to pay for having, presumably, highly developed powers of observation, and an acute awareness of the significance of non-verbal communication.

Inappropriate trainee attitudes can be conveyed through non-verbal means, for example through intimidating use of body language or eye contact. Alternatively a student may constantly interrupt others or dominate a group through persistent self-disclosure unrelated to the task in hand.

Trainers may become vulnerable to non-substantive complaints through their role in attempting to model counsellor qualities. Self-disclosing one's own weaknesses, mistakes, vulnerability or problematic attitudes, for example towards issues of sexuality, are normally received by a student group in the context of modelling the quality of congruence. However, for a student who is profoundly at odds with the ethos of counselling training, this material merely provides yet more evidence of the trainer's unfitness and incompetence, and provides supporting material for their intended complaint. The first casualty of this process is any developing notion of trust within the group. All members, including tutors tend to become increasingly engaged in defensive communication about behaviours and experiences, rather than about feelings and emotions.

In dealing with non-substantive complaints, the counsellor trainer in a sense, is hoist by their own petard. It is precisely the presumed qualities of heightened awareness, skills of interpersonal communication and sensitivity to meaning and nuance that equip him or her to become a trainer in the first place. When a student rejects the meaning of any joint communication, so that skills feedback is experienced as being malicious and humiliating to them, the trainer may really begin to question their own grasp of reality, at least initially. My own experience has been to be assailed by self-doubt, confusion and anxiety, leading to anger and blame. It is vital to check out your own perceptions of contested situations with other colleagues. In a group situation where there is a co-worker, this can be done fairly quickly as part of the constant debriefing which is part and parcel of counsellor trainer support and exchange. Where the contested situation has been a one-to-one tutorial, checking out the gap between intended and perceived meaning of a conversation with a student is much more difficult. It can also be the case that the originally agreed meaning of an event changes drastically over time, through a process of radical reinterpretation. The tutorial initially presented and experienced as being supportive is now seen by a student solely as being manipulative, bullying or abusive in intent or outcome.

The lack of a shared, mutually agreed meaning to events is a key aspect of non-substantive complaints. This is well beyond the differences in interpretation or understanding, which are part of normal everyday communication and mis-communication. A crucial component here is that the student's sole reference point becomes his or her own perception of reality, which cannot be contradicted.

## Understanding the process

It is very useful, therefore, for trainers to know something about abnormal group dynamics and about psycho-pathology, or to have ways of accessing such knowledge. The whole ethos of counsellor trainer is to question the labelling of individuals as being mentally ill, and to challenge the validity of psychiatric diagnosis, where it is applied in a mechanistic or insensitive manner. My own experience is that it can be extremely useful to develop a cognitive understanding of otherwise bizarre processes when being made the subject of a non-substantive complaint. Concepts such as borderline personality disorder, narcissism and projective identification begin to take on a different meaning when you experience unfamiliar feelings which have no identifiable origin within your own established emotional world. Without necessarily falling into the trap of seeking easy refuge in psychiatric labels, it can be enormously reassuring to learn that key aspects of your own rather weird interactions with a student are entirely explicable within certain psychiatric categories, such as that of personality disorder. The concepts of transference and counter-transference may still be relatively controversial outside psycho-dynamic circles, but may have a real value in explaining the peculiar emotional intensity of being the subject of a non-substantive complaint. My own experience is of waking up in the middle of the night, convinced I could smell smoke and that the house was on fire. I couldn't, and it wasn't, at least in material terms, but the sense of actual threat from a student complainant was absolutely real enough. What distinguishes this experience from other sorts of complaint is the feeling that the student has 'got right under your skin', and 'knows how to press all your buttons' with unerring accuracy. The result is a kind of crazily charged emotional dialogue, in which other participants can easily seem like remote and uninvolved bystanders. The only people who really seem to understand the process are those directly involved in the struggle to construct a valid, shared meaning to real-life events on the course.

At its most severe, the process of experiencing a non-substantive complaint seems akin to that of being the object of psychological 'stalking' in its intensity. The process of this has been well described by Robert Fine, a university sociology lecturer, in his book 'Being Stalked'. The student concerned attributed a sexual meaning to most forms of communication between herself and Fine, however impersonal. She eventually faxed 27 pages of complaint to the university about his alleged behaviour, and later claimed that the investigation was biased when he was cleared of unprofessional conduct. In common with my own experiences of non-substantive complaint, Fine observes that 'Mrs. M. attributed to my actions as a teacher an excess of meaning which always centred on herself' (1997: 21). The book makes some useful points about university being an unsafe place for a student with a fragile sense of self, and a weak sense of boundaries. This can arise from the very informality of communication styles, such as the frequent use of lecturer's first names, and the whole process of engaging in challenging discussion about academic topics. This lack of security is even sharper in the world of counselling training, where a spirit of constructive challenge and the opening up of personal material for exploration within a safe setting is a necessary part of the overall training process.

Some of the early warning signs of a non-substantive complaint by a student might include:
- inappropriate taping of teaching sessions, or suspicion of covert taping;
- displays of anguish, rage, distress or other emotions which seem somehow disproportionate to an experience or situation in the classroom;
- similarly extreme adverse responses to groupwork, feedback, personal challenge;
- overt and indirect challenges to your professional qualifications, management style, suitability for running courses of this kind;
- indications that the student is determined to gain personal satisfaction for slights endured;
- your own experiencing of a pervasive sense of personal threat, or acute sense of persecution.

The actual process of making a complaint takes the inner world of counselling training into the harsh spotlight of organisational procedures. In many cases, educational institutions have a real fear of potential litigation by students. It may seek to settle the complaint quickly, possibly at the expense of the integrity of the counselling course or its trainers. The complaint is often compounded by the presence of real features, which appear to provide legitimation for the complainant, in that the latter will seek to raise issues of discrimination and denial of their rights. The student's heightened sense of entitlement to special treatment may well be related to their actual status in terms of disability, ethnic origin or sexual orientation, which can lend apparent strength to their case. However, if there is no concrete evidence of discriminatory treatment as such, then the complaint will hinge on the 'attribution of meaning' to interaction with staff and other course members. The whole process of hearing the complaint is stymied from the beginning where there is no substantive evidence for the student's charge of harassment or unfair treatment. It may all depend on attributing meaning to a sequence of exchanges in a groupwork session, or to a challenge in a personal development group. In any case, the nature of the complaint forces the trainer into a somewhat defensive stance, in having to justify the purpose and meaning of their communications to an often sceptical senior management.

## Management responses

Management responses to non-substantive complaints can take a number of forms:
- *collusion* with the complainant: accepting the student's version of events without full investigation or proper consideration of the professional issues involved;
- *capitulation:* conceding to the demands of the student e.g. for a written apology by the trainer, taking disciplinary action against staff concerned;
- *coercion* of staff to refrain from certain forms of challenge or feedback activities on the course, to reassess contested assignments;
- *compromise:* accepting the substance of part of a complaint, while rejecting those aspects which cannot be proven either way;
- *counter-attack:* resistance to any veiled or open threat of legal action or adverse media coverage, rejection of student demands for refund of fees or financial compensation.

The response of management to organisational complaints against counselling courses will depend upon a number of factors. This could include the frequency and severity of such complaints, perceptions of the relative value of the counselling course provision within the overall training provision of the institution, and the degree of recognition and support for the special characteristics of professional training of this type. Courses which are seen to be successful, and compliant with established procedures of audit and quality assurance, may well win a more sympathetic response form senior managers than those which are seen to be maverick outfits, continually at odds with the rest of the organisation as a whole.

## Strategies for coping with organisational complaints

Given all of this, how can counsellor trainers try to survive, and even flourish, given the near-inevitability of non-substantive organisational complaints?

The need for a strong system of mutual support is absolutely crucial. If your own sense of belief in your own perceptions is seriously challenged, this needs to be checked out, and reaffirmed through support and discussion with your colleagues. As a rather late convert to the value of supervision of counsellor trainers, I now see this as a very useful adjunct to my work as a trainer. It helps me to see different perceptions of the same incident on a course, and to gain challenge, support and feedback from others. External consultancy for courses with a history of serious complaints may also be worth considering, although the issue of resourcing this as a non-teaching activity may require some creative accounting. Personal therapy for those subject to a non-substantive complaint can also be extremely useful.

It is vital to begin documenting your experience of a non-substantive complaint from the very earliest stage. Your intuition of trouble to come will usually be accurate. Often the first indications of future problematic behaviour or mis-attribution of meaning will occur on the opening residential, if you have one. Early warning signs or misgivings by colleagues should be fully discussed at team meetings. The whole process of documenting each contact with a student may well be tedious. However, the detail is often necessary to rebut allegations made at a later stage, when your memory of actual conversations, or the sequence of events, has become less clear with the passing of time. Recording your various contacts with the complainant should be factual, non-judgmental and accountable, in line both with the organisation's policy and with wider data protection requirements. The use of e-mail communication provides a readily accessible record of communication with the student, other tutors and management, but this facility does come at a price. It is quite possible for politically sensitive internal documents to become attached inadvertently to e-mail communication being sent to the student concerned. A good rule of thumb is, therefore, to avoid committing to paper or computer any comments, which you might have difficulty in justifying to others at a later date.

## Complaints systems

Within training or educational organisations, complaints systems will take the form of formal bureaucratic procedures. It is worth checking out carefully whether the student's complaint is actually a formal one, or simply a set of informal grievances. There is arguably a greater degree of protection for your own interests as a member of staff under formal complaints procedures. One stance may well be to decline to co-operate with any investigation, which does not invoke the organisation's complaints procedures on a formal basis. Under this system, an initial investigation may be followed up by a more formal hearing, with both sides able to present their case according to principles of natural justice. There will also be provision for representatives and support, who may be advocates or trade unionists, rather than lawyers. A crucial part in deciding the case will rest on course documentation. It is vital that the course is clearly documented, that the often implicit assumptions of counsellor training are spelled out in detail, as it is against this information that cases will often be decided. The course needs to be able to demonstrate clear criteria for selection, assessment, feedback and progression from one stage of the course to another. Decisions need to have been clearly recorded, for example in minutes of relevant meetings, tutorials, etc., in order to show the internal coherence of the course management. While this will prove to be an effective defence in many cases, there is probably no set of course documents on the planet which can withstand the relentless unravelling inflicted by a determinedly litigious student.

An understanding of psycho-pathology and of group dynamics is important for making sense of your own responses to non-substantive complaints, and the ensuing group processes. Once the complaint is made to a higher authority, complex organisational dynamics can result. Because of underlying boundary problems, complaints of this nature tend to draw in more and more people in the organisation. They also tend to move rapidly up and then outside the hierarchy, eventually including local councillors, Members of Parliament, funding bodies, and human rights organisations, in a dizzying spiral. In some cases, I have experienced the unfavourable regard of higher management as a further form of persecution, as senior managers perhaps seek to settle old scores, or rein in the 'mavericks' from the counselling section. In fact, the old, familiar dynamic of the senior manager acting as 'rescuer, to the complaining student's 'victim' can change very quickly. The manager, in turn, can rapidly start to become persecuted by a ceaseless barrage of phone calls, faxes, e-mails etc., as they begin to experience at first hand some of the bizarre behaviour of the complainant.

Surviving an organisational complaint may involve an attempt to inform senior management in more detail about the mysterious processes, which go on within counsellor training. They may well be more sympathetic than initially assumed, especially when course processes are closely allied to accepted educational processes (e.g. assessment of competency) and are consistent with organisational procedures (e.g. use of structured feedback forms for written assignments, etc.). It is also important, if appealing to professional norms to justify particular styles of training, such as the use of large group feedback, that trainers can demonstrate that they are, in fact, up-to-date with the best current practice. Counsellor trainers need to avoid any hint of professional isolation, by constantly appraising their own practice, and using all available opportunities for continuing staff development, and the use of external consultancy.

Survival in organisations can require a healthy sense of organisational politics. There may be unexpected allies to be found amongst senior management, perhaps due in part to the record of counselling courses as generators of income. Where counselling courses are isolated and under threat, trainers need to develop their skills in waging guerilla politics inside a larger bureaucracy. Given the experiential nature of counsellor training, and the likelihood that this will prove overly challenging and discomfiting for a very small proportion of students, it is inevitable that complaints will be made about matters which are based on subjective interpretation, rather than on substantive, provable fact. Counsellor trainers need to build their own support systems for responding to this kind of non-substantive complaint. Hopefully, these thoughts will be of some use to others who have succeeded like me, in surviving organisational complaints — so far.

## References

Berry, M. and Woolfe, R. (1997). Teaching counselling in universities: match or mismatch? *British Journal of Guidance and Counselling,* 25(4): 517–25.

Fine, R. (1997). *Being stalked: A memoir.* London: Chatto and Windus

Palmer Barnes, F. (1998). *Complaints and Grievances in Psychotherapy: A handbook for ethical practice.* London: Routledge.

Rana, R., Smith, E. and Walkling, J. (1999). *Degrees of Disturbance: The new agenda: The impact of increasing levels of psychological disturbance amongst students in Higher Education.* London: Heads of University Counselling Services.

# Chapter 5

# Some Underlying Psychodynamics of Complaints

## Michael Jacobs

The French analyst Didier Anzieu recounts the story of a patient to whom he gives the pseudonym Epimenides. Due to an assault upon this patient at work, he was unable to attend his sessions, so he rang Anzieu; and Anzieu said that he would cancel sessions until Epimenides was able to return — he simply had to let Anzieu know when. Three weeks later Epimenides resumed his analysis and in the session seemed to blame himself for the assault upon him. At the end he gave Anzieu the fee for the session, which Anzieu did not realize at the time consisted of payment for the three missed sessions as well. Epimenides then blew up, saying it was scandalous that Anzieu had forced him to pay for the missed sessions. Anzieu reminded him that he had *cancelled* the sessions, that Epimenides did not owe anything for them, and he promptly returned the overpayment. But this was not enough — Epimenides was still very angry. If Anzieu had intended that cancellation did not mean having to pay, he said, he should have made this plain. But since he did not make it plain he obviously did not mean it. Anzieu was simply trying to back out when he complained, and was making the word cancel mean what he wanted it to mean. Anzieu tried to deal with the situation by making an interpretation about what was happening, that Epimenides was projecting, and that he was now taking out the assault on himself on the analyst. But Epimenides just left the room. Anzieu was left feeling resentful, thinking that he lacked any ability to understand his patient and that his patient would not come back. Given his own feelings of hostility and inferiority he did in fact wish that the patient would disappear. But Epimenides turned up regularly in subsequent sessions, because, he said, he knew that Anzieu would be happy to get rid of him!

Such an episode may ring bells with other therapists and counsellors, particularly the sense that whatever you do you cannot win. It is not that the client has been obviously difficult, but that some small situation gets blown out of proportion, and both therapist and client suffer. Complaints sometimes, of course, concern what turn out to be fairly clear examples of therapist abuse or incompetence. Others stem from what in other circumstances might be thought of as trivial incidents. What is going on beneath the surface? Assuming that there is not deliberate or serious therapist error, how does it come about that issues which in other therapeutic contacts are handled by both parties satisfactorily, disrupt the course of therapy, and often lead to both parties feeling aggrieved, sometimes even to formal complaints procedures? The complaints procedure may indeed find for the complainant, and require the therapist to take more care in the future. But have the dynamics really been resolved?

There is a term 'negative therapeutic reaction' which is used in psychoanalytic theory and may throw light on such unfortunate conclusions to the therapeutic relationship. It carries several meanings, the most common being the way in which no change occurs, and therapy seems to enter a position of stalemate, often with critical comments on the situation coming from the client, and frustration on the part of the therapist. Such an impasse need not in itself lead to the client making a complaint about the therapist to the appropriate professional body, although, as I shall show, it may be one of the precipitating factors that leads to therapist error, which in turn may lead to a complaint. But 'negative therapeutic reaction' also refers to situations where there appears to be the makings of a real conflict between client and therapist, which can of course again lead to therapist error, or to the client seeking some pretext for 'picking a fight'. In using such an emotive phrase I intend no blame: one of the difficulties of psychoanalytic terminology is that it sometimes appears to be doing so, wrong-footing the client more than the therapist. There are awkward clients just as there are stubborn therapists: but my concern is to look at some of the reactions in both parties which lead in negative directions, sympathetically recognising the fragility of some therapeutic relationships, making them liable to go wrong when both parties were hoping that they would go right.

Anzieu describes one facet of this type of situation, in which he draws upon the concept of the 'double-bind' and 'paradoxical communication', a useful starting point for the type of situation which this chapter reviews. In the example of Epimenides he demonstrates how such a situation in the therapeutic relationship tends to mirror a feature in the patient's own life — more particularly in their childhood, when they also felt that they could not win. This feature is paradoxical communication, such as a mother constantly telling her little boy: 'You are a monster — only a mummy can love you'. This leaves the child with the dilemma, either not be a monster but then not be loved, which is tantamount to being and getting nothing; or else, to be loved and for that to have to become a monster (Anzieu, 1986: 529). In the example of Epimenides it appears that he was re-enacting with Anzieu 'the paradoxical situation in which his father used to put him when he was an adolescent, exacting from him perfection in his studies, while at the same time denying him the material means and the moral trust to carry this through' (Anzieu, 1986: 522).

Anzieu gives his patient the pseudonym Epimenides for a reason. He is the protagonist in the first and perhaps most famous paradox formulated in antiquity by the Greek sophists: 'Epimenides, the Cretan, says that all Cretans are liars. But Epimenides is a Cretan. Thus he lies when he says that Cretans are liars. But if the Cretans are not liars, Epimenides is telling the truth. In which case it is true that the Cretans lie. But then . . .' and so on. It is the no-win situation that is described by Gregory Bateson as the double-bind. We have also known it since Heller's (1985) novel as a 'Catch 22'. The therapist is presented with the problem of how to get out of a situation, where everything he or she does or says is liable to be interpreted by the patient or client as fitting the negative picture that the client has of the therapist. The therapy replicates an earlier situation, where the client could never get it right; but this is not simply being repeated in the present as an act of revenge, albeit towards another person, but perhaps in an attempt to put things right. Yet in the attempt on the part of the therapist not to respond as significant others may have responded in the past, and in the attempt by the therapist to look at things differently, this can be experienced by the client as an attempt to undermine the client's (fragile) sense of 'rightness'. It is this that, not surprisingly, can lead to a complaint being made in the first instance in the therapy, a complaint that is felt by the therapist as being unfair, and to a persistence with the complaint despite continued attempts on the part of the therapist to set things right.

Anzieu describes how he handled the situation with Epimenides and others more effectively than his initial attempt to make an interpretation. It is important to take the guilt out of the situation, especially any guilt about aggression; that is, to do the opposite of the client's family of origin who were continually making the child feel guilty. Anzieu also wishes to reassure the individual about the origin of the aggressive reaction by stating a general observation that when a person is placed in a paradoxical situation, such aggression is not only a normal reaction, but also often a necessary and vital means of protecting one's integrity. He also believes that changes need to be introduced into the setting. He gives the examples of moving to a face-to-face situation (and to appreciate the significance of this remember that Anzieu is a psychoanalyst), of using interventions to convey the therapist's personal experience, and of making re-arrangements as necessary to fees or schedules in order to ameliorate the persecutory feelings in the client. Anzieu does all he can reasonably do to remove the cause for complaint, rather than getting stuck in a battle of wills (see also the chapter by Hill in this volume). Taking such initiatives makes a lot of sense, because when a situation gets into a double-bind it could also be said to be knotted; and it is the therapist or counsellor who needs to cut through the knot, often by approaching the issue from a very different angle, such as a change in the usual response or technique. Some therapists (of whatever orientation) find this hard to do, caught as they are in the binding nature of their own training.

This example illustrates a number of features of the situation where a therapist or counsellor has a complaint made against them where it appears impossible to resolve it without the client wanting to extract some 'blood'. But if the double bind is one explanation of the dynamics of such situations, even more common is the basic ambivalence which is built into every therapeutic encounter. The pointer to this aspect of the negative therapeutic reaction is an observation by Freud shortly after he had identified what he called the super-ego (1923). 'There are certain people who behave in a quite peculiar fashion during the work of analysis. When one speaks hopefully to them or expresses satisfaction with the progress of the treatment, they show signs of discontent and their condition invariably worsens' (1923: 390). In this and later writings Freud suggests a number of explanations, such as an attempt to prove their superiority to the therapist, unconscious feelings of guilt, the need for self-punishment, masochism, that symptoms keep at bay the conscious awareness of the harsh criticism of the super-ego, and that change risks exposure to guilt feelings becoming conscious.

Freudian language such as this is not immediately attractive, although the suggestion that different parts of the person are in conflict as therapy progresses may be a valuable one. We do not have to accept all his explanations (such as masochism) to be able to appreciate that what he is suggesting is that in one way or another there is a potential conflict between different aspects of a person, which is not only a reason for seeking help, but which might continue to exert different forces within therapy as well. The obvious reason for wanting therapy is because there is some kind of unhappiness or discomfort, and people have positive reasons to continue in it: the alleviation of symptoms of one kind or another, personal development and growth, self-exploration, etc. But there are other feelings about change, self-knowledge etc. which might stand in the way of the stated aims, and lead to an ambivalent attitude to, and use of the experience of therapy.

Some of the characteristics of this ambivalence have been succinctly described in one of the 'classic' articles in psychoanalytic literature: 'Loss: a central theme in psychotherapy' by Heinz Wolff. His theme is not the losses which most clients have already experienced and which surely form a part of the material they bring to therapy, but rather that entering therapy itself involves a series of losses, which are also hard for the client to accept. Re-phrasing Freud's observation in more obviously acceptable terms, Wolff sets out his argument, that the client 'wants to change but all change implies the need to give something up: be this a symptom, a habitual behaviour, an attitude of mind, a value system or a particular form of relationship to another person. Giving up means losing something however stressful it may be; the change is thus desired and at the same time feared and resisted' (1977: 11).

Wolff's article describes the various losses which the client may experience at different phases of the therapy: (1) losses related to the decision to enter therapy; (2) losses to be faced during therapy; and (3) losses experienced in the relationship to the therapist.

Under the first heading he includes the need to give up certain illusions, such as that of being totally independent and not needing help, and having to acknowledge the need to depend upon someone else for help. At the same time this type of dependence is quite unlike most other helping relationships, because the therapist does not tell the client what to do, or does not alleviate their problems by simple measures such as a drug or practical assistance. The client has to become an active member of the therapeutic relationship, has to accept responsibility for her or his difficulties and for their resolution, 'whilst at the same time accepting that another person is needed to achieve this' (Wolff, 1977).

Although Wolff says that a client who is not willing to give up this illusion is unlikely to seek this particular form of help, this is too simple. Some clients go on struggling with this issue, unhappy about letting go of their independence, and therefore (for example) holding back strong feelings which make them vulnerable; or they continue to expect that the therapist will in due course make an authoritative statement that will effect a change for them; and as long as either feeling or illusion exists, the therapist is therefore seen both as a threatening or depriving figure and as a helpful one.

As in the double-bind, in some instances it is difficult for the therapist to respond in the right way. 'Damned if you do and damned if you don't.' Saying nothing helpful is depriving; saying something helpful may lead to certain negative reactions, such as those described by Karen Horney (1936). Client responses to a useful interpretation by the therapist can take the form of an attack, since the therapist's intervention may be perceived either as a stimulus to competition, or as a rejection, an accusation, a guilt-inducing reproach, or as a demand for the abandonment of all symptoms and the achievement of instant recovery. It is interesting that in the face of such reactions by the client Horney advises against the interpretation of the links with past dynamics and suggests instead the need for clarification and confrontation of what is going on between the therapist and the client.

Wolff suggests that the ambivalence may take the form of presenting practical difficulties about coming for therapy: he gives as examples excuses about being unable to afford the time or the fees, rendering the therapy ineffective by it being too short, or too infrequent. Some complaints concern such practical arrangements too, particularly about contracts. Perhaps it is the reluctance of some therapists to engage with the client's ambivalence that leads to contracts that are less than clear. In entering into a contract at all, a client almost inevitably has mixed feelings. Where there is uncertainty about boundaries some clients, in their anxiety, may take the opportunity to demonstrate their confusion, pushing at boundaries in order to seek clarification of just what they can expect and what is expected of them.

Under the second heading, that of losses to be faced *during* therapy, Wolff identifies several factors, such as having to give up out-dated beliefs about oneself and others, having to abandon rigid defences and attitudes, and having to acknowledge areas of oneself that are vulnerable. These are all aspects present from the beginning, but which have to be faced more obviously the longer therapy goes on. Owning less acceptable feelings and thoughts can give rise to self-criticism, and by implication a fear that the therapist is also going to be critical; yet it is the therapist who is promoting such self-exploration by the client, and the uncovering of different emotions and thoughts. The therapist therefore becomes a persecutory figure in the client's eyes, as well as being someone with whom relief and consolation can be experienced. There is also a loss of privacy as the client reveals more and more to the therapist.

It is axiomatic of all approaches to therapy that the therapist's ability to convey a non-judgmental and accepting attitude is a 'core condition', if not always given that name. Wolff (1977) observes that 'if the therapist himself has learned to own his inner fantasy world and personal hang-ups without self-condemnation he can more easily convey to his patient that he genuinely accepts him as he is and does not disapprove or reject him'. But it is easy to forget, especially for counsellors who place a very high premium on being non-judgmental and accepting, that despite all one's efforts, the client nevertheless feels exposed, and is perhaps still afraid that behind the velvet glove there lies an iron fist. Given that in complaints procedures the client often becomes a severe persecutory figure for the therapist (alleging that what is sometimes a relatively minor lapse in competence is a deliberate attack on the client), it is possible to see how the persecutory situation in therapy is turned upside down, and the client attacks as a form of defence. It is interesting that Wolff suggests, like Anzieu (and again he writes from within the psychoanalytic tradition), that it is helpful for the therapist to be more self-disclosing: 'In my experience, it is sometimes helpful if on such occasions [i.e. when the client feels the threat of condemnation] the therapist refers to the fact that he, too, has had to learn to accept similar aspects of his own personality' (1977). This is particularly helpful where the client idealises the therapist, seeing her or him as someone who has everything sorted, because this can lead to envy of the therapist, who is assumed to be 'sorted'. This envy can lead to destructive attacks, in the symbolic Kleinian sense of destructive envy attacking the bountiful breast. The Kleinian analyst Rosenfeld (1968) considers that in the negative therapeutic reaction a very primitive drive comes into play. It is appropriate that clients should at some point in the therapy recognise that the therapist has feet of clay. But sometimes one can have the feeling in complaints procedures that the client is determined, on discovering by accident (rather than through the therapist's intended disclosure) that the therapist is no longer the ideal figure, that the therapist should have her or his face ground in the mud.

Wolff identifies other aspects that need to be challenged and given up in therapy if the therapy is to be successful. He observes that many clients have previously relied on certain ethical values, and social, cultural or religious attitudes, some of which have been accepted in order to control feelings and impulses which the client feels are unacceptable. Moral standards and belief systems are likely to be challenged in therapy, particularly in respect of their being absolutes which can be applied in any situation. 'Such questioning of lifelong familiar standards and value systems will itself be experienced as a painful loss because rigid rules about what it is right or wrong to do, provide an outer authority on which to base one's decisions' (Wolff, 1977).

While of course it appears true (at least to the therapeutic professions) that giving up dependence on rigid ethical codes can lead to a greater sense of personal freedom and integrity, what is interesting here is that complaints procedures often involve detailed references, in a somewhat legalistic way, to as many clauses of a Code of Ethics and Practice as can be identified as vaguely relevant. Now it is the therapist's ethical code which is being used to challenge the therapist, who may have been experienced as threatening to undermine the client's accepted codes. Is there possibly a link here? Therapists can sometimes feel that they have had their own rule book thrown at them. It is as if the client, in being 'compelled' to question their own codes (by the very nature of the therapeutic enterprise), and perhaps to some extent having their own basis for being and doing undermined, may at times rebel against this by in turn using professional codes to undermine the whole basis of the therapist's work.

Again here it is useful to note that Wolff challenges the accepted wisdom of the discipline: 'It is important to note that therapists themselves will only feel free to follow their own intuition and to be flexible in their work with patients if they have freed themselves from unquestioning adherence to whatever school of psychotherapy they have been trained in, be this some form of psychoanalysis, analytical psychology, behavioural psychotherapy or any of the other schools of thought and forms of treatment available today' (1977). Therapists who adhere too strongly to the values of their own training may find themselves hoist on their own petard when the client wants to turn the tables in this way.

Another set of losses identified as being at the core of therapy are where clients may have to give up the illusion that they will find perfect happiness, and total satisfaction from a particular relationship or relationships in general. Included in this for some clients is the illusion that the therapeutic relationship is a perfect relationship, there to satisfy every need, a place where there should be no frustration or conflict. Yet, as Wolff observes, it is the nature of human life that there will always be disappointment, and it is impossible to return to a state of primal bliss. Some clients believe that 'they have a right to be given now and in the future what they missed out on in their childhood' (Wolff, 1977). In practice this can lead to a demand made upon other people, including the therapist, who feel so pressured that they are driven away, or become very defensive. Therapists can at such points hide behind technique and interpretations. As people realise that they are not getting what they want (and in some senses need, although it is unlikely they will ever be completely satisfied), their illusion turns to disillusion. At such points it is not surprising that complaints are made, first in therapy, and if not heard in therapy then against the therapy, driving the therapist still further away. In their ambivalence, the client drives the therapist away, yet wants closeness. Unfortunately if the pushing of the therapist away becomes a formal complaint, the very procedure (even if upholding the complaint) leaves the client feeling even more bereft — and the therapist unlikely ever to want to see that client again.

In the third part of his article Wolff concentrates on other losses experienced in relationship to the therapist. The client has to accept, for example, the imperfections in the therapeutic relationship, as well as the imperfections in the therapist. This loss can be better understood when we remember that therapists usually provide a relationship which in many respects is more consistent than any other (save perhaps early nurturing of the infant). Therapists aim to be reliable, to be present, whatever the emotional climate; and even if limited to an hour a week, that hour becomes deeply precious. The therapist is attentive to the client and their needs, is committed to them even if at times this can be experienced by the therapist as a burden. So when the therapist shows imperfections, these are liable to be experienced as more serious disappointments than if the therapist was unreliable, inattentive, and obviously rather useless.

Wolff (1977) suggests that 'provided he sets his personal limits and knows when to say "No" in order to take care of his own and his patient's needs, this apparent loss may lead to the reward of seeing his patient grow and develop in the relationship to him'. But of course, it is often at such times as a therapist says 'No' in this way that the client first feels consciously aggrieved, and all the unconscious discontent joins forces with the present feelings in response to the disappointment of limitations such as: 'I'm sorry, but I can't offer you another time between sessions'; 'I have to be away for a few weeks'; 'I think we now need to look at an ending', etc. There are many reasons why therapists, however sensitive and effective, will fail through falling short of the client's desire that they should be fully understood and cared for.

Wolff identifies some of the accusations clients might make: 'I am only one of many patients to you', or 'You don't really care for me as a person', or 'You expect me to tell you all about myself but I know nothing about you'. At this point in the paper Wolff links the losses in therapy to previous losses that have been experienced, so that failure on the part of the therapist is almost certain to replicate failure on the part of significant others in the client's life. Failure to realise just what the client is feeling, having to end sessions when there is more that needs to be expressed, breaks in the therapy because of illness or holidays, 'can all be experienced as severe and traumatic losses, often comparable to what a child goes through when he feels dropped, rejected or abandoned by his parents' (Wolff, 1977). Reich (1934) similarly links negative therapeutic reactions to failure on the part of the therapist to recognise such examples of what the psychodynamic approach calls the negative transference.

Wolff concludes by referring to the actual ending of therapy: 'It is especially when therapy comes to an end that all these disappointments and losses are likely to be re-experienced once more and to a heightened degree. Here separation and mourning become a reality; sadness and anger need to be expressed and worked through, alongside feelings of gratitude for the positive experiences of a shared relationship which hopefully has enabled the patient to grow so that he can take care of himself as a more independent adult' (Wolff, 1977: 19). It is perhaps not surprising that a number of complaints follow what appears to be experienced by the client as an unsatisfactory handling of the termination of the contract.

Although such inevitable failures whether they be actual or symbolic, can be used to therapeutic advantage, it requires a skilful practitioner to do this when the client is hopping mad, or deeply depressed. Failure to do so may lead to acting out of a legitimate complaint (in the sense of negative feelings) against therapists through a legalistic complaint made to their professional body. Wolff's article illustrates just how much ambivalence there is in the therapeutic relationship, and what cause there may be for having to act out negative feelings that are not identified and contained in the therapy itself.

The principal examples of negative therapeutic reaction in the literature pertain to the inability of the client to change — what we might refer to as 'stuckness'. Whatever the reasons for this — client defences or therapist ineffectiveness — it surely leads to tension in the relationship, examined in an article by Asch (1976) on problems with counter-transference in the therapist in such situations. Others have similarly examined these reactions (Brenner, 1959; Olinick, 1964; Modell, 1965; Kernberg, 1971). Asch puts the situation in stark psychoanalytic terminology, that 'counter-transference problems are the response to the covert sadistic component in the patient's masochism, which subtly but constantly belittles the analytic work' (1976: 399). While Asch comments on the patient's negative attitude as indicating 'disguised omnipotence', and 'arrogant narcissism', which 'wears away at the analyst', and on the 'provocativeness' or 'seductiveness', in the patient, these terms could as easily (perhaps more easily) be used of the therapist. It may be that in the face of clients who appear to make no move towards healthier ways of being the therapist assumes a more subtle omnipotence (as if trying harder to 'make' the client change) or becomes 'arrogant' (again subtly) in trying to push certain interpretations, or even 'provocative' or 'seductive' in order to try and elicit a different kind of response. So the continued suffering of the client (and it is this which Freud and some other analysts often mean by the client's masochism) leads to the therapist becoming more impatient, more forceful, and potentially therefore more dangerous. Add to this dynamic already described above, that the client is anxious about changing, and it is possible to see how a vicious spiral of withdrawal, therapist attack, and further withdrawal takes place, until the client turns and attacks the therapist who has been drawn into uncharacteristic behaviour or technique.

We may be less certain than Asch that clients deliberately or unconsciously provoke such attacks, or that they persistently try to wear down the therapist; but the effect of their withdrawal and fear of change may nevertheless be to lead to unwise responses on the part of the therapist, which in turn can then lead to a complaint. Brenner (1959: 224) suggests the need for a calm, observant understanding attitude in the therapist, that of 'an adult . . . dealing reasonably with a sulky, stubborn, provocative child'. The image is useful even if many clients do not demonstrate such behaviour overtly. Olinick (1964: 547) responds to this kind of statement by saying that to ask a therapist to stay calm and be understanding 'says too much in too few words'. The therapist 'is in a peculiarly vulnerable position. His "freely hovering attention", empathic identification, and the usual motivations that enter into his choice of profession tend to open his ego boundaries to the operations of the patient. This is necessary and useful, but, under certain regressive conditions, it may over-carry. The dominant-submissive axis of the therapeutic relationship is then reversed, with the patient dominant, although only in the temporary sense of a child in a tantrum' (1964: 547). Olinick suggests that sometimes the response to the destructive client is 'angry assertiveness against such . . . if it is tactfully motivated and timed, and clearly intended as the setting of limits' (1964: 547).

Asch is similarly aware that even then the therapist's patience can be exhausted, and that a transient defection from being calm and understanding sometimes has remarkable effects: 'paradoxically, the infrequent and isolated counter-transference reactions of the analyst may even help the patient to recognize his own inflexible internal standards. Mr. B. responded with audible relief to an unthinking, sharp comment of mine, saying, "At least I know now you are not as rigid and uncompromising as I am."' (1976: 401–2). Such responses cannot be planned (it is their very spontaneity and surprise appearance that breaks into the negative cycle), and they may of course backfire. Sometimes a therapist, as Olinick suggests, has 'to wait out the period of time':

> the analytic *pas de deux* must always be conducted with special, tactful attention to the patient's pace, rhythm, and capacity of expression, and here is one of those many areas in psycho-analytic practice where science and art have to be delicately combined. The analyst must sustain himself against the patient's ambivalent need to destroy, always recognizing the presence of the other side of the ambivalence, but interpreting only when the patient is, as one perceptive woman put it, "almost not saying 'No'" (1964: 547).

Perhaps one pessimistic conclusion that can be drawn from this examination of the negative therapeutic reaction, is that therapists are doomed to fail; that the odds are stacked against them, and that it is surprising, where such negative features abound, that anyone should gain from the therapeutic relationship.

However, as Novick (1980) reminds us, there is so much being written about the effectiveness of therapy, and about the criteria for successful work, that what can be forgotten is that therapists are actually experts at failing. They work with clients who have either failed in some parts of their life, and/or have been failed by key figures at different points in their life. Therapy is bound to involve the re-enactment of failure, and it is in dealing with this aspect of the work that therapists seek to become more confident. To do so, Novick concludes, 'the therapist too must learn to modify and adapt omnipotent fantasies; issues of therapeutic omnipotence or impotence can interact with the patient's need to make the therapist fail, to produce a negative therapeutic alliance. It is suggested that analysis can provide the patients with the experience that failure does not lead to destruction and, as with the "good enough mother", failure can lead to positive growth and development' (1980: 319).

Complaints are the most obvious examples of how things have gone wrong: that even if in the end the complaint is not upheld, clearly something has gone sufficiently wrong for things to get to such a point. We need to remember that there are many more examples of therapists and clients, who are able to work through the failures, and turn negative reactions in the direction of more positive outcomes.

## References

Anzieu, D. (1986). Paradoxical transference — from paradoxical communication to negative therapeutic reaction. *Contemporary Psychoanalysis*, 22: 520–47.

Asch, S. (1976). Varieties of negative therapeutic reaction and problems of Technique. *Journal of the American Psychoanalytic Association*, 24: 383–407.

Brenner, C. (1959). The masochistic character. *Journal of the American Psychoanalytic Association*, 7: 197–226.

Freud, S. (1923). *The Ego and the Id*. Pelican Freud Library, Volume 11. London: Penguin Books.

Heller, J. (1985) *Catch 22*. New York: Dell.

Horney, K. (1936). The problem of the negative therapeutic reaction. *Psychoanalytic Quarterly*, 5: 29–44.

Kernberg, O. F. (1971). Prognostic considerations regarding borderline personality organization. *Journal of the American Psychoanalytic Association*, 19: 595–635.

Modell, A. (1965). On having the right to a life: an aspect of the superego's development. *International Journal of Psycho-Analysis*, 46: 323–31.

Novick, J. (1980). Negative therapeutic motivation and negative therapeutic alliance. *Psychoanalytic Study of the Child*, 35: 299–320.

Olinick, S. L. (1964). The negative therapeutic reaction. *International Journal of Psycho-Analysis*, 45: 540–8.

Reich, W. (1934). *Psychischen Kontakt und Vegetative Stromung*. Copenhague: Sexpol Verlag.

Wolff, H. H. (1977). Loss: a central theme in psychotherapy. *British Journal of Psychology*, 50: 11–9.

# Chapter 6

# Therapeutic and Adversarial Relationships

## Derek Hill

Realism demands that counsellors should expect misunderstandings, moments of conflict, and even a complaint, as part of their working experience with clients. But many will have difficulty in imagining themselves locked into an adversarial relationship with someone they first met in the counselling room. At least two influences may be at work. First, an adversarial relationship is fundamentally at odds with the declared purposes of counselling since it implies the counsellor's commitment to prevail over the client rather than using their resources in the service of clients. Second, the existence of such a relationship challenges the belief that the supervised application of knowledge, skills and (self-) awareness is a potent agency for problem-solving and conflict resolution. However, adversarial relationships do arise from time to time in counselling and need to be understood in the context of that professional activity.

Writing about accusations of negligence, Samuel Knapp (1997) states '(they) come about when there is an unfortunate synergy of ill feelings towards the therapist and a perception of inadequate care'. Ill feelings can have many sources and will be considered later. 'Inadequate care' implies the client's sense of what adequate care would be, and invites us to explore the explicit and implicit bases of the counsellor-client relationship. As counselling has become recognised as a valued source of help for individuals, couples and families, so its nature and processes have been given more definite form. That formalization finds one expression in the codes of ethics and practice adopted by the counselling organisations. Most commonly, those codes adopt four key ethical principles as their core: Respect for individual autonomy; Beneficence; Non-maleficence and Justice (Bond, 2000). An examination of some of them (BAC[P], BASRT, COSCA) reveals that, in terms of relationships with clients, counsellors' compliance with those principles is linked with requirements to practice in a way which specifically protects clients from malpractice such as misrepresentation, breach of contract or of confidentiality, practice outside the area of competence, any form of exploitation, abandonment, and inappropriate relationships subsequent to counselling. Together, compliance with the principles and these aspects of a code of good practice make up the counsellor's *direct* commitment to the client. Other requirements in the codes to do with maintaining availability and effectiveness constitute the counsellor's *indirect* commitment. Strikingly, the codes leave the client's responsibilities largely implicit: to be a party to a contract for work, to attend counselling sessions, to make agreed payments.

It will be evident that, if used alone, the codes provide counselling clients with considerable scope to challenge the adequacy of counsellors' care while placing very limited responsibilities on the clients themselves for the nature and conduct of the working relationship.

A hundred years ago, analysts *required* their patients to comply with the analytic method, and *contracted* with them to provide a service for payment. Rogers (1942), Berne (1961), and Truax and Carkhuff (1967), all wrote about the therapeutic relationship in terms of trust, mutuality and genuineness and set the scene for the emergence of the practice of establishing a *negotiated* contract between client and counsellor. Counsellors with differing theoretical approaches have tailored the contracts they use to match their therapeutic strategies, but there were, and are, common characteristics — identification of the purposes of the therapeutic work to be done, establishment of the ethos of the therapeutic relationship and adoption of the necessary practical and financial arrangements. The primary justification for the adoption of such contracts is that they facilitate the processes of counselling and thereby promote the well-being of clients.

During the past two decades three new influences have arisen. Increasingly, counselling has become a business activity for individuals and organisations. Clients have brought growing awarenesses of their rights as consumers to the therapeutic arena. Evaluation of counselling services is becoming the norm, and counsellors and their organisations are more commonly being held formally accountable for the work they do. All three influences have been argued to serve the clients' interests by increasing the availability of high quality counselling services.

At the same time, growing efforts have been made to secure the recognition of counselling as a professional activity, and to protect the legitimate interests of the individuals and organisations providing counselling services. The latter has been achieved through self-regulation, formalization of complaints procedures and, where necessary, involvement in legal procedures. Generally, the rationale has been that the good name and viability of the profession, its members, and the associated organisations, is essential, if effective, ethical counselling services are to be available to meet demand. These changes, and the influences mentioned earlier, are welcomed by many but regretted by those who perceive commercial, bureaucratic and legalistic considerations to be distractions from the purposes of counselling and its client-centred ethos. In particular, these developments set competitive and openly adversarial relationships alongside those which are therapeutic, as elements of the working life of counsellors.

It has been proposed (Bond, 2000) that the four principles commonly regarded as the basis of ethical counselling practice should be augmented by adding one which establishes an obligation to exercise fidelity (the honouring of undertakings) and another which asserts the need to factor into ethical practice the *practitioner's* self-interest. It is unlikely that the introduction of the idea of fidelity will raise objections. The principle of self-interest may prove more problematic.

At first sight, the self-interest principle appears to be the means by which counselling can remove itself from the horns of the dilemma faced when the question is 'Do we now resort to a legal process in order to prevent (ex-)client X achieving their inequitable or damaging purpose?' In practice the principle relocates the problem because it would undoubtedly be argued that resort to a legal process is ethical only if *legitimate* self-interest is served. And it is interesting to speculate that, if the meaning of 'legitimate self-interest' can be determined, there may be circumstances in which a counsellor's practice is challenged because they have *not* adopted an adversarial stance.

It is important to note that the proposed principle may also affect the distribution of power between clients and counsellors in a subtle but advantageous way. Currently, the phrases 'in the client's interests' and 'so as to ensure access to effective, ethical counselling' are used to justify the ways in which *counsellors* set many of the ground rules for work with clients. This can add to the power imbalance which may exist when counsellor and client first meet; the client owning confusion, problems and distress and seeking help from the professional. Paradoxically, the counsellor's commitment to giving priority to the clients needs and to altruism, can set up the 'crossed transactions' (Berne, 1961) which make a truly mutual relationship difficult to achieve. Alternatively, if the principle of self-interest is invoked, the counsellor's needs and expectations of the client could be recognised from the outset. Although different to those the client has of the counsellor, they would then be seen to have a similar significance when the relationship-building and shared work of the two individuals is considered. This holds the promise of diminishing whatever power imbalance exists initially and could facilitate work to build the *mutual* regard and trust which underpins an effective therapeutic alliance. There is also a secondary benefit. Some of the arrangements that have been justified in the past as indirectly to the client's benefit can be recognised for what they are — acknowledgements of the counsellor's expectation to be treated with the same respect for autonomy, beneficence, non-maleficence, justice and fidelity that clients expect. It follows that counsellor and client have similar access to the means of redress if things go wrong.

If adopted, the self-interest principle would build into the ethical stance of counselling the even-handedness that counsellors and clients have long enjoyed under the law. In worst cases, counsellor or client might need to establish an adversarial relationship with the other while not stepping outside principled practice. That may be technically correct, but the argument is not consonant with the belief systems and the sense of vocation of many counsellors. These higher order sources of motivation encompass social conscience, prompt some to voluntary service, involve many different kinds of self-sacrifice, and are linked with attitudes that lead to them 'turning the other cheek' (Matthew 5, 39). Preoccupations with the rights, entitlements, and expectations of the counsellor play no part in such approaches to the counselling task. Some counsellors would never actively participate in an adversarial relationship and others would not initiate one. Many express great reservations about any formal declaration or mechanism which primarily protects counsellors' interests and thereby detracts from the focus on the well-being of clients.

Ultimately these issues are matters of conscience. Colleagues' differing attitudes and belief systems need to be respected. In particular, it is important to take into account the concern that codification of counsellors' self-interests could disadvantage clients and damage the reputation and the role of the profession in society. Several scenarios will now be used to explore the place of the practitioner's self-interest and adversarial relationships in ethical practice.

> *Clive had worked productively with his counsellor for eight weeks. After dealing with a personal crisis he had arrived 20 minutes late for his ninth session to find that his counsellor had left ten minutes earlier. His response was to write to the local newspaper, naming his counsellor and making it clear that he thought counsellors were charlatans who invited confidences but betrayed the trust put in them. With benefit of hindsight, the counsellor recognised that he had failed his client, was ready to admit that fact to him, and wanted to find a way to make reparation. Clive wanted no further communication with the counsellor and responded to a letter suggesting a meeting to resolve matters by letting it be known that, if not left alone, he would find other ways to attack the counsellor's reputation*

Here, an apparently satisfactory therapeutic relationship was disrupted by the counsellor's bad practice and, as a result, the client adopted an adversarial stance. The counsellor found no opportunity to take any reparative action before the client published information and opinions which were likely to do serious harm to the reputation of the counsellor and his colleagues. While concerns might be expressed about the conduct of the counselling before its breakdown, and about the counsellor's judgement in leaving the counselling venue before the end of the intended counselling session, the burning question is 'What should happen next?' There are many options available to the counsellor, including:
- Making a further direct approach to the client in an effort to find a way to minimise or repair the harm done by acknowledged bad practice;
- Seeking the involvement of an independent third party as a conciliator or mediator;
- Publishing an admission of fault and a conciliatory message to the client;
- Invite the client to make a formal complaint to the professional body;
- Refering the matter to those who deal with complaints in the appropriate professional body;
- Doing nothing which directly, or indirectly, affects the client;
- Making public a factual account of events together with information from evaluation studies which illustrate the benefits of counselling;
- Publishing an account of events, and of the client's response, which invites a critical assessment of the client's perceptions and judgements.

It may be that none of these options offers the most appropriate and ethical response to the situation faced in the scenario. They are listed to illustrate how diverse the counsellor's response might be. If faced with such a situation, the merits of options would need to be judged on the basis of the following propositions:
a) When malpractice occurs there is an ethical obligation to communicate that

fact to those directly affected, to inform them about action taken to avoid recurrences and, where possible, to take the action necessary to undo or minimize the harm done to the clients involved.

b) A client harmed by unethical counselling practice acts in accord with the purposes and ethics of counselling when seeking acknowledgement of that fact by those responsible, when securing an appropriate remedy from them, or in opting to have no further dealings with them.

c) Aspects of a counsellor's duty of care extend beyond the active phase of a therapeutic relationship, irrespective of the client's unwillingness to have further dealings with him or her, and also after the client's death.

d) [In the context of adoption of the self-interest principle] A counsellor's role in an adversarial relationship with an (ex-)client is ethical insofar as its purpose is to achieve a balance between serving basic professional needs and minimizing harm to, and constraints upon, the client.

These statements deserve careful consideration. Propositions a) – c) place the client's needs and well-being foremost and may result in the counsellor going to considerable lengths to ensure that harm to the client is minimized and benefits already gained are consolidated. Someone who is the subject of counselling malpractice might expect acknowledgement of that fact and a sincere apology from the counsellor concerned. They might also want the counsellor to do something which would directly reduce the harm already done, and that restorative or reparative action might be agreed. Both counsellor and client might see the need for another kind of action — that which would minimize the risk of malpractice recurring. This might involve change in business and administrative routines, or the counsellor's involvement in (re-)training or augmented supervision. All these responses provide scope for the counsellor's contrition and can have beneficial effects for all concerned.

Proposition d) shifts the focus and is an explicit recognition of the fact that, for any of a number of reasons, a client may act to cause harm to their counsellor, and to the profession at large. A client's retaliative or punitive response may stem from their sense of natural justice, or their wish to make use of the law. It is also likely to be an expression of the individual's hurt, anger and outrage. There have been situations in which a counsellor's sense of guilt and remorse led them not to resist such responses, and others in which the counsellor became adversarial. So what is the nature of the self-interest which should be taken into account in those circumstances? Earlier, it was suggested that there is the need to identify *legitimate* forms of self-interest. In an attempt at clarity proposition d) refers to 'basic professional needs', and maybe that should be phrased 'basic personal and professional needs'. There will no doubt be an on-going discussion about exactly which those needs are, but it appears reasonable to expect that the protection of the individual's private life, professional reputation, and access to clients, will be issues. The counsellor's professional status adds a complication since the individual has responsibilities to the profession and vice versa. It is thus a counsellor's responsibility to act in ways which preserve the profession's good name. That could involve a counsellor in defending their own reputation so as to avoid a slur on the profession at large.

That possibility brings into sharp focus another of the features of adversarial relationships. They almost invariably involve third parties and transform the private and confidential counselling relationship into one which is a more or less public. And those third parties may have interests or responsibilities which result in them disregarding the privacy of a therapeutic relationship and revealing personal information which would otherwise be protected by the counsellors commitment to confidentiality. It is the undisputed right of the client to waive confidentiality and reveal what they choose about themselves, but it is also acknowledged that counselling and other forms of psychological therapy are most effectively conducted as a private enterprise with no agenda other than the *private* affairs of the client. It is for this reason that Relate makes it clear to its clients that their commitment to privacy is required if counselling is to be offered, and that the organisation is unwilling to collaborate in work that is intended to result in reports being made to the courts or other authorities (Relate, 1996). An adversarial relationship between a client and a counsellor almost inevitably undermines the privacy and confidentiality of the original relationship and may open both the individuals involved, and the counselling process to exploitative publicity. This fact makes it important to keep in mind what the various codes have to say about the ethics of breaching confidentiality:

B.3.4.1 . . . Normally the decision to break confidentiality should be discussed with the client and should be made only after consultation with the counselling supervisor or if he/she is not available, an experienced counsellor.

B.3.4.2 Any disclosure of confidential information should be restricted to relevant information conveyed only to appropriate people and for appropriate reasons likely to alleviate the exceptional circumstances . . .

B.3.4.3 Counsellors hold different views about the grounds for breaking confidentiality, such as potential self-harm, suicide, and harm to others. Counsellors must consider their own views as they will affect their practice and communicate them to clients and significant others, e.g. supervisor, agency. (BAC, 1997).

The fact that an adversarial relationship frequently results in the counsellor's loss of control of confidential material is thus yet another factor which must be considered when the ethics of that course of action are being considered.

The origins of potential conflict between counsellors and clients are seldom single or simple. The following scenario reveals a client using false information to feed a preoccupation about a technical detail which triggers her own deep anxieties.

*Clare brought one word to her counsellor's mind when they first met — immaculate. Punctuality, dress, posture, speech and the precision with which she described her reasons for seeking counselling, all spoke of a woman who had 'got her act together'. Her 'concern' was that she was sometimes misunderstood by colleagues and acquaintances. Her counsellor was taken ill just before their third session and, by prior agreement with Clare, rang her work number and left a message with her colleague. 'Tracy (agreed false name) can't meet you tonight as arranged because she is ill.'*

*When Clare next met her counsellor she was angry. She believed that the phone message had communicated the fact that it was a counselling session that was being cancelled and she was outraged at that breach of confidentiality. She was offered an understanding response and reassurance that no breach had occurred. She would not accept that her information was incorrect; the counsellor had not recorded the message and could not prove her wrong. The last thing she wanted was that work colleagues believed that she had problems. Although Clare retained her composure throughout the session she would not once allow the subject to be changed. She subsequently wrote to the counsellor stating that, having made enquiries and been assured of the confidentiality of the process, she had decided to lodge a complaint with the body from which her counsellor had obtained accreditation.*

From Clare's point of view a very carefully considered *private* arrangement had turned a 'concern' into the stuff of her worst fears. Readers will have their own hypotheses about the influences on her behaviour, but there can be little doubt that her experience had been catastrophic. From the counsellor's standpoint there was no question but that what had happened was both ethical and a fulfilment of her duty of care.

What new issues have been raised by this rather complicated situation?

First, faced with a complaint, what weight should the counsellor give to her own insights into the influences which caused her client to respond in that way, and what could she do with that knowledge for her client's benefit?

The second has to do with the prospective role of the professional body. By what criteria does it judge the validity of a client complaint? Once accepted, are complaints processed in a legalistic way, putting client and counsellor in adversarial roles or, whenever possible, as a therapeutic engagement with the client?

Third, does the client's action in lodging a formal complaint leave the counsellor with any options other than to respond to the instructions of her professional body?

Each of those issues has sparked lively debate in the past and none has resulted so far in universally agreed practice. The following are the author's views and are offered as prompts for further consideration of the matters in specific situations.

Counsellors are trained to develop, use and refine working hypotheses about their clients' behaviours and problems as the basis for action, and there is no reason to believe that the practice should terminate when a client complains. Such hypotheses range between those well-grounded in recognised theoretical ideas, continuously refined in the light of carefully observed and experienced client behaviour and others which are idiosyncratic and based on brief contact. That is, some hypotheses are more robust than others. It is the counsellor's responsibility to make use of counselling supervision and other sources of professional support to ensure that working hypotheses are as apposite as possible and are under continual review and revision. It is also the counsellor's responsibility to evaluate the extent to which a hypothesis serves the client's purposes as against those of the counsellor — a firmly held hypothesis can be used to relieve a counsellor's uncertainties and anxieties, and excuse thwarted strategies. If, at a particular moment, the client's welfare becomes the responsibility of professional colleagues it is good practice to offer knowledge about the client to those others, *with the client's permission*. If that handover happens in circumstances in which the client may be seriously harmed it *may* be appropriate to communicate information without the client's permission (BAC, 1997, B.3.4.1).

As regards the procedures adopted by professional bodies, there is general agreement that the presumption must be that a client lodging a complaint believes they have a genuine grievance and that responses to it should be respectful, transparent and framed so as to help the client deal with the issue they identify. Typically, professional bodies are not empowered to use procedures with the force of the law. Most complaints procedures operate with an authority vested in them as a result of complainants and those complained against agreeing to be bound by their findings. The counselling ethos disposes such procedures to seek WIN–WIN rather than WIN–LOSE outcomes but they depend on the parties being like-minded. Those who involve themselves in the workings of complaints procedures are very aware of confidentiality issues, and of the risk of making a complainant's situation worse rather than better. Counselling supervisors should be regarded as a primary source of advice and guidance about these matters because it is becoming the norm for supervisor training programmes to include a consideration of breaches of ethical practice, and the strategies and procedures available to deal with them.

A counsellor's involvement in a client complaint does not deny them decisions about matters of conscience any more than it presumes the infallibility of the professional body involved. In very rare situations a counsellor's decision not to comply with the instructions of their professional body may be necessary for them, although it is likely to result in loss of membership. The ethics of professions like counselling have grown out of the principled stands of individuals

These considerations offer no direct response to the questions in the mind of Clare's counsellor. What if Clare was a celebrity, or if the counsellor specialized in RET (Ellis, 1973)? And what additional influences would be brought to bear if the counselling offered was provided by a managed care organisation? Each of those more closely defined situations may throw up issues which result in different priorities being given to conflicting ethical principles. Ethical practice has to do with making these finely balanced judgements based on a consideration of every pertinent aspect of the situation faced.

For the sake of completeness a final scenario will be considered.

*Neil requested individual counselling and met with a counsellor once. Ten days later a programme was broadcast on the local radio station in which a heavily edited audio-recording of the counselling session was used to portray counselling as a source of sloppy, antisocial, 'liberal' ideas which fostered an 'amoral cult of the individual'. No indication was given that the recording had been made covertly, or that it had been edited and used without the counsellor's permission.*

As many will remember, these things happen! From an ethical standpoint it can be argued that Neil (and that was not his real name) was never a party to a contract for counselling and that no therapeutic relationship was formed. The 'client's' primary purpose had nothing to do with gaining a therapeutic benefit and proved to be about serving the individual's political ends. An adversarial relationship had been planned by Neil from the outset and had been activated by his broadcast. The question faced by the counsellor, and by colleagues, did not result from uncertainties about the ethics of refuting a distorted account of counselling. It had to do with whether or not it was possible to engage actively in an adversarial relationship with Neil in a way that would benefit the reputation of the profession. The fact that there is no universal solution to that problem will come as no surprise! One of the less obvious factors to be considered is the balance to be struck when diverting the profession's limited time and resources from services to genuine clients.

The whole question of counsellors' engagement in adversarial relationships may appear so beset with difficulties that the appropriate, ethical approach to the issue is to adopt a form of defensive practice which minimizes the risk of such relationships, and equips the practitioner to avoid inequitable outcomes when they do arise. Readers will no doubt be able to identify a range of existing good practice routines which appear to accord with that approach. Indeed, some may have been attracted to this book by the hope that it would prove to be a manual of defensive practice. This author believes that an approach to therapeutic work with clients which is fundamentally defensive is in conflict with the philosophies and value systems which inspire counselling.

Although beliefs within the profession differ, and cultures give priority to different social entities — the individual, the couple, the family, the community — it is arguable that the whole profession is dedicated to the task of enhancing the well-being of humankind. That is, there is a shared belief that an essential feature of human-ness is the individual's relationships with others, and in the value of creative, collaborative interpersonal relations. A philosopher could elaborate on the origins and implications of those beliefs.

Significantly, it would be perverse of a profession committed to enhancing human well-being to adopt a way of working which is preoccupied by the need to defend against those it serves. The profession has no need for that approach because there are other elements in the social matrices in which it functions which attend to rights and justice. And if that is not universally true, then it is the task of differently defined groups to put those elements in place.

The alternative to defensive practice is the espousal of an approach best illustrated by one of the originators of the humanistic therapies.

The Basic Hypothesis

Effective counselling consists of a definitely structured permissive relationship which allows the client to gain an understanding of himself to a degree which enables him to take positive steps in the light of his new orientation (Rogers, 1942: 18).

This hypothesis led Rogers to write later about the 'necessary and sufficient conditions for therapeutic personality change' (1957) in terms of the counsellor's empathic understanding, unconditional positive regard, and self-congruence. These ideas set the context in which counsellors' define the nature of their duty of care, and that has to do with using themselves, their skills and knowledge, to offer clients authentic involvements in human interactions which address and mediate their experiences. Rogers' phrase 'definitely structured permissive relationship' also suggests that attention must be given to all those influences that could impinge on, and distort, an agreed structuring. That is to say, boundary conditions which locate, contain and nurture the therapeutic relationship must be defined and preserved. Although the counsellor's expertise may make it advantageous for him or her to take initiatives in the process of defining boundary conditions its achievement must be by mutual consent, and thereafter the preservation of those conditions is a shared task. There is no room for the counsellor's covert boundaries in the relationship with a client, both must dare to trust each other and the contract they have forged. Indeed, the creative process of the shared refinement of that contract is no small part of the therapeutic substance of the counselling.

This reasoning does not preclude an orderly approach to counselling, the putting in place of systems and routines that monitor the safety, effectiveness and the ethical nature of work done, or forethought about work to be undertaken. All these strategies can and should be recognised as elements of the counsellor's contract with the client. And if the client can come to play an active role in them there is therapeutic advantage to be gained. The mistrust, or lack of trust, which inevitably exists before the onset of an adversarial relationship results from the failure of the explicit, mutually agreed contract to enable those involved to tolerate the risks and anxieties which are an intrinsic part of the therapeutic relationship. The remedy — the way to provide effective counselling and to minimize the occurrence of adversarial relationships and their damaging consequences — lies in creating more effective contracts.

## References

BAC (1997). *Code of Ethics and Practice for Counsellors.* Rugby: BAC.

Berne, E. (1961). *Transactional Analysis in Psychotherapy.* New York: Grove Press.

Bond, T. (2000). *Standards and Ethics for Counselling in Action.* 2nd Edition. London: Sage.

Ellis, A. (1973). *Humanistic Psychotherapy: The Rational-Emotive Approach.* New York: Julian Press.

Knapp, S. (1997). Professional Liability and Risk Management in an Era of Managed Care. In D. Marsh and R. Magee (eds.) *Ethical and Legal Issues in Professional Practice with Families.* New York: Wiley: 271–88.

Rogers, C.R. (1942). *Counselling and Psychotherapy.* New York: Houghton Mifflin.

Rogers, C.R. (1957). The necessary and sufficient conditions for therapeutic personality change. *J. Consulting Psychology,* 21: 95–103.

Truax, C. and Carkhuff, R. (1967). *Towards Effective Counselling and Psychotherapy: Training and practice.* Chicago: Aldine.

# Chapter 7

# Complaints in Organisations

## James Greer

I'm sure, like me, most people would rather not contemplate the possibility of having to deal with a complaint in their organisation. Of course there is much that can be done to minimise the possibility of anyone feeling the need to complain in the first place, but we can never be immune from complaints being made against us. Indeed, in organisations, as in all of life's arenas, things do go wrong sometimes — mistakes are made, thus complaints are almost inevitable. The key issue is how will your organisation respond? What provision do you have to manage, deal with and learn from a complaint made against you?

The British Association for Counselling and Psychotherapy (BACP) have informed me that complaints made against their organisational members are proportionally higher than the number of complaints made against individual counsellors. According to the latest figures, approximately six per cent of the BACP's membership is made up of organisational members, yet organisational members account for about one third of all cases undergoing the BACP's complaints procedure. That means organisations, *proportionally,* have about eight times the frequency of complaints going through to the official BACP Complaints Procedure as compared to individual counsellors.

In this chapter I aim to highlight the kinds of organisational problems that can lead to complaints causing real damage — and make some suggestions as to what action organisations need to take to prevent, handle and, ideally, benefit from such an occurrence if it arises. In particular I hope you will be able to gain valuable insights from an organisation (referred to as 'Agency X') involved in voluntary telephone and face-to-face counselling. I worked as a consultant with Agency X and together we grappled with the sanctions imposed on them by the British Association for Counselling and Psychotherapy (BACP) following a complaints process which found them in breach of the BACP's Codes of Ethics and Practice. You will see how, despite some very painful moments, they not only survived the sanctions process but have now moved into being a far more healthy and mature organisation as a result. Agency X's story is told by their Chairperson and illustrates in a number of places in this chapter, the kinds of difficulties that organisations can encounter during a complaints process.

## Complaints in organisations can be complicated

Organisations can face a major challenge when they are complained against — it can be a very complex task to work out if and by whom an error has been made. Contrast this with how much more straightforward it seems when a counsellor is working alone in a private practice, where the number of people who are accountable for client work is usually limited to two — the counsellor or their supervisor. Any question of who has responsibility for unprofessional practice is likely to be relatively simple to work out, as the responsibilities for client work are fairly clear.

It isn't always quite so clear cut in organisations, as Agency X's Chairperson describes below:

> *For our organisation the situation we found ourselves in felt very complicated. If it had been a difficulty between two people, then it would probably have been much more straightforward. Even to this day, it is unclear as to where all the faults lie.*
>
> *There was a feeling amongst everyone, that something needed to be done, but no one person took control. Many people seem to have been involved, both within the organisation and externally. Everyone seemed to have a part to play and something to say. With hindsight, all this confusion seemed to contribute to the problems and made matters worse. It felt as if we were getting deeper and deeper into confusion, with no easy way out. At times it felt as if we were completely out of our depth, and it was at these times that we sought outside help, but to no avail.*

Organisations normally work by dividing up tasks between several job roles. A whole team of people may share in the responsibility for carrying out a particular aspect of activity. In a counselling organisation there may be receptionists, administrators, trainers, supervisors, managers, counsellors, directors or executive committee members and trustees. When a complaint is made to an organisation it may be about an incident which in some way relates to a number of these separate jobs, directly or indirectly. Many people may have some level of responsibility for issues affecting the complainant. This can make it hard to work out the exact cause of the complaint, who might be responsible and what might need to be done to put any wrong-doing right. This problem can get even worse if the different responsibilities of the different jobs in an organisation are not clearly defined, or where there is a blurring of boundaries between jobs. With so many people involved to some extent or other, it can become very difficult to see exactly who is accountable for what.

**Action to take:**
- test out if everyone has a clear and shared understanding of what they are individually responsible for;
- ensure the structure of your organisation is designed to avoid conflicts of interest;
- actively manage staff's performance (the good and not-so-good);
- ensure that organisational structures, though they may be flexible, enable effective leadership and clear accountability.

## People and systems in crisis

An organisation is a collection of people who come together to achieve a common goal. Effective functioning of the organisation depends on co-operation and a shared sense of purpose between everyone involved. Seen in this way organisations are in some ways like personal relationships — some are dysfunctional, in a chronic sense. Unresolved issues from the past, flawed organisational processes and systems, poor decision-making or lack of leadership are like cracks which begin to show when an organisation becomes under strain — just like the 'cracks' that can appear in a relationship when under stress.

And there is no doubt that dealing with a complaint, particularly a serious one which may have implications for several people, can be extremely stressful for an organisation. This stress serves only to add to the problems of effectively dealing with a complaint. Again, the Chairperson of Agency X, illustrates this point very clearly:

> *When a complaint was made against our organisation both individuals and the organisation as a whole found it very stressful. This was not something we had encountered before and we had very few systems in place to help us deal with it. People wanted to walk away and pretend it wasn't happening. Yet we knew for the good of the Agency, something needed to be done to bring back harmony. There was a core of people working towards this aim, however, as in most situations, people take sides and there were those who were clearly supporting the complainant as well as those who were not. This led to a split in the Agency, which was detrimental to the organisation, to volunteers and to our clients.*
>
> *People were too upset and stressed to see clients or receive telephone calls from them which became a grave concern for us. The Agency seemed to be disintegrating before our eyes. The atmosphere was strained and certainly not one that was healthy in a counselling environment. We were fighting to bring order back out of chaos and unwittingly this only seemed to make matters worse.*

Another issue worth considering is an aspect of organisational development which is often referred to as a 'systems crisis'. Usually most organisations start off very small: everyone knows everyone else; with so few people everyone 'mucks in'; job roles are more organic and flexible; standards of performance, communication and expectations, whilst they may not be written down are more likely to be understood and acknowledged by everyone.

As organisations grow and more people become involved, it becomes more necessary to divide up tasks — perhaps even establish a whole department to do the work which formed only part of one person's job in the early days. With more people involved, issues like communication become more difficult and decisions are taken which may affect many people who have played no part in the decision making process. Usually it is around this time that organisations suffer a 'systems crisis'. That is to say the old informal and organic ways of doing things in the early days no longer work effectively. Systems and processes need to be established to manage and control who's doing what and deal effectively and objectively with issues when they appear to go wrong. Of course the really smart organisations recognise the need to take action to avert their 'systems crisis' before it ever arises. However, quite understandably, many organisations are so busy doing the work that their organisation is there to do (for example counselling), that they do not realise the need to take action before it is too late. Something happens, like a complaint, or an accident and it becomes plain, with hindsight, that the necessary systems or policies were not in place to manage aspects of organisational life effectively.

**Action to take:**
- ensure everyone has a shared sense of purpose;
- be sensitive to emotional issues which may need a forum to be expressed so that they can be worked through effectively;
- agree clear standards of performance with all staff;
- develop a 'culture' or way of working that values and re-enforces ethical practice;
- create imaginative systems and processes that support your organisation appropriately for its size, age and history.

## Who can complain and how it can be so damaging

Another issue that organisations face in relation to complaints is that it is not just clients who complain. Supervisors, paid staff, volunteers, counsellors, trainees, trainers, external supervisors or those providing external consultative support, managers, trustees, funders — really anyone who has a connection with or a stake in the organisation (often referred to as 'stakeholders') may have a grievance which feels significant enough for them to make a complaint. Whether they go as far as taking their complaint to a professional association like the BACP probably depends on their perception of whether the organisation that they are complaining about will deal with their complaint in a fair, objective and non-punitive manner.

Of course there are all manner of reasons for people not trusting that an organisation will deal adequately with their grievance. Poor or confused leadership can create factions in an organisation which can alienate and embitter. Organisational politics, perceptions of fairness and issues of power and control become the wedges that can split the heart of cooperative working relationships. As in a pressure cooker with no release valve, frustration can soon become anger in an organisation where client or staff members feel they have not been heard and where there is no clear complaints procedure to follow. Ineffective or non-existent discipline or grievance procedures also open up a minefield of potential issues to complain about.

The Chairperson of Agency X describes how their complaint came from within their own organisation and how tangled it all became:

> *In our case, a complaint was made by a person who had a number of different responsibilities within our agency. Up to this time, I felt we had all been pulling in the same direction, working hard to enhance the*

*organisation, yet when this occurred, it nearly destroyed the organisation, and no matter what we did, the situation became gradually worse. It was a shock to realise that someone was so unhappy and that no matter how we tried to rectify things (and with the help of outside consultations) the problems couldn't be resolved. Things would seem to be getting sorted out and relationships more amicable, then just as things seemed to be settling down and getting back to normal, it would all come flooding back and we would be back where we started, only more frustrated and confused.*

**Action to take:**
- have a long hard look at your organisation and identify the kinds of stakeholder groups that might have a grievance with aspects of your work or practice;
- ensure there are ways in which such groups can effectively draw attention to issues of dissatisfaction without risking judgement or punishment;
- find out if complaints/grievance processes are ever used by anyone. If they aren't then they are probably not working;
- create accessible and pragmatic complaints procedures;
- create accessible and pragmatic discipline and grievance procedures and train staff to use them;
- ensure staff have adequate training and supervision;
- involve stakeholders in your organisation's development and generate a sense of ownership in decisions from those that are effected;

## Organisations have broad-reaching responsibilities

Organisations who adhere to a professional code of ethics have very broad reaching responsibilities for supporting ethical practice. It may well be the case that whilst individuals are well versed in their professional responsibilities, organisations are not. Certainly, as the Chairperson of Agency X describes below, having a very thorough understanding of the relevant codes of ethics is vital:

> *It was not until we were faced with the BACP sanctions, that we began to work on the Code of Ethics in such detail, and began to understand them fully. I am not sure if we could have reached this understanding, without the help of our consultant. Because of the nature of the work undertaken in any form of counselling, it is necessary to understand and adhere strictly to the codes laid down by the BACP. This brings me to the thought, that maybe it would be a good idea for organisations to have access to this kind of help when setting up, so that everything would be in place in case a complaint occurred.*

To illustrate this in a little more detail, consider Organisational Membership of the BACP and what responsibilities this infers on your organisation if you are a member. Organisations who are members of the BACP are required to have in place systems, processes and an approach to managing people which enable and support individuals in their organisation to behave in a manner which is consistent with the all the relevant BACP Codes of Ethics and Practice. It can be relatively easy for an organisation unintentionally to fall foul of such codes. Policy decisions can be made without enough attention being paid to the ethical and professional affects of such decisions. For example, by employing one of your supervisors or counsellors as a trainer or indeed as a manager, what effects will this have on their ability to be impartial (perceived or real)? If roles are in any way confused, does your organisation provide counsellors with access to 'independent consultative support'?

**Action to take:**
- read and properly understand the Codes of Ethics and Practice that your organisation has signed up to;
- consider carefully implications of the Codes of Ethics and Practice and ask how your organisation, its management style, its systems and processes, actively supports and promotes ethical practice;
- investigate your constitution and/or business plan and check they are congruent with current policy and ethical practice;
- identify areas where there may be issues (or potential issues) of conflict of interest. If you can't find any look again — there are almost bound to be some somewhere;
- ensure that every management or policy decision, before it is implemented, is scrutinised in terms of how it will impact on ethical practice. Then review the same once it has been implemented.

## Why complaints can be good for you

I've never met anyone who actually likes listening to a complaint made about them. Complaints are normally quite painful to hear. However as with a number of other aspects of life, despite the pain — there is a real possibility of gain. The Chairperson of Agency X describes how they have received some positive outcomes from their traumatic experience:

> *Though the complaints and sanctions process has been extremely difficult at times, the whole episode has been a great learning experience for us as individuals and for the Agency as a whole. It has enabled us to move on more confidently, knowing that all our paper work is updated and in order, with a far better understanding of running an organisation proficiently. It has made us stand back and take a good look at ourselves, made us realise that we got it wrong, although again I can honestly say not intentionally.*

## Complaints can be full of learning and opportunity

Several years ago I used to run training sessions for managers of small businesses on 'handling complaints' from their customers. I used to be met with incredulity when I used to urge them to *encourage* their customers to complain if they were dissatisfied in any way. The reasons for this are simple. If complaints are handled well: they lead to increased loyalty and respect from everyone involved; they may be full of information about how you can improve your organisation and the service you give to your clients.

Now I'm not suggesting you should encourage counselling clients to complain in the same way that you might if you were selling a product, but ensuring that everyone, including clients, know what they should do and who they should approach if they have a complaint seems to be crucial. People tend to complain when they haven't got what they expected. Often this dissatisfaction and unhappiness gets saved up for a while before it is released in the form of a complaint. Therefore complaints are often charged with angry, blaming feelings which are intended to punish. Not only can this make them difficult to hear at the time, but often in organisations the blaming tendency can be passed on — searching for a quick and easy scapegoat before the full picture is understood and a calm analysis of the facts made. Thus a vicious circle of complaint avoidance is established where organisations avoid complaints — which has the effect of bottling up complaints until they spill over in a destructive way — which, not surprisingly, makes them all the more worth avoiding in the first place.

Of course it is quite possible that with the appropriate skills and an objective yet compassionate process to follow, complaints can become a source of useful organisational and personal learning. In the next section I will suggest what some of these skills are and what an effective complaints process is likely to contain.

**Action to take:**
* have an accessible and practical complaints process (see next section);
* make sure staff have the skills and support to handle complaints effectively (see next section).

## Skills and processes for effective complaint handling

In the previous section I described a vicious circle of complaint avoidance which only serves to increase the damage that can be done as a result of complaints.

To break this negative cycle, people need to know that the organisation will take what they have to say seriously, and will listen and attend to it without defensiveness. This can be clearly signalled in two ways.

Firstly, the organisation can indicate to all clients and staff that it has a process in place which will ensure that any complaint will be acted upon quickly, confidentially, and objectively. A typical complaints process will describe, step by step, to whom a complaint can be made and how they can be contacted. It could also indicate timescales by which an initial response will be made to the complainant by the organisation and the time taken to conduct a full investigation. A description of who will be involved in carrying out the investigation and how any decisions are to be reached are also important pieces of information to include. Most complaints processes also explain details of any appeals process and what happens if there is still no resolution after an appeal has been heard. Often organisations will refer complainants on at this stage to an external professional body or mediator.

Secondly, those that are directly involved in hearing the complaint need to minimise the potentially destructive forces of a complaint by:
* avoiding getting defensive;

- discovering the full facts before jumping to conclusions;
- confirming that you are clear about all sides of the story;
- seeking agreement with the complainant regarding the next steps;
- following the organisation's complaints process to the letter.

The encouraging thing for organisations involved in counselling, is that many of the skills involved in effective complaint handling are very closely aligned to counselling skills. If an organisation has an effective process in place to handle complaints and deploys this process using appropriate skills, then most small complaints can be dealt with effectively, preventing them from turning into big complaints and spilling out of the organisation (for example involving the BACP).

If, after thorough investigation, a complaint is found to have been justified, part of effective complaint handling will involve taking some form of urgent action as a result of the complaint. From the complainant's view it may be extremely important that they are kept informed, in broad terms at least, of what action has been taken to put 'right' the 'wrong'. This will help them with closure and assist them and the organisation in moving on.

At times, if a complaint has highlighted wrong-doing on the part of one or more individuals, it may become necessary to take disciplinary action. This is of course where a clear and objective disciplinary procedure is vital.

**Action to take:**
- train staff in effective complaint handling skills;
- ensure everyone understands the value and contents of the complaints procedure
- avoid blaming at all costs;
- if it has been clearly established that your organisation has made a mistake say so, and don't forget to say sorry;
- if a complaint is upheld, take swift action and inform the complainant of what you have done;
- ensure you have a clearly established disciplinary procedure to follow in case you need it;
- carry out a review to ensure that after a complaint is made any learning that results is made use of.

## Closing comments

Complaints can be very damaging to an organisation. Complaints can also be full of learning and opportunity. Whilst it will never be possible to prevent complaints from occurring, the chances of them doing real harm can be minimised, and the likelihood of complaints being beneficial in some way can be maximised. An organisation's strategy for handling complaints needs to be *both* preventative and remedial.

The last words on this subject go to the Chairperson of Agency X. They have been through the complaints process in its most challenging form, with sanctions imposed by the BACP — and have emerged on the other side, to their credit. They have a re-vitalised and re-modelled organisation which has been designed to prevent such an experience from becoming so destructive in the

future. They've learned so much and we can all learn from their story.
　　Good luck to them.

> *We now have procedures in place to guide us through any situation with more knowledge and understanding. It is said that good comes out of bad, and certainly for us, we have ended up with a more secure future for the organisation.*
>
> *All our Policies and Procedures have been rewritten, including a document clearly defining roles within the Organisation. These are all in line with our amended Constitution. A new Complaints, Grievance and Disciplinary document is now operational, which we feel gives us a more solid foundation to work on in the future. All members have now been issued with a new comprehensive Handbook, so that everyone is aware of the changes made, and we have received very positive feedback from all our volunteers.*
>
> *We are confident that we are a more professional organisation now and have much more stable processes for guiding us through any complaints in the future.*
>
> *Only time will tell.*

Chapter 8

# Complaints: A challenge to the structures and practices of counselling organisations

## Derek Hill

This chapter discusses some of the essential characteristics of counselling organisations and explores the ways in which complaints can disrupt their structures and practices. Resources are identified which enable organisations to respond positively to such challenges, and some lessons that might be learned by independent practitioners are suggested.

For more than 60 years pioneers, practitioners, and more recently, business people, have devoted themselves to setting up and running organisations designed solely, or in part, to provide counselling services. Those involved, and others who have observed that activity, are inclined to comment that all that effort has resulted in the introduction of a new kind of professional support for individuals, couples and families facing problems. They are also likely to comment that the achievement has exacted what appears to be an unreasonable cost within the organisations: divisive conflict, disillusionment, burnout, distorted lifestyles, and the insidious effects of fickle public opinion. 'Physician, heal thyself' (Luke 4:23) seems apposite, as does an examination of the influences at work within the organisations.

Counselling organisations have been the focus of a number of extensive studies (Lago and Kitchin, 1998; Lewis, Clark and Morgan, 1992; Skynner, 1989; Tyndall, 1993; Woodhouse and Pengelly, 1991). The different perspectives of those authors assist in identifying several significant influences that demand attention if success in service provision is to be combined with the maintenance of organisational health.

There is no reason to believe that counselling organisations escape the problems discussed in any management textbook (Handy, 1990), but those general issues will not be considered here. The particular influences which have relevance to this chapter's discussion derive from the missions, value systems, activities and client communities of counselling organisations. Thus, the fact that counselling organisations tend to give an emphasis to operating in accord with particular value systems results in their workforces being constituted of individuals with strongly held beliefs. For example, numbers of counsellors in one charitable organisation regard a capacity to offer counselling free of charge for those without the means to pay for it as an essential feature of the service which they provide.

The consequence is that 'conviction politics' feature strongly in the life of the organisations and may, at times, give the external observer the impression that they are hotbeds of discontent and discord. The reality is that, when mismanaged, conviction politics can be profoundly divisive, but they have also been used to strengthen and clarify the missions of organisations. Palmer Barnes (1998) describes the differing approaches adopted by counselling organisations and Berne (1963) traces the development of ideas about social dynamics from Ancient Times to the 20th Century.

In counselling organisations problematic functioning which results from internal characteristics is added to by a distinctive external influence — the clients. A counselling organisation's task is to engage with the confusions, anxieties, conflicts and distress of those who use their services. Counselling itself can be regarded as a mutually transforming process, and the relationship between the organisation and its client community can be thought of in the same way. Ideally, the conflict resolution and problem-solving, and the growth in insight, awareness and understanding, which take place in counselling, will detoxify the content of casework for both client and counsellor. The reality is that those processes are commonly partial and the counsellor may end a case having benefited, but also having acquired or activated unresolved material. At the organisational level the cumulative effect of casework may be growth in expertise and capacity, but at the cost of a need to identify, contain and process effectively the unresolved material that is a by-product of service delivery. To understand the organisational implications of that by-product it is necessary to take a closer look at the characteristics of practitioner workforces.

In a paper originally commissioned by, and delivered at, the 1987 Annual Meeting of the Supervisors' and Trainers' Association of Relate (STAR), and later published (1989), Robin Skynner described what it was that motivated people to join the caring professions, and what the influences were which shaped their organisations. His earlier volumes, 'Families and How to Survive Them' (Skynner and Cleese, 1983) and 'Explorations with Families' (1987) described individuals' deprivation resulting from their parents' need for, and denial of, some form of parental care. That denial results in the apparently altruistic thought 'I want my children to have the things I didn't have myself' and the development of situations in which the children do not get what *they* need, but what *their parents* need. Skynner goes on to argue that some people join the caring professions to serve their denied needs in a similar way, and that in a given, specialised group of professionals individuals are likely to have the same denied needs. Professional bodies set up by innovators dissatisfied with existing ideas and methods tend to grow by attracting others with wider motivations — the prestige of membership, status, career enhancement — whose purposes are served by maintaining the currency of the founders' methodology. (Something of this can be seen in the almost religious commitment to the writings of key individuals.) What had been an 'open system' becomes a 'closed system', ideas become doctrine, and a rigid hierarchical structure develops. The capacity to embrace loss and change diminishes. To the extent that shared 'blind spots' are denied, the professionals will reproduce the dynamics of their families of origin in their institutions. Significantly, this involves the identification of, and engagement with, client groups which own, or can be invested with, the deprivation the professionals deny. Concentration on those being helped enables the professionals to avoid change in themselves, and the associated painful insights. Deprivation is thus perpetuated.

Skynner sees the key to healthy, 'open system' professional organisations to be open, two-way communication enabling the whole intelligence of the professional-client community to be used for learning and development. That open communication is aided by professionals who remain open to themselves and are pursuing growing self-awareness and self-acceptance. Another positive characteristic is a readiness to acknowledge and accept differences within the profession rather than the maintenance of a united front which conceals them, and locates jealousy in clients or students. Skynner describes his own insights as resulting from the influence of S.H.Foulkes' (1948) group-analytic method and an alertness to the different levels and systems in which individuals and professional groups are involved.

This view of professional institutions, and of counselling organisations in particular, gives a resonance to the aphorism 'Physician, heal thyself', but there is another kind of resonance to be considered: that which is set up in counsellors and their organisations by what were referred to earlier as the 'by-products' of the therapeutic process.

Woodhouse and Pengelly (1991) have built on work done by Isabel Menzies Lyth (Menzies, 1970) on the functioning of social systems in hospitals as a defence against their employees' anxiety. They explored the impact of anxiety on the dynamics of collaboration within, and between, the caring professions and write ' . . . that inter-professional collaboration across the whole network of services was permeated with the same dynamic tensions concerning triangular relationships and third parties that we were studying at close quarters in the marriage guidance field.' (ibid.: 37) They go on to illustrate the ways in which practitioners are exposed to the powerful unconscious dynamics within clients and their relationships, and show how the counselling organisations concerned are liable to be influenced by them. Two important ideas emerge. Firstly, practitioners' *behaviour* towards clients which indicates a recognition and understanding of their conflicts is probably as significant therapeutically as anything that is said to them. This proposition has importance in the counselling room, but also turns attention to the ways in which counselling organisations present and represent counsellors to (potential) clients. It suggests that the literature, the activities of lay support staff, and the organisation of the intake and appointment systems of counselling organisations have a more profound impact on the outcomes of counselling services than is sometimes acknowledged. Secondly, faced with clients' powerful unconscious dynamics, practitioners need an organisational setting which provides a holding environment permitting them to contain anxiety, understand its origins, and incorporate it purposefully in their work with the clients.

Woodhouse and Pengelly's study led them to conclude that conscious efforts to sustain the needed holding environment were typically paralleled by organisational practices acting as institutionalized defences. Among defences identified was a socially organised reluctance to establish robust intake and assessment procedures; those procedures being substituted by the 'decision-making' of individual counsellors responding to ideas about optimizing accessibility, and anti-discriminatory practice prevalent in their organisation. This defence reflects an avoidance of conflicts arising out of the different vested interests of the clients, the counselling organisation, and third parties such as referrers; the 'intruding third' in a triangular relationship. The disinclination of counselling organisations to work collaboratively, reinforced by the similar stances of other caring professions, is seen as another defence against the problems of triangular relationships, in this case made tangible by the tensions experienced between the demands for confidentiality and co-operation. This author's experience of couple counsellor's collective reluctance to give weight to, and address, clients' sexual interaction as an integral part of their relationships is yet a further example of an institutionalized defence against the primitive feelings and anxiety associated with triangular relationships.

Summarizing, it appears that alongside all the management issues with which every organisation must grapple, counselling organisations have at least five additional, different but inter-related internal tasks.

- They must put in place the means to sustain open communications, intrapsychically and inter-personally. That is, they must sustain their organisations as open systems or, in bigger entities, as assemblies of open systems.
- They must establish structures and practices which both assure and also define the permeability of the boundaries of their organisation's systems. A failure to maintain appropriate boundaries can result in loss of identity and differentiation, or isolate the systems from their environments.
- Their structures, staffing and practices must be shaped to ensure that clients experience organisational responses as well as counsellors' words which indicate a recognition and understanding of the conflicts for which they are seeking professional help.
- They must sustain for their workforces a holding environment in which the conflicted material acquired or activated through contact with clients can be metabolized and used for the mutually transformative purposes of counselling.
- Counselling organisations must be alert to their potential to evolve organisational defences within their structures and practices which act to protect them from the dilemmas and the anxieties that result from client casework and working relations with other caring professionals. Without those means there can be little hope that an organisation will remain healthy, creative, and effective as a service provider.

Lack of space prevents discussion of the different ways that those needs can be served. They are detailed in texts about the training of counsellors (Dryden and Feltham, 1994; Dryden, Horton and Mearns, 1995; Hildebrand, 1998; Jacobs 1991), their on-going professional development (Charleton, 1996; Johns, 1996; Relate 1999) and their supervision (Hawkins and Shohet, 1989; Holloway and Carroll, 1999; Hughes and Pengelly, 1997; Mattinson, 1975). Other sources which discuss the management of counselling organisations propose structures and practices which facilitate maintenance of those vital systems (Lago and Kitchin,

1998; Tyndall 1993). Together, the ideas and practices offered hold the promise of achievement of organisations which can make use of their service delivery role to learn, develop and attune themselves to change within their communities.

The scene is now set in which to examine the impact of client complaints on counselling organisations.

Over an extended period it has been the author's experience that only a tiny minority of client complaints are motivated by wishes to engage adversarially with counsellors and their organisations, and a similarly small proportion raise issues which may eventually result in disciplinary procedures being invoked. It is nonetheless true that the procedures adopted by counselling organisations differ widely in their nature — some are pseudo-judicial, others seek to sustain a therapeutic stance. The position taken here is that it is a counselling organisation's obligation to sustain privacy and to pursue therapeutic purposes to the greatest extent possible when addressing complaints made by clients.

The case study set out below describes events within an organisation that is trying to hold a balance between honouring its duty of care to its clients, and limiting the potential liabilities of the organisation. Liabilities might be increased by engaging a (potentially adversarial) complainant in open and frank communication intended to yield therapeutic benefit. Identifying details in the account have been changed.

> *Jean, the counselling centre's receptionist, took the telephone call just moments before the end of the day's working period. Expecting the caller to request counselling, or to make an enquiry about an appointment, she identified the centre and gave her name and role, but was interrupted by an angry male voice. He didn't want to speak to a receptionist, he wanted the manager. Uncertain whether the manager was in the building, Jean asked the caller to hold the line, checked, found the manager had left and, returning to the phone, said the manager was not available. She added that she might be able to help if told what the caller wanted.*
>
> *The offer was angrily dismissed and it was made clear that the caller felt fobbed-off. Jean assured him that the manager really had left the Centre, and repeated her offer of help. This was again refused. 'When can I get hold of the manager?' Told that the centre opened at 8.30 next morning, the caller rang off without further comment. Jean left a note on the manager's desk. 'I took a call from an angry man at about 8.55 pm. He wanted you and he knows you will be here this morning. Jean. 9.05 pm Monday.'*

The situation described will be recognised by many who work for counselling organisations. No doubt some readers will have anticipated the sinking feeling experienced by the manager when he reached his desk on Tuesday. It had to be somebody wanting to make a complaint. But who was the caller and why did he ring so late in the day? All in all, things had got off on the wrong foot. Jean was a very discreet and reliable receptionist who handled the centre's normal phone calls well, though she had never taken a call from a complainant before.

From the 'complainant's' perspective the call would have confirmed any prejudice he may have had about the centre's inefficiency. Though open, nobody in authority was available, and the impression had been given that the person receiving his call didn't know how to handle an important and urgent matter. It would almost have been better if he had been connected to a recorded message which suggested calling again during normal office hours. Though perfectly polite, the receptionist had failed in several important respects because she was unprepared. It was appropriate that a receptionist was present at a time when counselling was taking place in the centre. It was good that phone calls could be taken while the centre was open. It was understandable that the manager was not in the building. But it was self-evidently unhelpful, and possibly harmful to both caller and centre, that no contingency plan had been put in place to deal effectively with unusual, urgent or hostile phone calls which needed the absent manager's attention.

Such situations arise when an open system fails to recognise the implications of well-intentioned efforts to keep its boundary with the community permeable. Failure to have clear criteria which determine who and what can access the system, and when, and how denial of access (albeit temporary) is communicated to those concerned, is detrimental to the system and its environment. It results in messages being communicated which indicate that it does not know what it is about. The system's functioning is likely to be perceived as unfair, unreliable, or mindlessly arbitrary — not a safe system. In the longer term, it is also likely to result in the system being experienced as more closed — less accessible — than is intended. At the level of the individuals concerned it can generate confusion, distress, anger, and anxiety, unnecessarily.

Internally, a positive outcome could be secured by the centre if role boundaries were retained and refined, if anxieties were contained rather than discharged through blaming, if open communication between personnel was used to identify the root issues, and if realistic and reliable arrangements for the centre's boundary keeping were put in place. It should be added that boundary keeping arrangements require regular review. For example, the widespread use of mobile telephones might change thinking about a manager's accessibility. It certainly raises boundary keeping issues in the counselling room.

> Nick, the centre manager, sat at his desk at 8.30 on Tuesday morning and read Jean's note. Another over-full day had started with the prospect that planned jobs would have to be put aside because of an unforeseen call on his time. He was wondering what he could do to prepare for the phone call he now expected when the phone rang. Picking the phone up immediately, he gave the centre's name, his own name, said that he was the centre manager and asked who it was that was calling. That request was ignored. The male caller asked for confirmation that Nick was indeed the manager. Giving that assurance Nick again asked the caller's name and how he could be helped. The caller, a Mr. Follett, stated that he was not making a simple complaint, he was wanting immediate action taken to prevent his 23 year old daughter being placed in a situation that caused her to make a suicide attempt, as she had done the previous afternoon. Called to the local hospital as next of kin, Mr. Follett had found his daughter recovering from a drug overdose. He had gathered from Norma that having

*had an appointment with her counsellor in the early afternoon, she had gone back to her flat instead of returning to work, and had taken a considerable number of prescribed sleeping tablets. The alarm had been raised by a work colleague whom Norma should have met at 3 pm. Mr. Follett was clearly angry but very much in charge of himself. He wanted Norma's counsellor stopped from working with clients immediately. In particular, he wanted an absolute assurance that the counsellor would have no further contact with Norma.*

*Nick had been making notes as Mr. Follett spoke and, as soon as the opportunity offered itself, he acknowledged the caller's shock, distress and anger, and the very natural wish to do everything possible to prevent the recurrence of a life-threatening situation. 'That's fine, but what are you going to do about the counsellor? Where is he? What is his name? I'm quite prepared to get the police out to him!' It took some minutes for Nick to convince Mr. Follett that he was taking the matter seriously. It became apparent that the caller had very little further information, Norma had been barely awake when he was last with her. Norma had been kept in hospital overnight and Mr. Follett was on his way to collect her and take her back to the family home. Pointing out that no harm would come to Norma while her father was with her, Nick got Mr. Follett's agreement to speak again, later in the morning, when more information was available. Nick suggested that he would phone the Follett's home at 11 am and was given the number to call.*

*After scanning the notes he had taken, Nick phoned the centre's supervisor and asked her to come to his office immediately. He also rang the chair of the centre's management committee and left a message asking her to call back. Then he went to the reception area and began to search for appointments provided for Norma.*

The manager was the recipient of a 'third party' call. Confidentiality and respect for the client's autonomy require that such calls are handled with extreme caution. The expectation is that clients themselves will take any initiative necessary to protect their own well-being. That being the case, a 'third party' would normally be told that the existence of a counselling relationship can neither be acknowledged or denied, and that protection of individuals' rights to determine whether or not to make use of, to terminate, or to complain about, a counselling relationship is a practitioner's, and a counselling organisation's, first responsibility. Two matters complicate the situation. The 'third party' may have *direct* evidence that a counsellor's actions were bringing counselling into disrepute. Or they may have *direct* evidence that a client, a counsellor, or another person in contact with either client or counsellor, was at risk of serious harm. Such circumstances create dilemmas which must be resolved on a case by case basis. It appears possible that the manager, Nick, is faced with that kind of dilemma.

The account of events indicates that the manager acted with caution and skill. Any involvement with a third party caller offers hostages to fortune, but no acknowledgement of the existence of a particular counselling relationship was given, and no undertakings to intervene in a putative relationship were made.

The reported suicide attempt alerted the manager to the need for more information, and prompted the arrangement to speak again to the caller at a time when it might be available. It also bought the manager time in which to review the situation and identify ethical lines of action.

The account provides information which indicate some threats to the structures and practices of the centre:

- The manager's status (practitioner/non-practitioner), training and experience may, or may not, make him the most appropriate person to play a front-line role in the handling of complaints. Making that a function of a clinical manager may be more appropriate.
- The manager's 'over-full' days create conflicts of interest. The need to make moment by moment judgements about priorities may hazard the whole work of the centre.
- No reference is made to the manager making use of a written procedure or guidelines about the need to notify, consult with, or engage as lead worker, any other member of the centre.
- The manager's action in immediately arranging to talk with the supervisor appears constructive. Does the supervisor hold procedures or guidelines? If not, what will the supervisor's role be? Who will decide? What will be the purpose of that involvement?
- The manager's phone call to the chair of the centre's management committee also appears constructive. What was the manager's intention? To inform the chair about a potentially problematic situation or to seek the chair's direct involvement in handling the matter? If the latter was the manager's purpose, the risk exists that one of the potential benefits of the centre's structure will be lost since the chair's direct involvement from the outset would deny use of that person as a detached mediator at later stages.
- The manager's efforts to identify counselling sessions provided for Norma are a very natural response to the anxieties created by Mr. Follett's call. However, if successful, Nick would then have the name of the counsellor and access to other information which could easily distract from the primary issue — management of responses to a complicated third party intervention.
- The manager took notes when speaking to Mr. Follett but there is no mention of him keeping a log of all contacts and actions. That kind of record is an essential part of an 'audit trail', provides invaluable information for training, and would be a good source of learning for those involved in the situation.

Whether intentional or not, Nick's action ensured that he had some time to think and to talk to others. This benefit was obtained by risking that the caller would presume that his demands were reasonable, legitimate and were being acted upon. Complaints, demands, and other messages of a hostile nature, generate anxieties and a tendency to respond without careful consideration. The sense of urgency commonly communicated by those delivering such messages creates dilemmas for the recipient . How to balance the need for time to reflect against the need to alleviate threat or distress? How to frame a strategy that has thinking time built into it without creating misapprehensions in the caller about not being believed, not having a legitimate concern, or simply not being engaged with?

*While still searching through the appointment book Nick was joined by the supervisor. Having moved into Nick's office, Nick used the notes he had made to brief his colleague. 'This is a complicated situation. So what is it you want me to do?' Nick had not really thought that through and acknowledged that fact, inviting the supervisor to suggest what role she should play. Between them they analysed the situation. A decision would have to be taken about the centre's response to a third party call. Whose judgements and what advice should be taken beforehand? Who should seek those inputs and who should communicate the decision reached to Mr. Follett? Potentially, things became much more complicated after that stage. The supervisor pointed out that, even if the centre could not use information given by Mr. Follett externally, it was still in the possession of the manager and herself — and how should it be dealt with internally? This last point forced a recognition that even the limited information so far supplied by Mr. Follett must be kept in confidence and should only be available to those with a direct role in responding to the caller. At that point the chair of the management committee's call to the manager came through and, with nodded encouragement from the supervisor, Nick gave the chair a summary of the situation faced, without providing any identifying details. The chair's comment was that those directly involved should take whatever advice they thought necessary before reaching any decisions, and that she would like a brief report about action taken either when matters had been resolved, or as the situation developed from stage to stage.*

*Returning to the question about the roles people should play, Nick told the supervisor that he had decided that it was his responsibility to take advice, to reach a decision about the way to respond to Mr. Follett, and to act on that decision. He wanted the supervisor to go away for an hour and return with advice about how to proceed, based on consultations with her peers and her own supervisor.*

Has commonsense prevailed? Do organisations really need written procedures? The insight offered by the events described is that high quality personnel with good working relationships have a capacity to deal with crises. However, it is a hazardous strategy for an organisation to depend so heavily on the qualities of individuals — prudent management and governance demands that procedures are in place to deal with predictable critical events.

*The supervisor returned to Nick's office having been able to talk briefly with her own supervisor, but not having reached any of the others she might have consulted. She said that the first thing that she must acknowledge was that she knew about the casework involving Norma, and knew the name of the counsellor involved. Nick interrupted saying that he did not want to know any details before hearing what the supervisor's view was about responding to Mr. Follett. Staying carefully on matters of principle, the supervisor argued that a third party's genuine concern to get action taken to avert a threat to the life of a putative client placed an ethical obligation on the centre to gather information, even at the cost of breach of the individual's confidentiality. If the individual did prove to be a client, it would also be appropriate to discover whether or not the counsellor-client relationship was the source of influences, intentional or otherwise, which might lead to (self-)harm. Nick said that he had also taken advice, making use of an experienced EAP practice manager who lived locally. Among other comments, that contact had made the point that there was a body of professional opinion which asserted individuals' rights to take their own lives, though supportive of efforts which might be made to dissuade those concerned. Mr. Follett's view had been that counselling had precipitated a suicide attempt, and that further contact with the counsellor could do so again. Nick decided to make use of Mr. Follett's information to investigate the possibility that Norma had found contact with her counsellor a malign influence.*

*Nick put a call through to the Follett's home. He was surprised to hear a woman's voice answering and immediately asked to speak to Mr. Follett. 'My name is Norma. Are you ringing from the counselling centre?' Nick said that he was the centre's manager, that he had made a commitment to speak to Mr. Follett, and that he thought it best for Norma to bring Mr. Follett to the phone. 'I know what my dad did, we have talked about it. He is happy for me to speak to you and I want you to understand things from my point of view.' Nick suggested that he be given the chance to check that out with Mr. Follett, he would then be ready to listen to Norma. What emerged from Norma's statement was that she had asked for counselling because she had been feeling suicidal more and more of the time. The counsellor had worked hard to help her make sense of her life and to find reasons to go on living. They had worked to a schedule which was intended to put her on a 'positive path' and make her independent of counselling by its end. Things had gone very well until the last week or two, as the end of counselling got closer. Counselling had ended on Monday despite Norma's unspoken misgivings. She had thought that her only option was a 'cry for help' and had taken the tablets confident that her work colleague would raise the alarm. Norma very much wanted counselling to resume. She apologized for her father's action — he had got the wrong end of the stick.*

*Checking his notes as he spoke Nick told Norma's story to the supervisor. As he did so he realised that the questions forming in his mind about the nature and appropriateness of the counselling received by Norma implicated the supervisor herself. 'I have given you the facts as I understand them. You will realize that I must investigate the casework done with Norma, and that includes inputs from supervision. I want you to do two things. First, I want your undertaking not to speak to anybody about the situation, especially not to the counsellor. Second, I must ask you to be ready to discuss with me, or someone I select, your understanding of Norma's counselling and what you believe should happen next.' The supervisor left, aware that she had spent no more than ten minutes with the counsellor talking about the work with Norma. Subsequently Nick rang his EAP clinical manager contact to ask whether she could devote two or three hours on the following day to some work to determine how the consequences of a complicated piece of casework should be handled. He felt angry and punitive, and at the same time realized the importance of some prompt action to ensure Norma got the help she needed.*

Had the client not intervened, the manager would have acted on a decision that might well have been disputed in any subsequent review of events. Dilemmas commonly result in courses of action which are not entirely satisfactory (BAC, 1997 B.1.6.3), the critical issue is whether or not decisions were taken in the light of all the available facts, having taken advice, and after a careful review of the other available options. The events described suggest that a number of favourable factors contributed to the process in which the manager was involved. Are there ways in which the centre could organise and manage such events so as to put less reliance on good fortune?

The client's statement drew attention to two issues. Had she received safe, competent counselling? What should the centre offer her in the future? It also resulted in the manager redefining the supervisor's role in the handling of the situation. Was that the precursor of a judgemental investigation in which the supervisor would have to justify her actions, or was she being offered the space in which to reflect on the therapeutic work done, and to be done? Did the plan to involve an outsider who had specialist skills indicate a readiness to engage in adjudication, or an acknowledgement of the limitations of the centre, and the benefits of skilled case management? Lastly, did the supervisor's recall of only ten minutes devoted to the client's case indicate the inadequacy of the arrangements for supervision, or the weaknesses of supervision in which the counsellor chooses the material to be addressed.

*Wednesday morning. Nick, the manager, and Tricia, the EAP clinical manager, had spent half an hour reviewing the events connected with Norma. Tricia was becoming increasingly concerned to know more about the nature of the counselling Norma had received. Nick had prepared for the meeting by assembling details of the sessions which Norma had attended. The centre's practice of keeping all formal casenotes in a locked cabinet in the counsellors' room had permitted Nick to collect those relating to Norma. Twelve sessions were recorded. Norma was reported to have described herself as 'depressed' at the outset, but there was no specific mention of suicidal feelings or intentions. In session two agreement to structured counselling was recorded. There were notes identifying a variety of life events and a number of preoccupying thought patterns which had been the focus of attention. By session nine the counsellor reported evidence of Norma's more positive thinking and improved appearance. It was in that session that the intention to end the work after twelve sessions was noted. No record of any expression of misgivings on Norma's part was found in notes on sessions ten, eleven or twelve. The last line of the notes on session twelve stated 'Norma realizes that she needs to stand on her own feet and she left, quiet but determined'.*

*There was no record of supervisory input, consultations with the client's GP, or consideration of a referral.*

*Notes from the supervisor stated that the counsellor, Rory, had discussed his work with Norma in terms of the multiple losses she had experienced and her fears that her parents would die 'too soon'. There was no mention of habitual suicidal thinking, or of his adoption of a fixed term contract. The supervisor stated that she had thought the counsellor well -equipped to work with Norma, he had recently completed a postgraduate diploma course. She owned herself shocked by the differences in the accounts given by Norma and the counsellor, and by Norma's statement that the work had been focused on freeing her from habitual suicidal thoughts.*

*Tricia's view was that more needed to be known about the counselling done and that she would like to speak directly to Rory. It may be that he needed a period of intensive supervision of his casework — had the depth of Norma's depression and the intensity of the distress associated with her suicidal thinking been recognised?*

*Nick reached into a desk drawer and took out the centre's disciplinary procedure, but Tricia wanted to discuss the options available to the centre when Norma was next contacted — she had asked for her counselling to be resumed. Tricia saw that as being potentially problematic.*

*On Wednesday afternoon Norma spoke again to Nick. Her father had arranged a private consultation with a clinical psychologist for her that morning. The outcome had been that she would be attending a series of sessions with her, starting immediately. She would not want more counselling by Rory for the moment. She asked the manager to tell Rory she was sorry.*

The reader, like the clinical manager, will be left with a catalogue of concerns about the centre's systems and procedures. What may have appeared at first to be an effective organisation was left questioning the ways it had allocated roles and resources to supervisors, counsellors and lay workers; about accountability for casework; about its structure and whether it provided for all the functions necessary to handle the predictable contingencies of work with clients; and about procedures and guidelines for client complaints, for collaboration with the other caring professions, and for referrals. A single instance of a challenge to the centre's workings had threatened the working assumptions of its key personnel, and was likely to have substantial repercussions for all concerned.

Stokoe uses psychoanalytic thinking in a discussion of the nature of therapeutic organisations' responses to client complaints (Stokoe and Fisher, 1997). Use is made of Bion's concepts of container and contained (1962), Winnicott's concept of a holding environment (1965), and that author's own experience of complaints procedures. Clients seek help because they are unable to contain their own unresolved material. Therapy offers that containment and analytic work is done when the meaning of the impacts of the client's material on the therapeutic container is understood and fed back into the therapy. Those impacts on the container constitute risk for the therapist. When the therapist is caught up or damaged by an impact there must be a further source of containment available to provide therapeutic responses for *both* client and therapist. Stokoe asserts that risk, being caught up in the client's material, and being damaged by impacts are occupational hazards and that it should be a therapeutic organisation's *obligation* to ensure that this additional kind of containment is in place from the outset, and is known to exist by the client. He sees a client's complaint as an appeal to a third person to put right what has gone wrong for client and therapist — an appeal to 'Daddy' in the Oedipal triangle. To be effective in this sense the third person needs to be known to the client from the outset, and known to be engaged in a continuing, appropriate (confidential, professional) dialogue with the therapist. So defined, the third party can serve as both the source of secondary containment and, as a part of that function, the agency through which therapeutically oriented thinking is applied to a problem presented in a complaint. Stokoe's argument is based in the belief that it is profoundly inconsistent to trust in work based on therapeutic principles up to the point at which the client complains and then to switch to a pseudo-judicial framework thereafter. More than that, he argues that it is to the client's detriment if that happens. His colleague, Fisher, takes the argument a step further. It flies in the face of experience to assert that, in situations in which complaints are lodged, both client and therapist are functioning as detached, mature, autonomous individuals. In the generality of cases client and therapist are enmeshed and engaged in roles with one another other than what Berne (1961) might call Adult—Adult. That is, client and therapist are engaged in 'acting out' the emotional dynamics of the therapeutic relationship. This makes it vital that the initial response to a complaint — to the fact that therapist and counsellor are, together, in difficulties — is one based on a therapeutic framework for thinking and action. In this way the needs of both client and therapist can be understood, and questions about unprofessional conduct resolved by those with highly developed practice skills.

These ideas will be persuasive for psychodynamic practitioners. It is likely that they can be paralleled by propositions based on the conceptual frameworks of other approaches — a task left to those better versed in those forms of practice. The question is whether they can be translated into structures and procedures which will allow counselling organisations to handle client complaints with a congruence and creativity which will serve the clients', the counsellors' and the organisations' own needs.

The primary requirement is for a source of secondary containment with which clients have contact as they enter counselling, and which is also known to be engaged in a continuing 'background' professional dialogue with their counsellors. Clients should understand that, if they have concerns about their counselling which cannot be dealt with in the counselling room, the secondary container is their first source of help. In particular, it should be apparent that this resource is devoted to providing *therapeutic* responses to issues that arise in counselling through the consistent application of good practice, underpinned by counselling ethics. In themselves, the functions described do not add up to a job description, but they do point to the need for highly experienced practitioners. Supervisors, clinical managers, and intake and assessment specialists all have skills which suggest their involvement. Those familiar with training methods used in Family Therapy may see the consulting group behind the one-way mirror as an ideal source of secondary containment. Numbers of counselling organisations have arrangements in place which go some way towards providing the resource described. In order to make ideas concrete, and to highlight key features of a practical arrangement, the centre featured in this chapter's case study is referred to. The changes proposed are:

a) First and foremost, the establishment of the principle that a counselling organisation needs *both* managerial supervision and counselling supervision for its practitioners. Managerial supervision is the means by which the practitioners are held accountable for the duties they undertake as employees, and by which the organisation can be held to its responsibilities to provide a setting within which effective counselling can be delivered. Counselling supervision ensures that counselling is undertaken with the benefit of availability of the secondary containment of which Stokoe wrote (Stokoe and Fisher, 1997). These are discrete functions and it should always be the case that those concerned are in no doubt about what form of supervision is being undertaken. This last point is of particular importance when individuals have responsibilities for both counselling supervision and managerial tasks in the same organisation. This principle informs the changes which follow.

b) The job description of Nick, the non-practitioner manager, is rewritten to exclude direct involvement in client complaints, or in the determination of good practice guidelines for lay support staff in contact with clients. He is charged with responsibility for disciplinary procedures applicable to all centre staff. He will convene meetings with the supervisor and practice manager and be responsible for taking recommendations and proposals for the operation of the centre to the management committee for its approval.

c) A widely experienced counsellor is appointed Practice Manager charged with responsibility for a system providing pre-counselling (assessment) interviews and allocation of clients to counsellors. That system is staffed by experienced counsellors. Collectively, Practice Manager, pre-counselling interviewers and supervisor have responsibility for the *therapeutic* work of secondary containment. The Practice Manager has responsibility for determining, and providing training in, good practice for lay staff in face to face, or telephone, contact with clients.

d) A written procedure for handling client complaints is adopted.

e) All staff are briefed about new appointments, changes in job descriptions, new procedures, and their purposes.

f) Literature given to clients on first contact with the centre includes a statement referring clients to the Practice Manager if they have concerns/complaints about their counselling.

g) The Supervisor role is extended by the requirement to act as a channel of communication between the counsellors and the secondary containment group, and to use that group as a resource when dealing with case management issues.

h) A review of structure, procedures and the functioning of secondary containment is scheduled in six months time.

It is not intended that the arrangements described should be regarded as a model for widespread adoption. It is hoped that they will generate discussion and creative efforts to install what has been called secondary containment where it has not previously existed.

Some thought must be given to the counsellors themselves. Experience shows that being the subject of a client complaint can prove a frightening, de-skilling and isolating experience. Colleagues can be experienced as judgemental and many of an organisation's normally supportive structures take on self-protective qualities. Secondary containment separates the processes used to deal with problems in counselling from those which , from time to time, are necessary to deal with disciplinary issues. That is, it ensures that counsellors have a supportive professional environment within which to do their work and deal with their problems, particularly when the work is at its riskiest and anxieties run high. Secondary containment put in place after a complaint has been lodged can never perform with the same beneficial results as that which had been a feature of the counselling from the outset. Its belated introduction changes the rules by sharing responsibilities which counsellor and client had formerly believed to be the counsellor's alone with the potential consequence that the client's trust in the counsellor is further undermined.

This chapter has concerned itself with counselling and complaints in organisational settings. An independent counsellor may have read it happy in the belief that their practice is not complicated by the need to understand and use sometimes complex structures and procedures in order to serve their clients. The reality is that a well-developed private practice must have arrangements in place to provide all the resources discussed above which facilitate safe, effective counselling and promote the counsellor's professional development. And that includes secondary containment. All too often the supervisor who in some sense undertakes that function in untroubled times proves unable to contain counsellor *and* client when difficulties arise because they are inaccessible, and an unknown quantity, to the client. Nor is a remote professional body able to step in effectively, since the on-going professional dialogue on which secondary containment is based is seldom sufficiently developed. Stokoe (ibid.), writing about psychoanalytic psychotherapists operating independently, suggests that clients who are assessed by one practitioner and referred to another might be encouraged to regard the assessing therapist as 'Daddy' and that both therapist and client could benefit from that form of secondary containment. Perhaps counsellors in private practice need to put similar arrangements in place?

## References

BAC. (1997). *Code of Ethics and Practice for Counsellors.* Rugby: BAC.

Berne, E. (1961). *Transactional Analysis in Psychotherapy.* New York: Grove Press.

Berne, E. (1963). *The Structure and Dynamics of Organisations and Groups.* New York: Grove Press.

Bion, W. (1962). A Theory of Thinking. In *Second Thoughts: Selected Papers on Psychoanalysis.* (Reissued by Karnac [Maresfield] 1984).

Charleton, M. (1996). *Self-directed Learning in Counsellor Training.* London: Cassell.

Dryden, W. and Feltham, C. (1994). *Developing Counsellor Training.* London: Sage.

Dryden, W. Horton, I. and Mearns, D. (1995). *Issues in Professional Counsellor Training.* London: Cassell.

Foulkes, S. (1948). *Introduction to Group-Analytic Psychotherapy.* London: Heinemann. (Reissued by Karnac [Maresfield], 1983).

Handy, C. (1990). *Inside Organisations: 21 Ideas for Managers.* London: BBC Books.

Hawkins, P. and Shohet, R. (1989). *Supervision in the Helping Professions.* Milton Keynes: Open University Press.

Hildebrand, J. (1998). *Bridging the Gap: A Training Module in Personal and Professional Development.* London: Karnac.

Holloway, E. and Carroll, M. (1999). *Training Counselling Supervisors.* London: Sage.

Hughes, L. and Pengelly, P. (1997). *Staff Supervision in a Turbulent Environment: Managing Process and Task in Front-line Services.* London: Jessica Kingsley.

Jacobs, M. (1991). *Insight and Experience: A manual of training in the technique and theory of Psychodynamic Counselling and Therapy.* Milton Keynes: Open University Press.

Johns, H. (1996). *Personal Development in Counsellor Training.* London: Cassell.

Lago, C. and Kitchin, D. (1998). *The Management of Counselling and Psychotherapy Agencies.* London: Sage.

Lewis, J., Clark, D. and Morgan, D. (1992). *Whom God hath Joined Together: The Work of Marriage Guidance.* London: Routledge.

Mattinson, J. (1975). *The Reflection Process in Casework Supervision.*

Menzies, I. (1970). The functioning of social systems as a defence against anxiety. In *Containing anxiety in institutions: selected essays.* Volume 1. (1988) London: Free Association Books.

Palmer Barnes, F. (1998). *Complaints and Grievances in Psychotherapy: A Handbook of Ethical Practice.* London: Routledge.

Relate (1999). *Student Handbook. Postgraduate Certificate, Postgraduate Diploma and Master of Arts Degree in Couple Therapy.* Rugby: Relate/ University of East London.

Skynner, R. (1987). J. Schlapobersky, (ed.) *Explorations with Families: Group Analysis and Family Therapy.* London: Methuen.

Skynner, R. (1989). J. Schlapobersky, (ed.) *Institutes and how to survive them.* London: Methuen.

Skynner, R. and Cleese, J. (1983). *Families and how to survive them.* London: Methuen.

Stokoe, P. and Fisher, J. (1997). An Invitation to a Dialogue about a Model for a Complaints Procedure. *Society of Psychoanalytic Marital Psychotherapists Bulletin,* 4: 51–5.

Tyndall, N. (1993). *Counselling in the Voluntary Sector.* Buckingham: Open University Press.

Winnicott, D. (1965). *The Maturational Processes and the Facilitating Environment: Studies in the Theory of Emotional Development.* London: Hogarth Press.

Woodhouse, D. and Pengelly, P. (1991). *Anxiety and the Dynamics of Collaboration.* Aberdeen: Aberdeen University Press.

# Chapter 9

# Complaints, Boundary and Training Issues: Comparisons between Britain and America. An Adjudicator's View

## Rob Hooper

### Introduction

'Could it be me?' My guess is that these are the words that form in the minds of most practitioners and educators of counsellors when the subject of 'complaints' is raised. This is both from the point of view of the safety and well being of our clients and trainees and of saving our own skin. My own increased focus on complaints within counselling has certainly been sharpened in the four years that I have been an adjudicator for the BACP complaints procedure. I have been involved as an adjudicator with three cases where both training courses and boundary issues have been involved.

This chapter will focus on boundary issues for counsellors and trainers and how we might develop good practice in order to avoid complaints. Despite our development of good practice, however, it might not be possible and would not be ethical to prevent the possibility of complaints. It is also possible that such complaints will increasingly be taken to the courts. Since America frequently precedes us in the development of our professional work, I will be looking briefly at American law in this respect and considering how far this might apply to the future for therapists and counsellor educators in this country.

### Three complaints about boundaries and training

In the following examples the facts have been changed significantly in order to protect confidentiality.

> In the first case a female trainer, Pauline, at a University in the South of England had fallen in love with a male student many years younger than her. The two had interacted socially whilst they were trainer and trainee and had begun a sexual relationship in the Spring vacation following Pauline having terminated her role as a trainer in the course. The relationship was no passing fancy as soon afterwards the couple became engaged and later married. However, fellow students on the course felt that in the early stages of their relationship trainer and trainee had not

*been transparently honest. Though this was not verbalised it seemed that they experienced some feelings of jealousy and/or feelings of favouritism. I and the other adjudicators had sympathy for both sides in this case. Nevertheless we considered that there were breaches of ethics and boundaries and sanctions were imposed against Pauline.*

*In the second situation a male consultant to a training course, Mark, accepted an approach by a trainee to provide personal therapy. It transpired during the therapy that the trainee was not only an alcoholic — which she had concealed from course tutors — but also had mentioned emotional problems which Mark felt were so severe as to make her unfit to take up a counselling placement for her training. Not only did Mark attempt to block the placement, but he also discontinued therapy rather abruptly. Although the student appeared to agree at the time with the appropriateness of this, she afterwards became angry about it. Some clear breaches of boundaries had been made in this situation and also the ending had not been worked through responsibly. The adjudicators found against Mark and action was taken.*

*The final case concerned a young man on a course at a college, who was well respected by his tutor, Rebecca, and formed a platonic but very close relationship with her. For him Rebecca could do no wrong and she was very much looked up to. Unfortunately, Rebecca had to leave the college due to an entirely unrelated disciplinary matter. Stanley, the course director who assumed responsibility for the student at this stage, did not have the same regard for this student as his former tutor had. He not only made this clear, but in a written response to an assignment submitted by the student, made it clear that he had not had the time or the patience to read every word of what he implied was a long winded essay. The student was furious with this treatment and was advised by his fellow students to make a complaint through BACP against Stanley. The college had attempted to deal with the situation appropriately with its procedures for dealing with complaints, through formal meetings with all the course members. The student was not satisfied with the outcome and decided to make a complaint to BACP, against the college and not against the tutor. However, he had not followed through the college complaints procedures correctly and because of this the adjudicators were unable to uphold the complaint even though they felt that in many ways it seemed justified.*

It may be seen that all three of these cases involved a combination of issues of boundaries being breached and also of students having high expectations of tutors leading to misunderstandings on both sides. Fiona Palmer Barnes (1998: 47) makes a division of bad practice applicable both to training and therapy. She suggests that distinction should be made between:

- mistakes          unintended errors or slips of practice
- poor practice      practice not of the highest standard either unintended or intended

| | |
|---|---|
| • negligence | lack of due care and attention to good practice |
| • malpractice | practice which is intentionally abusive either emotionally, financially, physically or sexually. |

Aspects of the three cases outlined above undoubtedly fall into the first three categories. Roger Casemore (1999: 95) has suggested that if counsellors could only acknowledge mistakes, apologise, and make attempts to improve their practice then many cases would not reach what is usually a lengthy complaints process that is often damaging to all concerned. Often, he suggests, those making complaints have only wanted some admission and acknowledgement of wrong-doing, some understanding of the distress caused and a statement that the mistake would not be repeated.

In terms of the cases outlined above it is probable that had these sentiments been communicated the cases would not have gone forwards. Too often the parties move too quickly into defensive positions. Casemore believes that to be open in this respect would be more in line with the ethics of counselling. This might well be the case though our legal colleagues might be giving us different advice. Certainly aspects of the cases discussed have made me feel 'This could very easily happen to me' and have given me cause for further reflection. This is also true of all the adjudicators I have worked with, all of whom are experienced therapists and educators who have been in practice for a number of years. It is easy to see how the impact of jealousies about perceived uneven dealings with students could develop out of all proportion. In the small world of counselling, the division of consultant/educator/supervisor/therapist roles can become a little cloudy and the essential contract of confidentiality in therapy and the separation and containment of different roles requires vigilance. The written word in particular can easily cause unnecessary offence or be misconstrued.

Next I wish to look briefly at the situation in America where counselling has been in existence on a large scale for much longer than it has been here and where there is a larger bank of experience to draw upon. This is not to say that the American experience can automatically be transferred to our situation in this country, and matters may develop in different directions here.

## The American situation

It is important to look at counselling and counselling training in relation to the law in that BACP or other complaints procedures may become preliminaries to legal action being taken. Adjudicators of the BACP complaints process became very aware that once a complaint is made it seems to gather strength and as the complainant talks to friends and colleagues about what is happening the whole process gets into a higher gear, to gather additional factors, often becoming out of proportion to the original grievance. This could result in the complainant taking further action through the courts — even with a complaint that has not been upheld by the professional body concerned. How this has developed in America could be a useful pointer to what might develop in this country, and the American experience of establishing practices which are ethically sound and professional offer useful pointers to practice and training here.

A good understanding of the situation in America can be found in the last monograph of the legal series published by the American Counseling Association (ACA) entitled *Avoiding Counselor Malpractice* by Robert Crawford (1994). I add to this my perception of how this relates to counsellor educators according to my experience in this country.

Legal practice is more complicated in America because of separate national, state and local systems, however there is in existence a large body of American case law as a result of dramatic rises in recourse to the law and increased government regulations coupled with increasing numbers of codes of ethical standards provided by various professional bodies. Crawford urges counsellors to join their appropriate professional associations and to be active in them, so that counsellors are not passive recipients of legal standards but take an active part in influencing them. The American experience shows that counsellors are at risk of legal liability under criminal court actions, but are more often at risk of civil court actions, under the law of Tort relating to individual rights. The law of Tort is concerned with personal wrongs in which it is alleged that one person's conduct (the counsellor or trainer) cause a compensatable injury to another person (the client or student). Crawford states that 90% of actions against psychotherapists and counsellors are through Tort law. In America counsellors are particularly concerned not to give 'advice', not only because of theoretical considerations in support of this but because 'advice' can be misconstrued. This makes the position of counsellor educators probably more vulnerable than that of counsellors as giving advice within training is not only acceptable but an essential part of the process. Crawford's chapter on 'Reasonable Standards of Care' (1994: 35–46) is particularly useful in looking at how a counsellor can provide a high quality legally acceptable service and it is briefly summarised here, with added applications for counselling training institutions.

First, in establishing the relationship, the therapist needs to establish appropriate contracting with the client and monitor the work as it proceeds. Likewise in counsellor education there needs to be constant monitoring to ensure that the training is the most appropriate for the trainees needs. For both client and counsellor and for trainer and student the relationship needs to be kept within professional boundaries. Confidentiality needs to be constantly maintained for the client and for the trainer, and crosscutting roles such as teaching, consultation, supervision and personal development facilitation need to be clearly delineated. For work with both clients and students there is a need to follow specific legal requirements. With clients this would include, for example, appropriate child-abuse reporting. Within educational contexts there are requirements for academic standards and attendance as well as ethical considerations.

In situations where there is no clear legal guidance, consideration should be given to adherence to different sources of standards including those set in place in the community, in the institution and by professional bodies. These of course might conflict, so openness to discussion of these standards could be vital. In grey areas the standards set by the profession are the most significant and would be taken most notice of by the courts. So strong notice should be taken of codes of ethics and practice for counsellors and for trainers. Evidence of recourse to legal advice by professional bodies would be considered as important — another reason for belonging to a professional body. Also important is the obligation to consult with other professionals who have experience of similar situations.

Finally, counsellors and trainers should be aware of consequences of alternative courses of action, to have an understanding of what should reasonably be known, and to constantly reconsider working practices. The client/student relationship should be carried out in the most appropriate manner in order to be consistent with the law of Tort. (i.e. 'conduct is wrongful if the burden of alternative conduct that could have prevented the harm is less than the foreseeable probability and gravity of the harm' (Crawford, 1994: 44).)

In addition to his 10 point plan Crawford adds some specific practical advice. Headed notepaper should not be posted to clients in therapy and great care should be taken when responding or making telephone calls in relating to changed appointment times. Care should be taken in allowing untrained staff or family members to answer the telephone. When special abilities are claimed by counsellor and educator, the standard of care is established in the light of 'reasonable conduct' which could be expected of a professional in similar circumstances, according to professional guidelines. Counsellors, Crawford suggests, should use a systematic approach for diagnosis such as the DSM IV categories — and students should be aware of these categories or similar ones and of their own competence to offer help with clients when on placement.

With respect to satisfying the condition of 'informed consent' Crawford suggests (1994: 59) that for many counsellors it is important to have a written document that can provide evidence that there is a contracting process, participated in by the client. He adds that where a printed form is used the client should make a hand-written statement confirming that the document has been considered carefully. This similarly applies to students in training — a clear signed contract could establish exactly what staff and students are preparing and continuing to engage with. Once the counselling relationship is established it should be conducted strictly in formal terms. Any other behaviour, such as offering cups of tea or helping with transportation can be misconstrued and perceived as exploitation of the client for personal satisfaction. Such rules perhaps do not need to pertain so strictly between tutors and trainers but here also a certain line needs to be drawn and the trainer should not be dependent on the student for friendship or any other personal need.

Crawford further establishes crucial elements of good counselling practice with respect to beginnings and endings (1997: 61–7). There should be clear procedures and a recognised pattern for establishing relationships with clients, including their assessment, which is made clear to clients at the beginning of therapy. The same applies in the interviewing procedures for counselling students, there should be clear discussion of the risks of working in a therapeutic relationship including an awareness that the work could increase pain, vulnerability and mood swings. Students should be informed at the outset, that they will experience this through the requirement to engage in their own therapy, in their personal development groups, and in the wider challenges of the whole community group. There should be discussion of possible alternatives to counselling for example self-help groups or no therapy at all.

The way in which the counselling or training relationship ends is absolutely crucial and many complaints centre on where this went wrong. The end of therapy is a vital transition point, which requires all the counsellor's awareness and sensitivity to manage it appropriately. Similarly the ending of a training relationship needs to be very sensitively handled. In some explanation of the burgeoning of complaints against counsellors in America, Crawford writes:

> The discomfort, pain, guilt and grief that causes clients to seek counselling can have overtones of anger, displaced aggression, and projection that increases the likelihood that clients will make legal and ethical complaints. In addition, it is not surprising to counsellors that some persons have unreasonable expectations of the counselling process and subjectively blame the counsellor for circumstances that anyone should know were not caused by the counsellor (1994: 81).

Similarly students in training have often experienced some pain or emotional distress that has led them to consider entering the world of counselling themselves. These emotions often surface during training as a result of the emphasis that training courses put on personal development groups and continued therapy. These emotions can, as with clients in counselling, be redirected by trainees towards the trainers. The business of counselling and counselling training in America is becoming increasingly hazardous in terms of complaints leading to court action.

## Complaints and the law in the U.K.

I now turn to the situation in the U.K. and look at how elements of the professional complaints and legal process in America are replicated in this country and how some factors in this country are rather different.

Two important authors in this country on matters relating to counselling standards, complaints and the law are Peter Jenkins and Tim Bond. Jenkins (1997) highlights possible abuse of power already seen in the American system, such as sexual abuse of clients by counsellors and issues of possible fostering of false memories of childhood abuse. This is also a major concern for Tim Bond (1993: 108–9) who gives examples that in the U.S.A. sexual contact occurs between male therapists and clients in about 11% of cases and between female therapists and clients in 2 to 3% of cases. Whilst it is not clear what the incidence of this kind of abuse is in Britain, this is a not infrequent complaint taken to the BACP complaints procedure and it is likely to be even more common with practitioners who do not ally themselves with any professional body or code of ethics.

Whilst codes of conduct make it clear for counsellors that sexual relationships with clients are not acceptable in ethical terms, there is not always such a clear cut rule with the issue of relationships between trainers and their students. It might be argued that mutually agreed relationships between adults might be acceptable. Nevertheless the existence of inevitably unequal power relationships, and in particular the factor that other trainees might develop feelings of jealousy about special relationships, makes this not advisable. The BACP Code of Ethics and Practice for Trainers in fact strictly disallows sexual relationships between trainers and trainees. Difficult feelings can surface if there is even any suggestion of this, as may be seen by my own example of Pauline, at the start of the chapter.

Both Jenkins and Bond pinpoint confidentiality as a major area of concern, which can cause difficulties in ethically grey areas and between institutions and individuals. Bond suggests it is of critical importance to avoid the use of names or of 'personally identifiable information during supervision or if cases are discussed in training' (1993: 52). He stresses that a breach of confidentiality is actionable in law. Confidentiality is perhaps one of the most critical responsibilities of counsellors and places a heavy burden upon them. It is not difficult for counsellors to be seduced into accidentally breaching the rule of confidentiality or to break it with the belief that so doing could be in the client's interests. Rules of confidentiality need to be carefully established and maintained when working with counselling students.

Bond echoes the principle outlined by Crawford that there is a strong legal imperative for counsellors not to give advice. This is not only an underlying principle of many approaches to counselling — apart from cognitive behavioural approaches which might typically include a large element of teaching and such advisory features as 'bibliotherapy' and the giving of homework tasks — but it is also advantageous legally since the giving of advice brings with it clear legal responsibilities. It is not difficult for a client to bring an action against a counsellor for providing inappropriate advice. Bond goes on to claim that although failure to advise of risks of treatment can be as actionable as giving bad advice, there is no professional requirement that such risks ought to be discussed (Bond, 1993: 51). In contrast to this there can sometimes be a situation where a counsellor may feel it is their responsibility to suggest that the client should make contact with some specialist for help other than counselling — for example contact with a medical practitioner — though the grounds for doing so are likely to be moral and ethical rather than legal.

Both Bond and Jenkins underline Crawford's understanding of the American situation by suggesting that written contracts are advisable. In addition to the clear benefits of avoiding misunderstandings, which might lead to complaints and/or legal action, such contracts help to ensure good practice and promote autonomy in the client. This should be no less applicable to the situation in training courses. It is clearly of benefit for trainees to have a clear understanding of what is required of them, what is offered to them and what the responsibilities of the trainers are in relation to them, through the use of a written contract. Whilst recognising that contracts cannot cover every eventuality or possible cause of misunderstanding and conflict, they can offer a good base level of protection for client and counsellor, trainee and trainer.

There are inevitably many other areas of good practice in relation to avoiding complaints, which cannot be covered in this chapter. However a central issue which cannot be neglected is how this issue is covered in training courses. Jenkins is concerned about what he sees as an inadequate coverage of complaints and legal issues on training courses. He quotes a survey of his own in which 'In a small sample survey of 60 counsellor training courses at Diploma level or above, a third had no specific coverage of legal issues' (Jenkins, 1993: 13). It is of great concern that future counsellors might not be as aware as they need to be of these issues which might well cause great distress for themselves and their clients.

So how does the situation in the U.K. relate to the larger American experience? Whilst therapists here are increasingly more dependent on European Community directives, the American experience could offer considerable learnings for us coming from a system which, though it has differences to our own, is broadly similar to ours. Jenkins suggests that, as the movement towards statutory recognition of therapy gathers strength, and with it increasing demand for training and accreditation of practice, so this goes hand in hand with an increased legal dimension to our work. He suggests that 'the more visible therapists become through legal recognition, the more vulnerable they also seem to become in a litiginous environment' (1997: 13). That the governmental requirement for regulation is gathering pace is underlined by Sarah Browne in an article in the Counselling and Psychotherapy Journal where she suggests that regulation could come into force soon after the year 2003 under the aegis of the Health Professions Council (Browne, 2001: 4). Even so, Jenkins gives us some cause for comfort in his belief that there are enough differences in the systems to make it likely that the huge influx of legal action might be slower to reach us than is often feared.

Even in the U.S.A. where there is a great deal of case law in existence, there is a low risk of successful litigation. He quotes figures of almost 90% of malpractice cases being settled out of court, and most of those which continue to trial are won by therapists (1993: 83). So far in Britain very few cases have come to court. A large part of the reason for this is that there are considerable difficulties for our clients to prove their therapist has been guilty of malpractice on account of the particularities of the law of Tort in this country and the lack of existing case law in this country. Jenkins suggests that the greater emphasis on litigation in America has had a long history, and we will not necessarily replicate what is happening with respect to complaints and the law in this country. He feels that there is no evidence of a malpractice explosion at the moment.

We can perhaps learn from the American example to try and ensure that this does not happen. One reason why there are so many complaints in America is the myriad codes of conducts in fields related to counselling by different professional organisations. Our own codes of conduct have become quite complicated — for example the BACP codes have been continuously revised over the years and have had many additions. I and my fellow BACP adjudicators have often felt that in many of the cases we are dealing with, the 'letter' of the codes has become more significant than their 'spirit'. This is unfortunate. Accordingly BACP are at present considering ways of simplifying their codes so that the broad principles of acceptable moral and ethical conduct, and of good practice, become more significant than more narrow precepts. By revising the codes in this way we might do something to prevent the damaging litigious atmosphere that prevails in the United States. Coupled with this, however, and of more importance, we need to continually monitor our own behaviours and practice in counselling and training to ensure that our ways of working are of the highest standard possible.

## The three examples in relation to the discussion

I would like to return to the three cases of boundary and training issues with which this chapter began, to the situations of Pauline and Mark and Stanley, and to look at these in relation to our brief examination of complaints and the law in the U.S.A. and Britain. It is my belief that in none of these cases was there serious malpractice, but that in all of them there was some poor practice and negligence, which might have been obviated by careful consideration of the suggestions outlined above.

Pauline fell in love with her student and subsequently married him. It would be a cold-hearted legislator who felt no sympathy with this situation, but the tutor's behaviour subsequently could have been different. When the tutor and her student began to feel that there was something more than a professional relationship developing between them they were unwise to go to social events together where they would be seen by other members of the group and set the scene for jealousies to arise. Also, before an intimate relationship was allowed to develop, Pauline would have been well advised to cut off all connections with the course whilst her student was continuing the training. Yet it seems harsh to judge them severely for what occurred. In considering the feelings of the other students, however, I remember as I write this my own jealousy when, in my training, the leader of the course took into her own home a student who needed accommodation and support. This jealousy increased when that student secured a new job before I did and I inevitably felt that more help had been offered to her than to me. No serious crime was committed in either case, but with the situation being discussed here different social and professional behaviour could have diminished the feelings of being less cared for, experienced by the other students. If Pauline had stated clearly to the other students that she understood their feelings, that her behaviour had been unwise, and that action had been taken so that there could be no possible effect on their chances of success on the course, then perhaps the case would have not come to the complaints board. Most of Crawford's 10 points seem to have some resonance here.

In the second case Mark, a consultant to a course who was also counselling a student on that course, attempted to block a placement and discontinued the therapy suddenly. Whilst not a trainer on the course involved he was clearly involved with it and therefore it was unwise of him to be counselling one of the course students. If he had seriously considered that his client was in danger of causing serious harm to others by his placement there, he would have had a responsibility to break the confidentiality, but this is not completely clear and in any case the issue is about inappropriate boundaries between his role as a therapist and as a consultant on the course. In addition to this, a frequent cause of complaints is that endings are not worked through appropriately. The client had agreed initially that an ending was appropriate but on further consideration felt aggrieved that this had happened. Not enough time had been given for reflection on what was felt by both therapist and client to be the right course of action.

Again a 'holier than thou' attitude can easily prevail. As a trainer on a person-centred course I am constantly aware of the dangers of working with students in ways which — though very clearly and specifically are not a counselling relationship — enter into very personal and often 'therapeutic' arenas. This work has to be clearly delineated from the academic and professional judgements that need to be made constantly. Also, if a decision was made that a particular student was 'not in the right place' to be on the course, the professional decision could easily be seen by the student as a personal judgement, and the ending of the training relationship would need to be very carefully worked through. Even if it was the student's own decision to discontinue, care needs to be taken that the student feels that the lines of communication remain open for exploring feelings and perhaps for consideration at a later date of returning to the course for completion. In this particular case Mark did not blatantly transgress boundaries, but there were enough areas of discomfort around the boundaries of the relationship, and certainly in relation to the manner in which counselling was terminated to lead us as adjudicators to consider that some reparation needed to be made. Again, many of Crawford's 10 points summarised earlier concerning boundaries have echoes here, in addition to his, and to Bond's and Jenkins' considerable emphasis on the importance of dealing very carefully with endings in counselling relationships which apply clearly also to trainer/trainee relationships.

Finally I turn to Rebecca and Stanley. This kind of scenario is frequently a big issue in courses where a trainer leaves suddenly in the middle of a course, where close relationships have been built up with students, and the transfer is difficult to achieve satisfactorily. This might also have been a factor in the difficult relationship between Pauline and her students. I remember a situation with a course where a much respected course leader died suddenly, causing much distress to students and the remaining staff. It was certainly unwise of Stanley to appear to devalue his student's work by accusing him of long-windedness. At the same time it is not difficult to see how easily a written comment, however respectful of the student's work, might seem to be uncaring and harsh within the context of a changed relationship and I have occasionally experienced students extreme distress concerning evaluations that I have made, particularly those students who have recently returned to the world of education and who have made life changing sacrifices to enter the world of counselling.

## Conclusion

With the three cases discussed here there are few clear cut issues of malpractice, more of errors of judgement and things that could have been done differently, but all indicate practice that needs to be considered and improved. In our therapeutic practice and in our training roles for counselling we would be well advised to look carefully at the wide experience that American practice and case history has to offer, without assuming that it has automatic application to our own culture. As we become involved in our professional associations we would certainly be wise to look carefully at how we might achieve a different development in some respects from how things happen in America and to take on any useful suggestions for improving our own practice. We need always to keep in mind that the prime purpose of this should not be to preserve our professional skins, but to offer the best possible experience to our clients and students. Palmer Barnes reminds us that in any complaint there is an element that speaks of some organisational or professional difficulty that we need to attend to. She understands that it is never easy to make a complaint, that such actions take considerable emotional energy and should be regarded not as a source of anxiety but as an opportunity for taking on new learning and changing our own practice or that of the institutions with which we work. She further states that 'it is much easier to close down on a bad experience. Pathologising the patient or colleague who has made a complaint is all too easy, and unfortunately it happens all too frequently' (Palmer Barnes, 1998: 113).

Engaging with individuals for their personal therapy or acting as educators and trainers for those who wish to take on these roles is dangerous territory, which may make us the focus of strong feelings of passion and of anger from either clients or trainees. It certainly needs to be made clear to clients and to trainees that, in addition to embarking on a journey of discovery that may be beautiful and life-enhancing, at times they will also experience entering dangerous waters and hidden reefs, where they may be vulnerable and at risk. As trainers we must ensure that we offer our trainees the best possible guidance and maps of the oceans they are entering. As therapists, we must ensure that we offer our clients the strongest vessels of containment that will enable them, and us, to withstand the highs and lows of our journeys of adventure into the self and into deeper relationships with others.

## References

Bond, T. (1993). *Standards and Ethics for Counselling in Action*. London: Sage.

Browne, S. (2001). Regulation Coming Soon. *Counselling and Psychotherapy Journal*, March.

Casemore, R. (1999). Why can't we own our mistakes? *Counselling*, 10 (2): 94–5.

Crawford, R. L. (1994). Avoiding Counselor Malpractice. *American Counselling Association Legal Series, Vol. 12*.

Jenkins, P. (1997). *Counselling, Psychotherapy and the Law*. London: Sage.

Palmer Barnes, F. (1998). *Complaints and Grievances in Psychotherapy: A handbook of ethical practice*. London: Routledge.

Chapter 10

# Scapegoats and Sacred Cows: Towards good enough conflict resolution

## Nick Totton

### Introduction

I believe that psychotherapy and counselling have taken the wrong road in their approach to conflict between practitioner and client, saddling themselves with a set of assumptions and corresponding structures which benefit neither clients, nor practitioners, nor organisations, and which frequently create more misery from already miserable situations. This has happened, I think, because we have taken over from other fields — in particular, from allopathic medicine and the legal system — inappropriate models for addressing conflict, which ignore and even contradict our understanding of human relationships and attitudes. And this in turn has happened because we have failed to address our own anxieties in relation to client-practitioner conflict, choosing instead to project them outwards.

My claim is that, by drawing on our everyday therapeutic experience and understanding of relationships, we can quite rapidly develop approaches to client-practitioner conflict which reject bureaucratised procedures of blame, scapegoating and avoidance of responsibility, and address the primary needs of hurt and frustrated clients and practitioners. I shall sketch out one existing attempt to create such an approach, and look at its strengths and weaknesses.

You may already be asking what practical help this chapter can offer, given that you have to operate in the existing context of complaints procedures. One answer — which I think deserves serious consideration — is that you can choose a different context, by joining a different sort of validating body. Another answer is that the ideas I present imply an approach to conflict with clients which should minimise the chances of a formal complaint ever being made. Above all, this is about offering clients the one thing which they usually most want: an apology.

### The Independent Practitioners Network

I have written elsewhere (Totton, 1997) about the Independent Practitioners Network (IPN), in which I participate. Since I shall be referring to IPN's practice

---

This chapter draws on two previous articles, referenced as Totton, 1999 and Totton, 2000b.

on practitioner-client conflict resolution, I will briefly explain its structure. The basis of IPN's practitioner validation is the peer group of five to ten practitioners, who directly know about and stand by each other's work. Typically the group will use peer supervision to underpin this mutual validation. Each full member group has its process monitored by two other groups, which are also available for support and facilitation. For a client who is unhappy about their practitioner's work, the first port of call will probably be the nearest IPN regional contact person, who will try to find out what the client wants and needs to have happen; a conflict resolution process will be created in response to the unique situation, and will draw on other members of the practitioner's group, on the link groups, and if necessary on any or all IPN participants.

I shall be describing some of IPN's procedures in more detail as I go on, and explaining what seem to me to be the strengths of IPN's approach, as compared with those of some other organisations.

## The culture of complaint

Most people who have personal experience, in whatever role, of most current complaints procedures are deeply dissatisfied. This statement is not based on research evidence (though see Clarkson, 2000), but on personal conversations with a number of complainants, complainees, adjudicators and others, plus my own direct involvement, in a variety of roles, with four complaints concerning members of various organisations. I have so far not encountered *one person* who was even broadly satisfied with how a complaint was handled. Many have expressed profound and bitter disappointment and resentment.

How can it be that large numbers of generally competent, interpersonally skilled and well-intentioned individuals — as I believe most practitioners to be — create and administer such a disastrous system? The reasons cluster around the ongoing process of 'professionalization' and regulation which besets psychotherapy and counselling as it does many other aspects of our culture (Postle, 1998, 2000; Totton, 1999).

Professionalization has its own dynamic: once a group decides to carve out a niche as a profession, it inevitably seeks to make boundaries around itself and to control admission (Larkin, 1983). This means laying claim to a body of expert knowledge (Cant and Sharma, 1996; Giddens, 1991). The fundamental motivation involved is quite simply self-interest. Like many social phenomena, however, the drive to professionalization is seldom conscious of its own dynamic: it holds false beliefs about itself, for example that it is motivated by the good of the client — that professionalization will protect the public from dangerous, incompetent and perhaps unscrupulous practitioners.

This belief is virtually unsupported by evidence. Mowbray (1995; see also Hogan, 1979) details the practical and theoretical reasons for doubting that professionalization and accompanying regulation safeguard the client. There are constant reports of abusive practice in the 'well-regulated' medical and legal professions (Stacey, 1994). Every insider knows that abuse occurs not just on the wild fringes of each profession, but in its most senior and respected circles; for example, a past president of the American Psychiatric Association and the

American Psychoanalytic Association, and honorary life president of the World Association for Social Psychiatry, drugged and raped a number of patients (Noel and Watterson, 1992). Such cases seldom get publicly reported.

The professional posture of expertise, wisdom and unimpeachability produces the standardised 'complaints procedure', using an adversarial, quasi-legal structure inappropriate to most situations which arise in psychotherapy and counselling. Grinding on for month after month, fitting the client to the structure rather than the structure to the client, and producing at best a largely irrelevant verdict of 'guilty' or 'not guilty', complaints procedures are often disastrous for all involved.

What unhappy clients often want most is an apology, an acknowledgement of hurt; and this is the one thing that the professionalized complaints procedure prevents them from having. The client seldom feels that the practitioner has said 'Sorry'. How can they, if it will be treated as an admission of guilt? Of course any practitioner is going to regret a client's suffering, the breakdown of the relationship, even if they feel no guilt at all. But in an environment which assumes that no one is trustworthy (Thorne, 1997:147), few practitioners will dare acknowledge error.

In a remarkable act of self-mutilation, practitioners have amputated their own understanding of psychological processes. We know a lot about the projection of shadow figures; yet we go on talking about dangerous abusive therapists 'out there', and creating ways to hound and expel scapegoats — as if this will resolve our own feelings of resentment and even hatred towards our clients, for stirring us up in so many painful ways (Winnicott, 1947), together with our corresponding fear of *their* hatred and how it might destroy us.

Is there an alternative? Can we approach client-practitioner conflict in a way which responds to therapeutic needs? I believe so, but it isn't easy. It involves letting go of several comforting and familiar ways of doing things: sacred cows which block the road to an effective, appropriate and respectful way of facilitating conflict.

## Sacred cow 1: Complaint

The biggest single obstacle to resolving client-practitioner conflicts is the idea of 'complaint' itself — very deeply embedded in most practitioner organisations, and resting on assumptions which are hard to articulate. Here is an attempt: 'The client-practitioner relationship is contractual, aligned with and ultimately guaranteed by the social contract. The practitioner has professional responsibilities towards the client, including but not limited to a duty of care, and these are defined by the scope and appropriate activities of their profession: just as a lawyer's profession is to carry out legal activities on behalf of and at the request of their clients, so the therapist's profession is to carry out therapeutic activities on behalf of and at the request of *their* clients. Any breach of professional responsibility is thus appropriately the subject of complaint to the practitioner's professional organisation, which establishes and polices these responsibilities.'

The fundamental difficulty with this picture is that it in no way reflects the specific characteristics of psychotherapy. It is an 'off-the-peg' approach, which treats therapy as one form of professional service alongside others such as medicine, law, architecture, accountancy and so on. From a certain point of view, in fact, it is part of an attempt to 'tame' the activity of therapy, to make it fit or appear to fit into a particular social contract with which, in some ways or at some moments, it actually conflicts (Totton, 1997b; cf. Totton, 2000).

An alternative picture starts with the proposition that the psychotherapy relationship is intrinsically *about power*. In the classic setting, two people sit in a room and explore their different interpretations of reality; frequently, they clash in various ways about whose interpretation is to be accepted. 'Why did I say that?' 'What do I truly feel about you?' 'Is my partner really as I describe him?' These clashes and negotiations are the very stuff of psychotherapy; and running through them is a central issue about *who has the power to decide*. The feelings and attitudes which come up in the client and practitioner around these issues are a reflection of the client's (and sometimes the practitioner's) early life, the ways in which adults traumatically denied or attacked the child's experience.

The power struggles of therapy, then, are what transference and counter transference are made of; and also the point at which transference and reality meet. Typically, the client's feeling-memories of childhood oppression will arise in response to *real* mistakes, misunderstandings and insensitivities on the part of the therapist (Casement, 1985; Smith, 1999). Hence the struggle for power to define reality is perhaps the biggest arena in which real therapeutic change can take place. To have one's experience acknowledged instead of denied is a deeply healing experience.

A complaint, then, is 'therapy conducted by other means'. The context for a complaint will develop when these real mistakes, misunderstandings and insensitivities — which may be very small on an 'objective' scale of things — are not sufficiently perceived and acknowledged by the practitioner (Sands, 2000). The cumulative effect is that the client feels they have exhausted all means of asserting their own reality within the therapeutic space: they feel that their only recourse is to appeal to other points of view besides their own and their therapist's.

It is important to see that *the client cannot be wrong about this*. They can be wrong, quite obviously, in what they think reality is; they can be and often are 'oversensitive' by average standards — and of course therapy by its structure encourages such sensitivity (Sands, 2000). But it is only when therapy becomes an experience of having my reality denied that I will seek reparation. This, ultimately, is what any client is complaining about. Clearly they may also be complaining about being sexually seduced, bullied, ignored, ripped off and so on, and all of these things are wrong. They are also extreme cases of the denial of the client's reality, or of the therapist's collusion with the client's *self*-denial. So long as I feel there is space for my experience within the therapy, I will not need to go outside it.

From this point of view, when things go wrong in therapy it can best be considered as a *conflict,* appropriately addressed through *conflict resolution*. The primary problem is that the client and therapist have ceased to be able to negotiate reality, as happens constantly throughout successful therapy. The client (and possibly also the therapist) has reached a point where they feel dominated by the other person's version of things, so that their own truth is excluded. They need help in exploring whether and how negotiation, and hence safety, can be restored. While the complaint model tends to drag any problem out of the therapy relationship and into the courtroom, the conflict resolution model holds at least the possibility of re-containment within the therapeutic dyad.

This does not exclude the idea of wrongdoing on the part of the therapist. (By 'wrongdoing' I mean anything ranging from actual abuse to technical clumsiness.) However, the way to clarify this is by working to restore as much as possible the therapeutic dialogue between client and practitioner — even if this can no longer take place within the dyad. If the client can start to feel heard again by the practitioner, this will include the experience of having their grievances heard; and the road will be opened to whatever reparation or correction is required. Even if the therapy relationship as such cannot continue and even if, in the extreme case, the therapist ends up being excluded by their peers because they are unable to recognise their own shortcomings, a therapeutic experience for the client may have been facilitated.

Hopefully this all clarifies why complainants consistently say that what they want is an apology. Apology is the first stage in recognition of the other person's experience. If I feel wounded and mistreated by someone — especially someone whom I have related with intimately — then how can I believe that they accept my experience unless they tell me they are sorry about it? Apology is not about blame.

The Independent Practitioners Network has based its approach to client-practitioner conflict on the use of conflict resolution. (IPN is not quite alone in this: the Association of Humanistic Psychotherapy Practitioners has recently introduced such an approach.) IPN does not use any single model of conflict resolution, but is building up a body of knowledge and expertise in the area; what is clear is that the key to successful resolution is for both client and practitioner to feel supported and listened to.

This view of psychotherapy does place specific demands on the practitioner, however. She or he has to recognise that *the client cannot be wrong* about important aspects of the situation. Specifically, the therapy *has* broken down; and we cannot blame the client for that ('The operation was a success, but the patient died.') It may well be no-one's fault — failure of the therapy does not equal failure of the therapist; but attempts by therapists to pathologise clients for pointing out that the therapy is failing are all too common, and wholly unacceptable.

Typically, the complaints model jerks the relationship between client and practitioner out of a deeply deferential mode into a crudely egalitarian one. It imposes a picture of client and practitioner as 'equal in front of the law', so to speak, two individuals with a contract. The reality of the relationship has probably been very different. The client and practitioner are indeed peers, but at the start of therapy the client generally does not know it. She or he is trying to fit the therapy into one or another model of a hierarchical relationship, casting the therapist as parent, expert, teacher, healer, guru. When therapy works, it does so through the therapist's gentle but firm resistance to these roles. My strong suspicion is that most complaints originate in the therapist's complaisant acceptance of hierarchy.

## Sacred cow 2: Commandments

By 'commandments', I mean the lengthy and exhaustive ethical codes which are *de rigeur* for most practitioner organisations. There are several major drawbacks to an approach which tries to specify the details of acceptable practice; and the first one is that, like any set of commandments, it can never be exhaustive — someone will always invent a new way to sin! But such codes are used to silence the victims of therapeutic misbehaviour which has not been anticipated. The first move in standard complaints procedures is to investigate whether or not the alleged behaviour is a breach of the code of practice — not the much more important question of whether or not it is *acceptable*.

The even more important question, however, is whether or not there is a conflict between client and practitioner; which there clearly is, since the client is contacting the organisation in the first place. The emphasis on wrongdoing and punishment leads many bodies to treat a whole class of client-practitioner problems as irrelevant or outside their scope, simply because no 'sin' is alleged. As I am arguing throughout, the core task is to hold and facilitate conflict, not to sit in judgement on sinful practitioners.

For traditional complaints procedures, if it is established that the alleged behaviour breaches the code of practice the central question becomes: Did it happen? A crude emphasis is suddenly placed upon 'the facts of the matter', in striking contrast to the necessarily subtle and flexible attitudes towards 'facts' which characterise therapeutic work itself (Scott, 1996). In rare situations there will, finally, be a need to establish a consensus view on whether one person is crazy or another person is a devious liar. But this point comes far, far down a road which generally does not need to be travelled at all.

Exhaustive ethical codes can damage therapeutic work in a more subtle way. They allow a fantasy to develop between client and practitioner, along the lines that 'Really they want to have sex with me/be my friend/have me live in their spare room; but they're not allowed to'. This is a common style of fantasy, in my experience, and it needs to be vigorously challenged by the practitioner, owning their choices and substituting for the imagined 'therapy police' their own judgement and responsibility.

In IPN, each member group creates an ethical statement which is circulated to other groups for scrutiny and challenge. Some of these are quite long and detailed, others very short and sweet. I often feel pulled towards believing that we must all have a shared code, must agree explicitly on some things — that otherwise we will be impossibly vulnerable to external criticism. But a single code to which we all sign up guarantees nothing except appearance. Whatever we all *say* we agree to, what we *do* may be different; and monitoring what people do, in both cases, depends upon the courage to challenge. There is a mass of evidence that in professional bodies, this sort of challenge very rarely takes place, even when someone's unacceptable behaviour is well known (Clarkson, 2000).

In IPN, challenge is a face to face process of saying 'I don't accept that', rather than a matter of pointing to a list of commandments on the wall. No list will ever be long enough — and every list will be too long: every list will forbid things that in *some* situations are good practice, and allow things that in *some* situations are bad practice. As Calvin Coolidge pointed out, we are all against sin; but this is very different from living, or working, in an ethically alive way.

I want to reproduce here the ethical statement of my own IPN peer group — with trepidation, because I imagine some people will be shocked by its brevity and generality (some other IPN groups have statements which are much longer and more detailed). However, I believe that both of these qualities are positive rather than negative: we need to give our clients a document which concisely indicates the ethical *context* of our work, rather than precise details of what is or is not 'appropriate', and which makes clear that *any* problem the client experiences can validly be brought forward for resolution.

## Burley Group Ethical Statement

As practitioners, we endeavour, each in our own style of work, to respect the individuality of our clients and the responsibility of power within the therapeutic relationship.

As a group, we commit ourselves to standing by each other's work, with all its inevitable imperfections. We will continuously examine and challenge our own motives, methods and models, and will process whatever problems and conflicts arise within all aspects of our work.

[This is followed by a list of group members, and a contact number in case of conflict.]

## Sacred cow 3: Confidentiality

Here my iconoclasm is only partial: I agree that the client must be protected from disclosure which may simply magnify their experience of abuse. It is up to them how much of their experience is made public, and in what way; they may even need encouragement to be more cautious and self-protective. But does the same go for the practitioner? I take what may seem a harsh position: that by occupying the role of therapist or counsellor — in many ways a highly privileged one — we largely abdicate our right to privacy around what we do in that role. The need for transparency is a higher priority than the need to shelter practitioners from the public gaze.

It is widely agreed that practitioners should never ask their client to keep any transaction secret — and that if this happens, the client should hear an alarm bell ringing. Sometimes, during an interaction with a client that I fully believe to be appropriate and therapeutic, the thought pops up 'How would this look/sound to an observer?' Sometimes what happens in therapy would indeed seem weird or dubious to an outside view. So we can limit what we do by these external (and in a sense imaginary) standards — or we can take our chances. What we cannot do is ask the client to keep what has happened secret — or to refrain from sharing their view of us, however good or bad this may be. And even less do we have this option when the client is in public conflict with us. Asking them to keep secret their view of what we have done — their 'complaint' — is essentially the same thing.

Our enormous privilege as therapists must be balanced by equally great responsibility. IPN seeks to discharge this responsibility by working counter to the powerful gravitational pull of privacy on Planet Therapy. To be a part of IPN means to share one's work in a profound way with at least four other people, and to have another ten people check that this is happening. Even in IPN we are finding that we struggle around the implications of transparency, especially in a concrete situation where there is a question of exposing a therapist's shortcomings to view. A very deep sense of intolerable vulnerability emerges. Does this mean that practitioners do indeed need protection; or does it mean that we need to work more deeply on our own emotional material and how it affects our ethical stance?

Arnold Mindell, whom I regard as a great therapist, has said on workshops that there is ultimately only one way to deal with criticism: to be shot so full of holes that there is nothing left to be attacked. In other words, the only true defence against criticism is endless humility: a continuous awareness of our own imperfection. At which point we can hear the mooing of the next sacred cow.

## Sacred cow 4: Perfection

Attachment to the illusion that we can be perfect — either in our work itself, or in conflict resolution — is deeply counterproductive. Several theorists have written about the key role in therapy of 'creative mistakes', which very often constitute symbolic re-enactments of the client's past trauma (e.g. Casement, 1985: 90ff). If the therapist can acknowledge the error, apologise for it, and at the same time encourage the client to explore its meaning, then a mistake can frequently deepen and strengthen the therapeutic relationship, as well as enabling the client to understand their core issues. In trying to smooth out the possibility of such rough edges in the work, we risk losing something essential.

Similarly, we need to accept that therapy necessarily involves disappointment. It faces the client (and often also the practitioner) with the impossibility of getting some needs met, of completely healing some wounds. Too much emphasis on grievances can give clients the false impression that disappointment and imperfection are avoidable — that if they experience these things, someone has let them down (this is part of the general growth of the 'blame culture' and litigation as a solution to pain). A successful conflict resolution process doesn't mean everyone will be delighted; it will often end up highlighting disappointment. However, we can still look for a sense on all sides that feelings have been heard and needs recognised. Sometimes, perhaps, the end of the process will be for everyone to grieve together: to hold grief rather than grievance.

Accepting our human imperfection — even treasuring it — can enable us to become less defensive in response to clients who let us know how much our behaviour, naturally and inevitably, sometimes hurts them. The reality is that we have nothing to protect — or nothing worth protecting — except the truth of the matter. If we can respond with sympathy and empathy, followed by an exploration of the interaction which has produced these feelings, then we are unlikely ever to need a conflict resolution process, let alone a complaints procedure. But then, as I have said, we are imperfect . . .

All of this implies very strongly the need for an approach to conflict resolution which abandons perfection and tries instead to be 'good enough', in exactly the same sense that therapists and practitioners try to be 'good enough' — as an extension of Winnicott's original description of the 'good enough mother' (e.g. 1949). The key qualities of a good enough conflict resolution structure are very similar: they include holding, responsiveness, and self-correction. However, just as one baby's good enough mother is not the same as another baby's, every conflict resolution process will be unique, and will need a unique structure to contain and facilitate it.

## Sacred cow 5: Expulsion

The unrealistic demand for perfection leads to a wish to expel what is imperfect — a wish which shows up very strongly in the current drive to professionalization, with its fanning of public anxiety about who is a 'safe' therapist. This involves a chronic fantasy that we can get rid of all the messy, dirty, chaotic aspects of therapy and counselling — as Emmy van Deurzen, former chair of UKCP, puts it, 'cut back' the weeds, the 'sprawling plants' that 'obscure each other's light and deprive each other of nutrients' (van Deurzen, 1996). This scary metaphor raises spectres of infantile envy and hatred — a sibling rivalry which wants to throw out the new baby along with the dirty bathwater we would so much like to deny. But the dirtiness is intrinsic to the baby; and the baby is what we will, as therapists and counsellors, always be left holding! (Totton, 1999: 321). To give this difficult and imperfect baby good enough holding, we have to give up the temptation to project outwards onto other people both the 'criminal' and the 'judge' — recognising that both these positions are part of our selves.

## Good-Enough Conflict Resolution

As Winnicott says about good-enough parenting, 'what releases the mother from her need to be near-perfect is the infant's understanding' (Winnicott, 1949: 245). I am not equating the infant here with the client, as so often happens in therapy; rather, both infant and mother, like judge and criminal, are aspects of our own being. We can release ourselves from the need to be near-perfect by understanding the twin origins of that need: on the one hand a genuine love and caring for the client, but on the other hand a fear and hatred of the client's capacity to be left unsatisfied, unhelped, unhealed.

I do not believe that either this article or IPN offers a perfect solution to the issue of client-practitioner conflict. But perfection is not required. What is most urgently needed is a *therapeutic* approach, rather than a legalistic one: an approach which hopes to use therapeutic skills and understandings to re-facilitate the relationship between the people involved, even if this relationship is limited to apology and parting. This attempt may fail; but it is essential that we try — if for no other reason than to bear witness to our belief in the project of psychotherapy.

## References

Cant, S. and Sharma, U. (1996). *Complementary and Alternative Medicines: Knowledge in practice.* London: Free Association Books.

Casement, P. (1985). *On Learning from the Patient.* London: Tavistock.

Clarkson, P. (2000). *Working with Ethical and Moral Dilemmas in Psychotherapy.* London: Whurr.

Giddens, A. (1991). *Modernity and Self Identity.* Oxford: Polity Press.

Hogan, D.B. (1979). *The Regulation of Psychotherapists.* Cambridge, Massachusetts: Ballinger.

House, R. (1997). Participatory Ethics in a Self-Generating Practitioner Community. In R. House and N. Totton (eds.) *Implausible Professions: Arguments for pluralism and autonomy in psychotherapy and counselling.* Manchester: PCCS Books, 321–34.

House, R. and Totton, N., eds. (1997). *Implausible Professions: Arguments for pluralism and autonomy in psychotherapy and counselling.* Manchester: PCCS Books.

Larkin, G. (1983). *Occupational Monopoly and Modern Medicine.* London: Tavistock.

Mowbray, R. (1995). *The Case Against Psychotherapy Registration: A conservation issue for the human potential movement.* London: Trans Marginal Press.

Noel, B. and Watterson, K. (1992). *You Must Be Dreaming.* New York: Poseidon Press.

Postle, D. (1998). The Alchemist's Nightmare: Gold into Lead — the Annexation of Psychotherapy in the UK. *International Journal of Psychotherapy,* 3 (1): 53–83.

Postle, D. (2000). Statutory Regulation: Shrink-wrapping psychotherapy. *British Journal of Psychotherapy,* 16 (3): 335–46

Sands, A. (2000). *Falling for Therapy: Psychotherapy from a client's point of view.* Basingstoke: Macmillan.

Scott, A. (1996). *Real Events Revisited: Fantasy, memory and psychoanalysis.* London: Virago.

Stacey, M. (1994). Collective Therapeutic Responsibility: Lessons from the GMC. In S. Budd and U. Sharma (eds.) *The Healing Bond: The patient-practitioner relationship and therapeutic responsibility.* London: Routledge, 107–33.

Thorne, B. (1995). The Accountable Therapist: Standards, experts and poisoning the well. In R. House and N. Totton (eds.) (1997) *Implausible Professions: Arguments for pluralism and autonomy in psychotherapy and counselling.* Manchester: PCCS Books, 141–50.

Totton, N. (1997a). The Independent Practitioners Network: A New Model of Accountability. R. House and N. Totton (eds.) *Implausible Professions: Arguments for pluralism and autonomy in psychotherapy and counselling.* Manchester: PCCS Books, 287–93.

Totton, N. (1997b). Not Just A Job: Psychotherapy as a spiritual and political practice. In R. House and N. Totton (eds.) *Implausible Professions:*

*Arguments for pluralism and autonomy in psychotherapy and counselling.* Manchester: PCCS Books, 129–40.

Totton, N. (1997c). Learning by Mistake: Client-practitioner conflict in a self-regulated network. In R. House and N. Totton (eds.) *Implausible Professions: Arguments for pluralism and autonomy in psychotherapy and counselling.* Manchester: PCCS Books, 315–20.

Totton, N. (1999). The Baby and the Bathwater: 'Professionalisation' in psychotherapy and counselling. *British Journal of Guidance and Counselling* 27 (3): 313–24.

Totton, N. (2000a). *Psychotherapy and Politics.* London: Sage.

Totton, N. (2000b) Beyond Complaint. *Self and Society* 28, (1): 9–12.

Van Deurzen, E. (1996). Registration: What it will mean to you as a counsellor. 5th St Georges Counselling in Primary Care Conference, Keynote Address. Quoted in Postle 1998: 73.

Winnicott, D.W. (1947). Hate in the Countertransference. In D.W. Winnicott, *Through Paediatrics to Psychoanalysis: Collected Papers.* London: Hogarth Press, 1987: 194–203.

Winnicott, D.W. (1949). Mind and Its Relation to the Psyche-Soma. In D.W. Winnicott, *Through Paediatrics to Psychoanalysis: Collected Papers.* London: Hogarth Press 1987: 243–54.

The Independent Practitioners Network can be contacted through the website at http://www.ipnet.org.uk.

# Chapter 11

# Managing Boundaries — It's the little things that count

## Roger Casemore

Some time ago, I was counselling a young woman (I'll call her Marguerite) who had moved to England from Germany with her job in a large engineering company. She had referred herself to see me with acute depression arising from her loneliness, her very low self-esteem, sexual difficulties and a history of difficult childhood experiences in her family of origin. Several months later, when I was still counselling her, a young German, (I'll call him Max) who came from a different region in Germany and was working in another part of the same company, referred himself to me with very similar presenting problems. No mention was made of any connection between them and because the company they worked for was so large, I had no reason to suspect that they might know each other, just because they were both from Germany. During the following year I continued to work with them both, developing what seemed like good therapeutic relationships and experienced them both making some progress in different ways.

Then in one of our sessions, the young man began to explore some painful feelings he was experiencing in a relationship at work, and making a connection between those feelings and emotions he had experienced as a child. Seeking to clarify those emotions and to be empathic, I checked out the connection describing an incident in his childhood which I thought he was referring to. 'That was when you . . .' ( I won't describe the details).

'No', he said. 'That wasn't me. I think that must have happened to Marguerite!'

I blushed scarlet, immediately filled with guilt and a sense of having made a monumental blunder. In fact I had made at least three. I had mixed up my two clients' histories, I had broken a confidence by one client to the other and I had worked on an assumption that they did not know each other. I apologised immediately and said how stupid I was to have made such a mistake and that it clearly should not have happened. Max accepted my mistake with some laughter and said he was very glad to discover that I really was human and could get things wrong. He then went on to tell me that it was Marguerite who had given him my details when he was looking for a therapist and he also told me that they had recently begun to meet from time to time, to discuss their progress in therapy. He agreed not to tell Marguerite what had happened until after I saw her the next day, which would give me the chance to tell her first and to apologise for the slip up. The session ended well and in fact the event seemed to add something to our relationship, which ended some twelve months later when he returned to Germany.

I spoke to Marguerite the next day, telling her what had happened, how I had felt at the time and how Max and I had dealt with it. I apologised to her for inadvertently breaching her confidence and she was very accepting. She also said that she was glad to discover that I really was human and added that she also needed to take some responsibility for not letting me know that she knew Max and that they were meeting to share their experiences in their therapy with me. The incident seemed to add something to our relationship as well and I continued to work with her for a further two years by when she was fully recovered.

It may seem like a very small slip that I made, but it could have resulted in a breakdown in the relationship with either or both of my clients and could so easily have resulted in either or both of them taking a complaint out against me. Owning the mistake and apologising had enabled us to stay in a therapeutic relationship instead of moving to what Derek Hill, elsewhere in this book calls an 'adversarial relationship'. I know that over the thirty plus years that I have been practising as a therapist, there have been many, many occasions when I could have done things differently to the way I had done them and I guess that quite a number of those could have led to me being the subject of a complaint. I don't think there is any way that any therapist can completely guard against that. None of us is the perfect therapist and none of us is safe from either a valid complaint or a specious or vindictive one.

I really don't want to write about the big or serious mistakes made by therapists, the deliberate abuse and exploitation which occurs on a not infrequent basis or the serious incompetence and lack of knowledge which has often been demonstrated in complaints which have been dealt with by BACP or BPS. I want, instead to draw attention to the simple every day mistakes that can happen through lack of awareness, carelessness and misunderstanding which have the potential to draw the counsellor and client into conflict, causing pain to them both, and often causing lasting professional damage to the therapist and the profession.

I wonder why it is that so many therapists don't ever seem to consider that they might become the subject of a complaint? Is it that they have an implicit belief that because they are involved in a caring process in which their intention is to help, that as a result, nothing can go wrong — and that even if it does there won't be any unpleasant consequences? Is it because the subject of complaints rarely, if ever, gets raised in therapist training? Is it because we as therapists have such faith in our own congruence and stability that we develop an intrinsic and false belief in our own invincibility? Is it because we are working all the time with clients who are incongruent or unstable, stressed or distressed, chaotic and vulnerable, that our potential to make mistakes gets forgotten. My suspicion is that most experienced therapists pay little attention to this possibility and therefore it is no surprise that trainees and newly qualified therapists do not do so either. Sadly, they are likely to be even more vulnerable to mistakes and complaints, through their lack of experience.

I don't know the answers to the questions above, all I do know is that the number of complaints against therapists continues to run at an unacceptably high level and that so often, the therapist is shocked and surprised that a complaint has been taken out against them. Evidence from other professional fields and from everyday life seems to indicate a change in the nature of our society, with a steadily increasing inclination to enter into litigation, perhaps encouraged by changed attitudes in the legal profession, with lawyers advertising for clients who feel they have been wronged or mistreated in some way and encouraging them to take legal action. In addition, increasing numbers of clients are more knowledgeable about the purpose, nature and methodology of counselling and are more likely to be aware when therapists have made mistakes, or acted inappropriately.

Each year, on average 45 complaints against therapists are being heard by BACP. This may not seem, a great deal to some readers. However, this figure needs to be seen within the context of the number of enquiries from people wanting to make a complaint. In the period March 2000 to February 2001, there were over 270 enquiries from individuals wishing to make a complaint. In addition, in the same period there were 25 complaints under the BACP Complaints Procedure — 'Article 4.6' (BACP, 1999), against therapists whose activities have been deemed to bring the counselling and psychotherapy profession into disrepute.

A substantial number of complaints heard over the past few years by BACP have clearly begun with minor acts or omissions, a lack of clarity about contracting or small breaches of boundaries, that have led almost inexorably to a substantial change in the nature of the relationship between therapist and client, resulting in complaints of exploitation or abuse by the therapist. 'Poppy', writes elsewhere in this book about the tiny acts by her therapist which created a relationship of dependency leading almost imperceptibly to her seduction and continuing abuse.

Deborah Lott (1999), suggests we should 'Forget sex, it is the smaller intimacies, sometimes even commonplace courtesies that present the biggest dilemmas between clients and therapists'. She further states:

> After years of media scrutiny, we have all got the message that sex between client and therapist is wrong. Not only is an affair an ethical transgression on the part of the counsellor, it is also often a psychological disaster for the patient. But there are countless subtler — and no less consequential — boundary dilemmas that confound clients and therapists. These dilemmas centre around the smaller intimacies, even the commonplace courtesies, that normally mark people's everyday behaviour. In a psychotherapeutic setting, however, they often take on deeper symbolic meanings (p. 1).

Her article, which I would strongly recommend all therapists and trainees to read, can be down-loaded from the Internet. She gives a number of examples of ordinary, everyday acts by therapists, (including acts that were intended as kindnesses) which were experienced by the client in a very different way to that which the therapist had intended and all of which led to serious breaches of the therapeutic boundaries.

Breaching boundaries is one of the most common causes cited in complaints to BACP and sadly, these seem to prevail far more in complaints against therapists who describe themselves as 'person-centred' than those from other modalities. Most therapists and trainees learn quickly the importance of having a good contracting process to establish firm but gentle boundaries which will enable clients to feel contained, held and safe. Although the theoretical importance of this is taught well in most training courses, in reality the importance of it is something that can only really be internalised through the experience of getting it wrong and learning from the consequences of that. I have always believed that practising as a therapist is a risky trade and the risk is substantially higher for trainees and newly qualified therapists. So often it is the small acts committed in a naive, almost unknowing way that lead to therapist downfall and complaint. Examples such as: lending a cold client the therapist's cardigan, offering a client a cup of tea, giving a hug, lending a handkerchief instead of providing tissues, sending a birthday card or holiday post card, stopping to talk and exchanging pleasantries in the street, extending the length of counselling sessions without negotiation, visiting a client in hospital, complementing the client's dress or hair, telling the client how well they are doing, accepting a small gift from a client, are just a few of the small steps that can begin a slide into real danger for therapist and client. These acts, whilst seeming harmless and acceptable in themselves in every day life, are likely to carry a different meaning within the special nature of the therapeutic relationship. Even such apparently minor shifting of the therapeutic boundaries in these acts, carries with it the promise of providing far more than the act itself and these acts will assume greater symbolic weight when clients are at their most vulnerable or, disastrously may actually cause the client to become more vulnerable to the therapist.

Boundaries do not get set or appropriately maintained automatically, they have to be deliberately activated and monitored by the therapist. In order to do this, and to be both safe and ethical in their practice, therapists should adopt a discipline of observing and questioning every intervention of whatever kind, that they want to offer to their clients, both within the therapeutic hour and outside of it. As Deborah Lott says, 'For therapists — and clients — who are struggling with boundaries the paramount question must be: Does this action serve the patient's therapeutic interests? If an act or an encounter threatens that goal, it is suspect, even if its exploitative potential is not obvious.' (1999: 1).

I recall, some time ago, discovering from a supervisee, that he had begun to offer his clients a cup of tea or coffee when they arrived at his consulting room. His explanation was that they often travelled long distances to see him and that therefore he should offer them some sustenance. When we explored his reasoning further and his feelings about what he was doing, it became clear that he also had a need to demonstrate his capacity to be caring and nurturing of his clients. It also became clear that a pattern was developing in his work, of an increasing inability to challenge his clients effectively or to offer them 'tough love'. Neither had he considered how his clients might be experiencing his 'hospitality' and he recognised that they could be experiencing him as patronising them, parenting them or offering them 'tea and sympathy'. He also recognised that he was providing a built in opportunity of 'resistance' to engaging therapeutically at the start of each session, for both himself and for his clients.

We agreed that he should end this practice and that he would need to work towards this by 'coming clean' to his clients and re-negotiating the boundaries. It was also really helpful for us to spend some time in supervision, exploring his therapeutic intent. Why was he a therapist, what was it he was setting out to do? And also how might his clients be experiencing his therapeutic intent and his actions? It became clear that underneath his rationalised reasons for becoming a therapist he had a strong altruistic drive, rooted in heavily introjected parental values that he must help others less fortunate than himself. His underlying therapeutic intent was to 'help others', to 'make them better', to 'get them to feel better', rather than his rationalised, stated intent of helping others to help themselves.

The question of 'What is my underlying therapeutic intent?' seems to me to be a critically important question for all therapists to be asking of themselves. Whilst a degree of altruism is desirable and necessary, it should not be so strong and uncontrolled that it sabotages the therapeutic process. It is important that we are aware of the strength and level of our altruistic drives and the values they are rooted in and that we do not let them take over and change the nature of the therapeutic relationship.

Cohen (1994) writes strongly about the importance of evaluating therapeutic intent, in all interactions with a client and goes further to state the importance of the therapist checking out with the client, the client's perception of the therapist's intent. She quotes Carl Rogers' opinion that '. . . there can be no substitute for the continual checking back and forth between purpose or hypothesis and technique or implementation'. (Rogers, 1951) He further states:

> But as I study my specific behaviours in an interview, I detect implied purposes of which I had not been aware, I discover areas in which it had not occurred to me to apply the hypothesis, I realise that what was for me an implementation of one attitude, is perceived by the client as the implementation of another (ibid.: 26).

This leads me to the element of boundary setting and breaking, which is perhaps most contentious within the ethos of counselling and psychotherapy, to do with the validity of touch in the therapeutic relationship. At the start of the academic year, I say to all my students on the counselling courses I run: 'Watch my lips. Do not touch your client, even if they ask you to. The very most you should do is to shake their hand when they arrive and when they leave — and you will need to check out if that is acceptable to them.' I tell them that this also includes when they are working with each other as counsellor and client in the practice periods within the course. We then explore the reasons and the rationale behind this, on a number of occasions throughout the course. I also make a note of the date and time I do this and tell the students that I have done so, in order that if a complaint is ever taken out against them as a result of their touching a client, they will not be able to claim they were never taught not to do that. Trainers might like to reflect on the fact that they could be actionable by a client of a student to whom they have given a qualification, if they have not ensured that students are fully cognisant of their legal duty of care towards their clients and their duty to ensure client emotional and physical safety. Courses and trainers who do not clearly and explicitly teach their trainees what they must or must not do put their trainees and themselves at risk of legal action in addition to complaint via BACP or other professional bodies.

Personally, I hate to take this line because in some ways it seems so antithetical to the therapeutic ethos. I am by nature, a tactile person. I like to give and to receive affection and to touch and be touched when that seems appropriate and seems to meet my needs and the needs of the other person. In my everyday social world that seems to be perfectly acceptable. I also know touch is not completely acceptable in our society and that in some sectors of my professional life, I and what I do, are described as 'touchy-feely', with the inference that I and what I do are somehow soft or weak and unacceptable. What I also know is that whatever I do as a therapist is very likely, in some degree at least, to be experienced differently by my client. Whilst, as a person-centred therapist, I may be concentrating strongly on my phenomenological approach and desperately trying to avoid interpreting anything my client does or says, my client has no such strictures on them. I must remember that they can and will interpret any and everything that I say and do within the context of their experiencing of their reality, within which they are meeting and experiencing me. It is likely that there will always be at least three realities of experiencing within the therapy room, mine, my clients, and that which we share. It is a foolish therapist who forgets this and assumes that all is as it appears to be in their eyes.

I suspect the therapist in the incident I am now going to describe had no idea of how the client experienced what the therapist did:

Jo was a young counsellor who referred himself to me for a one-off supervision session, to informally check out his experience of a recent incident that had happened in his own therapy with an experienced male therapist. He explained that he felt he could not take this to his regular supervisor, as that person knew who his therapist was. He had entered therapy to help him deal with a developing drink problem, some generalised feelings of depression and the onset of minor panic attacks. In the third session the therapist had enabled him to get in touch with some fairly deep feelings and he had begun to experience a fairly severe panic attack. The therapist suggested that he lay down on the floor and try to breathe gently and slowly, using his diaphragm. The therapist kneeled on the floor beside him and started to stroke his temples and his shoulders and arms. He also put his hand on the client's diaphragm, talking to him in a gentle voice and encouraging him to calm himself. The client began to experience strong erotic feelings and immediately felt that the therapist wanted to have sex with him. He calmed down from his panic attack fairly rapidly but instead was overcome with feelings of fear and loathing towards the therapist. He terminated the session on the basis of feeling unwell and left rapidly without making another appointment and had since written to the therapist to say that he would not be coming to see him again. Some two weeks later he was still fearful of what had happened and wondering if he should take a complaint out against the therapist. In the end he decided not to do that and entered into therapy with someone else, making it clear in the contracting that under no circumstances should the therapist attempt to touch him, no matter how distressed he might become.

In talking this experience through with me he identified the impact this was going to have on his own practice, as he had never considered how his touching a client with the most appropriate of intentions might be experienced so differently by the client. He recognised that what he experienced might well have been a transference from the therapist or a projection of the therapist's desires. He also recognised that the therapist's intentions may not have contained any sexual intent whatsoever and really were intended to calm his panic attack and keep him safe and that the feelings he experienced might have come solely from within himself.

I believe that the 'counsellor-client' who came to see me, took some real learnings from that situation and I certainly received a real reminder of why I avoid touching my clients. He never told me who his counsellor was, so I was not left with the dilemma of what action I should take. If I had been told who the counsellor was and had been given permission to contact him, I might have had to consider taking out a BACP member to member complaint. I am left with some ambivalent feelings about not being able to do that, particularly when I remember the pain my 'one-off' supervisee experienced.

I have had many supervisees and trainees come to me with the question of what they should do when either they feel they want to hug a client or a client asks them for a hug and they feel that they want to respond positively and not reject the client. I have a number of responses to that:

- Usually the first is to ask them to say in what way they think hugging the client will be in the client's therapeutic interest and in what ways might it be harmful?
- The second is usually to ask them what need of theirs will the hug be meeting and should that need take precedence over their duty to act responsibly and ethically as a therapist and to maintain appropriate boundaries?
- Third I will ask them what else they think the client might read into them hugging the client, even at the client's request?
- Fourth I will ask them what they think the next challenge to the therapeutic boundary will be and how they will resist that?
- Fifth and finally I will ask them if they would hug their doctor or if their doctor would hug them?

I will suggest that if they do agree to the hug, the client and they, will know the boundaries have shifted. If a hug has become acceptable, then that automatically means that something that was even more unacceptable than a hug before this event, is now likely to be more acceptable after it. If the client could ask for a hug and get it, they can now believe that they can ask for something else and get that. If they believe they can ask, then undoubtedly, they will! I think the same will happen for the counsellor. Having discovered that they can hug and that they like it, the possibility of the next boundary being broken becomes less remote, more likely and more easily justifiable, even for experienced, well grounded therapists. In some way the client-therapist relationship will have changed or become distorted. Touch in the therapeutic setting is unlikely to be a simple social act and will always be open to substantial interpretation (accurate or otherwise).

That is not to say that in reality clients should never be touched. There are bound to be times when it will be appropriate, for example sometimes when a client is uncontrollably distressed, a calming hand on the arm or the shoulder may be necessary, or, at the end of a long therapeutic relationship, a brief parting hug may be an important symbol of the ending of the relationship, a client who becomes physically ill may need some physical attention in order to protect or assist them in some way. What I am suggesting very strongly is that any sudden or recurring temptation to touch a client or to offer physical contact of any form should be carefully thought through before it is acted upon and ideally should be taken to supervision for consideration as to how it should be dealt with. Ideally, each of us should be using our internal supervisor to ask a series of questions like the five questions I have outlined above, which I ask my students and supervisees, and that we really take the trouble to reflect on these and listen to ourselves.

Finally I would like to briefly consider an aspect of complaints which may bring a shiver to us all. Above I have largely written about situations where clients can be seen to be in a therapeutic alliance with their therapist. Things can and do go wrong in these situations but there is some possibility of recovering from mistakes if they are owned and apologised for. Experience within the BACP world of complaints has shown that most clients who take out complaints want their complaint to be acknowledged, to feel their grievance has been heard, sometimes to receive an apology and to have an assurance that the same mistake is unlikely to occur again.

There are other complainants for whom there will be no satisfaction other than the crucifixion or immolation of the therapist, even when the therapist is completely innocent. Highly disturbed, vexatious clients are an ever-present danger to therapists and carefully maintained high standards of practice and even a commitment to low risk clients is no guarantee of protection. Many trainees and newly qualified counsellors can be very unaware of how dangerous clients can be and can often fail to take account of the impact that clients can have on the therapist and their immediate close circle of family and friends. I learned the hard way, as many of us have to, from the following situation.

John had been referred to me for counselling, with generalised feelings of depression and concerns about his obesity. In his early thirties and a practising counsellor he seemed intelligent and articulate and to have a supportive family. I became aware in the first session that he seemed to be dissociating from his feelings and to be having some paranoid thoughts towards his work colleagues. I was a little concerned by this but as a fairly young therapist, I wanted to stretch myself and convinced myself that 'I could cope with him'. I did not realise how much I would regret those words, which I have take directly from my notes at the time. How I wish now that I had noticed what my unconscious was saying. Not that I was competent to work with him but that I could cope with him!

During the second session I soon realised that he was far beyond my competence at that time. That he was seriously psychologically disturbed and really needed to be hospitalised for his own safety and the safety of others. Fortunately he seemed quite well disposed towards me and agreed that hospital might be a good idea and asked that I should accompany him to see his doctor. After a brief conversation with me (with my client's approval), the doctor took control of the situation. I stayed with my client whilst another Doctor was involved and in a fairly short space of time my client was sectioned and admitted to hospital. He left me in a calm and friendly way, to go in the ambulance and I returned home to carry on with my life.

For six months, I heard nothing and in fact had quite forgotten about him, when I received my first letter. In this he wrote at length about his perception of me as both the devil incarnate, the cause of all his problems and also the only one who could help him and rescue him. Foolishly I wrote back a brief, and I hoped, empathic letter making it clear that I could not take him on as a client. Then began the increasing torrent of letters, rising rapidly to one a day and getting longer and longer and more and more bizarre in their content. Mistakenly, I replied to the first couple of letters reiterating each time that I was unable to help him. Then wrote saying I would not be replying to any more letters from him and that I would return them unopened, which I did for several months. He stopped writing for a short time and then began again and also started to telephone me at home and at work. He also started to make some fairly serious threats against my family. At this point he was released from hospital and began to turn up at my home and at my office, being very abusive and threatening violence. All the time his plea was for me to heal him and undo all the damage I had done to him.

This had a huge impact on me, my family and my colleagues at work, none of whom were aware that I practised as a therapist in my spare time. At that point, I asked for help from my supervisor and was put in touch with a group of therapists who offered support to therapists who were being abused by disturbed clients. With help from them, I learned to stop blaming myself, to manage my fear of him and to detach myself from any emotional engagement with his feelings towards me. His letters, which by now were arriving two or three times a day with fifteen to twenty pages written in red ink, were put straight in the bin, the telephone number was changed and made ex-directory and an injunction was taken out to prevent his harassing me any further. Difficult stuff for the 'tender' therapist to learn to do and for me, a real demonstration of 'tough love' both for him and for myself. He was then sectioned and hospitalised again and the problem disappeared for over fifteen years. Then, out of the blue, I received a letter with red ink on the envelope. I thought I knew the writing but couldn't think who it might be and opened it. Yes, it was from him, fifteen pages of the same content written as though there had been no intervening years. You can imagine how the fear came flooding back. However, with some swift telephone calls, I was able to check that he was still in hospital and it was extremely unlikely that he would ever be released. I did read his letter though and it had a sting in the tail for me. In the final paragraph he threatened to take out a complaint against me through BACP and to ensure that I would suffer for all that I had done to him and he would make sure that I would never be able to practice again.

I know that there is no likelihood of him being able to do that, however I do know that there are a lot of therapists practising to day, including myself, who have clients who are extremely disturbed and can become excessively, negatively, obsessively fixated on their therapist. BACP and the other therapeutic associations can be quite good at spotting complaints from clients like this, but not always. Disturbed clients do make complaints of bad practice, which are legitimate and should be heard and dealt with. Sometimes disturbed clients make vexatious complaints against therapists who have done nothing wrong and sometimes those complaints have to be pursued all the way through the complaints process to prove the therapist's innocence. The impact of such an experience on the therapist, their family, friends and colleagues can be enormous and very debilitating.

In one way, we can do little more than be aware of this possibility. In another we can do a great deal to be more effective in our assessment and diagnosis of clients and ensuring that we work as much as we can within our known levels of competence and that we do not stretch those too far. We certainly need to catch ourselves if we are feeling concerned about a client and decide that we can 'cope' with them, rather than knowing that we are sufficiently competent to work with them. 'Caveat Emptor' (let the buyer beware) is a principle in English Law, which warns the customer to be cautious about the services or goods that they are buying. Perhaps we should have a similar slogan for therapists, 'Caveat Concillarius' to warn us against just accepting any client who walks through the door or is referred to us.

To return to my theme, I think it is important to notice in the last situation I described, that it was a really small and well intended action on my part, which really started the process which damaged me quite considerably. The therapeutic relationship ended when the doctors took over responsibility for the client. I should have maintained the totality of that ending boundary and not diffused it by writing to him in reply to his letter. I've never written to a client or former client since. It is the little things that count, so watch out for them.

## References

BACP (1999). *BACP Complaints Procedure*.
Lott, D. (1999). Drawing Boundaries — Recognising structure and boundaries in patient-therapist interactions, *Psychology Today*, (http://www.findarticles.com/cf_1/m1175/3_32/54504419/print.jhtml)
Cohen, J. (1994). *Person Centred Journal*.
Rogers, C. R. (1951). *Client Centred Therapy*. Boston: Houghton Mifflin.

# Chapter 12

# Working Safely:
# Counsellor competence

## Moira Walker

Those with experience of complaints procedures, and who have adjudicated on complaints panels, know only too well that complaints by clients against counsellors arise from many sources of client experience. Some clients clearly have had dreadful and abusive experiences at the hands of counsellors who are unprincipled, unethical, and abusive. Practitioners who have worked with clients following such experiences know only too well the damage, the pain and the anguish caused — this in addition to the original distress that took the client for help initially. Other clients have reacted badly to a therapeutic error that in itself does not appear major but for a variety of reasons escalates out of control and cannot thereafter be contained. Other complaints are unfounded, a few are simply vicious, and conscientious counsellors are caused unnecessary anxiety, disruption and worry. In some cases there is a major discrepancy between what the client and practitioner perceive as counselling and its boundaries and consequently misunderstandings arise and grow.

There are also instances where counsellors, however well intentioned, struggle with clients who are presenting issues and behaviour that are not within their levels of competence in terms of their skills, knowledge, or experience. Sometimes, which greatly exacerbates the difficulty, the work is not within the level of competence of their supervisor either. I would note that this is very different from counsellors who are actively, and at some level, intentionally, abusive to clients. In my experience these are all too often extremely experienced and highly qualified practitioners who hide their actions frighteningly well from colleagues and supervisors. Such therapists tend to be predominantly male (Rutter, 1990) and have professional credibility (Strean, 1993). It is not this area, but that of working within individual levels of competence that I will address in this chapter, noting that the situations I describe are generally not ones of intentional bad and abusive practice but more often arising from benign intent backed by insufficient knowledge and experience. The saying 'the road to hell is paved with good intentions' springs to mind. Where distressed and needy clients are involved, who reasonably trust that the counsellor knows what they are doing, good intentions in themselves are not good enough.

The question immediately arises of how does a counsellor know if they are working within their level of competence? There are perhaps two questions here: how does the individual counsellor assess their own level of competence? And how do they assess whether the client they work with fits this closely enough? This is further compounded by the reality that levels of skill develop as time goes on and do so in the light of new therapeutic experiences with new clients presenting with more complex issues. It is also recognised that research indicates that beginners are as successful in terms of outcome as experienced therapists (Macdonald, 1992). So it is not an easy or a straightforward equation but it is in part the recognition *in itself* that this is complex that helps counsellors work within their limitations. Over confidence is dangerous as is a desire to learn too much too quickly with an 'interesting' or 'challenging' client as the unfortunate guinea pig.

Examples of both good and bad practice can illustrate the dilemmas and assist in focusing on other questions related to competence that extend beyond the individual counsellor's responsibility. The first is of a counsellor still in training and in a placement where initial assessments of all clients were undertaken by very experienced practitioners. Cases were then matched according to the level of expertise assessed to be required. This counsellor took on a young man assessed as suitable for a beginner . The assessor felt short term counselling appropriate for a presentation of a late adolescent transitional difficulty in a client who related well and easily and although troubled was not deeply distressed. The case was discussed in supervision prior to the first session and all concerned felt it suitable. However in the first session a very different scenario emerged. The client was extremely distressed; at times almost incoherent and spilled out in a highly uncontained way a history of terrible abuse and acting out behaviour including self-harm. Reporting the session afterwards the counsellor said she felt like a duck swimming against the tide — calm on the surface and paddling madly underneath. She had however contained the client and the session well commenting that she had resisted an urge and curiosity to want to know more. She felt slightly ashamed of this but this recognition of, and an ability to work with, a problematic counter-transference served her well. She intervened, calmly but firmly, twenty minutes before the end of the session and acknowledged empathically his dreadful experiences and the pain he was currently feeling. She continued by saying that she wanted to help him come back to the present, to see how he felt now and to look at how he was going to cope with the coming week. This worked well and he left quite calmly, thanking her, and with a plan of action for his week.

In supervision she commented that she knew not to try anything clever but to work in a way that she could manage and that was safe for both counsellor and client. There is not space here to describe in detail the supervisory discussions that transpired in the supervision group and the discussions that the supervisor had with other experienced colleagues. But considerable work went into reaching a decision. The counsellor herself felt torn between passing the client on to a colleague with considerable specialist experience, and her sense that she had made good contact and felt able to contain him, provided she was contained and supported enough through supervision. It was finally agreed that in any case she should see the client for the next session and explore with him alternative routes of help. In this session she first acknowledged with the client how different he had been in the assessment to the first session with her. He explained that in the assessment he had said little of significance, knowing he would not see that person again. He commented that he had spent a life-time living with secrets, covering up and pretending — it had not been hard to do. She explained that she was still in training; that she was not experienced in the issue he was bringing, that there was more experienced help available, and that if they did agree to work together they would have to learn together how to proceed and that may be at a very slow pace. She explained about supervision and that if they were to work together she wanted the client in contact with the GP and would want permission to talk with the doctor.

As a result of these discussions this client and counsellor decided to work together within a very clear contract. It was arranged in the agency that supervision would be in place shortly after each session and that in the event of the supervisor's illness or absence another supervisor would be available. The work was closely supervised and was ultimately very successful. In this example a trainee counsellor was able to work successfully with a complex case because she recognised her own limitations and worked with caution; she was in touch with her own process and able to use supervision which was effective, frequent and reliable; the agency acted as an effective container for the counsellor and the client; the contract was clear and the client understood its parameters and had been involved in its creation. Although the original filter of assessment had not worked nevertheless good agency practice effectively intervened.

This compares with another instance with a less happy outcome. This involved a newly trained counsellor desperate to find a job in an area where these were few and far between. She finally started work in a very reputable agency which had decided to extend its remit to include counselling. She was confident that she could cope with the range of work that would present. There was an expectation that she would see twelve to fifteen clients a week and would be solely responsible with some administrative back up for organising her work including the assessment of clients. She was extremely enthusiastic but the other roles of the agency meant that the work would inevitably be complex including people with an extensive history in the psychiatric services. She had no training in mental health issues and no back up from specialist services — it was up to her to put in place what she needed. She felt strongly that the labelling of people with mental illness labels was discriminatory and unhelpful. Whilst in itself many would be in sympathy with this statement it can be a dangerous oversimplification if it detracts from good and objective assessment.

An early case was a woman with a history of multiple abuse, with episodes of profound dissociation who was possibly multiple personality. The counsellor had little knowledge on which to base her work but felt that she would learn from this client and that it was the challenge she needed at this stage in her career. She was genuinely committed to working with her; wanted to give of her best; read widely on the subject and gave much time and thought to the work. It did prove uncontainable: she gave more and more time to the client, sessions became longer and longer, telephone calls were frequent, including to the counsellor's home, and the counsellor became completely overwhelmed. The case had been mentioned in supervision but had not been discussed in depth or regularly. The counsellor felt that the supervisor would not approve of the way she was working and had been confident that having formed a close working relationship with the woman that she would be able work successfully. But in the event it was this very alliance that facilitated the expression of powerful negative and destructive feelings from the client to the counsellor who could not manage them. She felt frightened, attacked, hurt and defensive and began to dread seeing the client. She terminated the work with little warning as she could not cope with continuing. The client was re-admitted to hospital and did complain to the agency. As neither the agency nor the counsellor belonged to any professional organisation the complaint came to nothing. But considerable damage was done to the client and the counsellor too felt demolished, de-moralised and exhausted. It was a very steep learning curve for her but at what cost to the client?

The case raises a number of issues. There are obvious dangers for any counsellor with this level of experience taking on a post of this nature unless they have previous and considerable relevant expertise. It is a one person service, in an agency where the main focus is not counselling. The agency did not know the issues or needs involved, from their perspective they were employing someone qualified who did. In this situation the demands are inevitably considerable on any lone counsellor. The need for a job overcame other considerations but it could be considered irresponsible for a newly qualified practitioner to take on this type of work without prior relevant experience. In addition there appeared to be a discrepancy between what the agency perceived as her qualification and the actual content of her training. The agency assumed that she would be competent to assess complex presentations and would have a working knowledge of mental health issues. This, they felt, was what a professional qualification in counselling implied. In fact neither were true — her training had not included assessment; the placement she had been on would not allow trainees to do these; and neither had she any knowledge related to mental health. Additionally, her training had apparently not been rigorous regarding the number of counselling hours actually undertaken; there had been a problem with placements, resulting in her having worked in total less than a hundred hours in client contact.

So there are several layers of responsibility which need to be recognised in ensuring that counsellors work within their levels of competence. Employers may need to check out more thoroughly what counsellors are actually qualified to do in terms of their training and by their experience. However I have known employers who vigorously resist this. They argue that it is the responsibility of training organisations and professional bodies to ensure uniformity across courses and to match course content with the needs of the workplace. So what is the role of training courses in this scenario? Is there sufficient match between training and the needs of those who employ counsellors? How much variation is there between what is apparently the same level of qualification? Is there sufficient emphasis on counselling practice and a breadth to this experience? Have course syllabuses shifted sufficiently in terms of recognising the needs of clients who now present for counselling? Counselling courses are numerous and as Palmer Barnes points out: 'the current proliferation of counselling courses of differing length and content mean that individuals can complete a comparatively basic, academically related course and immediately move on to further qualification . . . without having had any real experience of therapeutic practice.' (1998: 22).

The need for sufficiency of training is especially relevant in today's world. Those who have worked in the profession a long time, particularly those with previous experience in mental health, know that many counselling clients of today would have been seen in mental health settings in the past. In some ways this is an extremely positive and hopeful move but only if the skills are available to ensure safe working practices. The answer to these questions relating to courses is, of course, as variable and varied as the courses themselves. Some are truly excellent and many highly competent. Others have areas of weakness, and some are simply poor and insufficient, but the resulting qualification appears the same. This remains highly problematic both for those deciding to train (which is often prescribed by where you live rather than what you might like to choose) and employers who often, and quite reasonably, take at face value the qualification being proffered.

Clearly in both the cases described above the role of the supervisor was significant. In the first the supervisor looms large as a containing and supportive figure who is taking an active role both in ensuring a good service for the client and that the counsellor works appropriately, whilst enabling the counsellor to safely develop her skills and offer effective and safe help to the client. In the second instance readers may wonder about the supervisors role. As previously noted supervision was provided in accordance with professional guidelines and the agency was paying. It should be remembered that this counsellor believed she was doing a good job and was very committed. She would not have worked unsupervised. But here questions are raised about the nature of supervision, the experience of the supervisor, and the match between that and the work undertaken. This supervisor was highly qualified and experienced. The counsellor had chosen him on that basis. But he worked primarily in private practice with little experience of agency work. They had agreed that the counsellor would maximise her knowledge by presenting two cases regularly and in depth and the case in question was not one of them. This was partly because the supervisor had stated clearly at the beginning that it was not the type of case he would take on and that he was sceptical of the dissociative disorder diagnosis. There the discussion appears to have ended reinforced by the counsellor's determination that she could and would work with the client even if her supervisor felt differently.

Supervisors understand the process differently. Most would agree that the role is clearer when counsellors are in training but after that the waters are muddy. In my experience when working with trainee counsellors with only a small number of cases, supervisors feel that they should have a clear overview of all of them, and trainings often make this clear. When a qualified counsellor is working with a busy caseload this can feel an impossible supervisory task — it cannot be done within a few hours a month and may be seen as a very unhelpful way to proceed. The extent to which supervisors are, or are not, responsible for the practice of their supervisees is reflected in the lack of legal clarity . At present the question of the legal liability of the counselling supervisor seems unclear and it has been argued (Page and Woskett, 1994: 151) that the possibility of liability is likely to be limited. However it remains untested. Jenkins notes that 'the potential legal liability held by supervisors for therapists under their charge seems to be a major area for misunderstanding and potential confusion' (1997: 68). It is clear that supervision is a multifaceted task ,which can have many functions and purposes. (Hawkins, 1989; Kadushin, 1976). It is not uni-dimensional and the same supervisor may define it variously in relation to different contexts and with different supervisees.

However another question arises here which is one of the match between context and counsellor and supervisor. In the second example two features are noticeable. One is that it is a job in a very particular setting, and yet the supervisor has little experience of it. How appropriate is this? One view might be that skills are transferable, that a good supervisor works well within any context. Yet many supervisees who are considerably more experienced prefer a supervisor who has specialist knowledge of their field and their context. This has certainly been my experience within the field of abuse: there is a knowledge base and a skill base that is specialised, and in both selecting a supervisor, and being selected myself this is a significant factor. The other feature relates to the lack of an overall view of the counsellor's workload: again there is a question of whether a supervisor should be assisting the counsellor in managing their caseload and in ensuring their work is of an appropriate level and amount. What is clear in this instance is that as a relatively inexperienced counsellor she needed this input from someone and did not get it. However the supervisor himself was clear and honest regarding the parameters of his role — it was to increase clinical knowledge by exploring the same cases regularly — so whose responsibility was it to ensure such assistance was in place? The argument is circular because the counsellor only recognised the need after she became deeply and dangerously embroiled in work she could not manage or contain.

So what of the counsellor — what in retrospect would have enabled her to work within her levels of competence, rather than exceed them so dangerously. It seems evident that the job itself exceeded her level of competence: she was effectively running a counselling service with all that involves — generally a job that would be taken by a senior practitioner. However having taken it the situation may have been rendered more manageable rather than the opposite by the counsellor acting somewhat differently. In working with the client described she did seem overtaken by that dangerous combination of evangelical zeal, inexperience and lack of knowledge. Perhaps a rule of thumb is if a powerful desire to rescue and heal takes over, particularly where a history of such disturbance is evident, this is a clear contra-indication to the work. If it is undertaken — and I think generally it should not within that scenario — it should only be after careful consultation and supervision; within a clear contract; with proper professional back-up from other services and after a close examination of personal motive and ability to cope with potentially strong negative feelings.

Even with a less serious presentation than the one described here this counsellor should have given considerable thought to the sufficiency of supervision. Sometimes specialist supervision can be a helpful adjunct to an on-going arrangement. Supervisors themselves can suggest this and may be a good source of knowledge of other personnel available. If the supervisor was not himself prepared to oversee her work as a whole then it was crucial that this role was formally taken on by someone. The counsellor should also have sought advice at an early stage from a practitioner in a similar post. Reinventing wheels is a tedious and often unnecessary task, and a painful one when you end up entangled in the wheel. Time taken to network, to link in with other services, to seek information is never wasted. Not only does it prevent mistakes and dampens dangerous enthusiasms it lessens isolation and creates a supportive and containing world — very important in such a potentially lonely job. As we saw from the first example given in this chapter it is clear that beginning practitioners can be extraordinarily effective, but this must only be attempted within a carefully thought out therapeutic plan. It is always important to recognise that taking on complex work early in a career means entering very stormy waters that can, given the right conditions, prove a moving and invaluable experience for both those involved, but equally can do so much damage to both.

Another area of great concern is where counsellors move into private practice with very little experience. Most of us know of so called counsellors who set up with impressively glossy brochures when their training is minimal; their experience exceedingly limited, and their knowledge base startling in its inadequacy. Paradoxically, their confidence level is often frighteningly high. I once exchanged increasingly heated letters with someone who had undertaken a ten week counselling skills course — with no prior related training. He went into private practice; sent me a beautifully designed brochure and became extremely angry when I both refused to refer clients to him and told him he was acting unethically. Such practice is often based in the practitioners home where there is no support and where private counsellors can be particularly vulnerable even when highly experienced. This is the area of incompetence which is most stark and deeply concerning — it is simply unethical and unacceptable and is likely to continue until the profession is regulated. It is more widespread than many realise and as many of these people do not belong to a reputable professional organisation there is no protection or redress for any clients. The damage that can be done to clients in this situation is considerable as those of us who have worked with people who have suffered at their hands know only too well.

Another scenario is when students on counselling training courses offer themselves privately (often at a low fee) when they are unable to find placements. Courses that are reputable would generally not allow this practice in their trainees and any course that is BACP accredited is stringently assessed including its placement policy. The responsibility for bad practice in this instance extends beyond the individual to the course itself and its staff; to the institution (if there is one) that approves the course, and to those who supervise in this context. Supervisors may argue that in this situation it is better that such bad practice is supervised rather than leaving the person as a therapeutic loose canon. However another course of action where training courses are involved is to refuse to collude in such bad practice; to complain to the course organisers, inform the professional organisations, and, if the course is within an educational establishment, contact them explaining the ethical issues involved, requesting that they investigate.

This situation is very different from one that arises from a counsellor responsibly taking on work that initially seems within their area of competence but over time develops into something much more complicated, demanding and difficult than could reasonably have been foreseen. This relates in part to the first example given in this chapter but that situation quickly became evident and it would have been relatively straightforward for the case to have been transferred to a more experienced practitioner if that had been the clinical decision. It was a first session, the therapeutic relationship was in a very early stage and it was rapidly clear that the presentation was far from straightforward.

However that is not always so and an example illustrates how problematic this can be. A counsellor with some experience was given a case of a woman experiencing a mid life difficulty involving several simultaneous losses and changes. Everything indicated that she was suitable for this counsellor. She was in an apparently supportive marriage; she was working part-time; had friends and interests, and related well in her initial assessment session. She was depressed but appropriately so to her situation. She was able to express this and appeared to experience some relief from talking. She had to wait for an appointment and although she expressed concern about this she seemed to cope during the waiting period. The work seemed to progress quite well although the counsellor always felt slightly anxious and uneasy and was puzzled by this — she could not locate the source of the feeling and the client appeared to be working usefully on her recent bereavements and losses. These included the death of her elderly father whom she had described as warm, loving and a very dear person to her.

After about four months work, at a point in which a good therapeutic relationship was thoroughly established, the picture changed drastically. On the anniversary of her father's death the client seemed to literally fall apart in the session. It was barely containable and the client went on to experience a serious psychotic episode. A history of very severe abuse emerged, plus a history of suicide attempts and periods of extreme disturbance. This client was so used to living with unspeakable secrets and she so successfully dissociated that it had not been possible to recognise what lay behind the more obvious presenting persona. In this example this counsellor did not ultimately continue working with this client — she was transferred to a psychotherapist working within the mental health services. The transfer was fully discussed with the client, when she was able to absorb this information, and an ending period was agreed in which to conclude the work with her counsellor and introduce her to the new therapist. The client, although distressed by the disruption, did accept the other therapist who was able to work long-term with her both on her past history and on losing her counsellor. Although not ideal this change was seen as unavoidable by all those concerned — the counsellor, the supervisor and the agency all agreed that the case was not within the competence of either the individual counsellor or this particular agency. Although short-term distress and disruption to the client was unavoidable it was felt that this was a more ethical course of action than continuing and the client was involved as fully as possible and her feelings validated and acknowledged.

It is indeed a dilemma for the counsellor, however experienced, when an unexpected and unpredictable change in the work occurs and there are occasions when it has to be recognised that the counselling has to cease — that it would be inappropriate to continue. And yet ending without sufficient warning to the client is also to be avoided and in itself can be a cause for complaint. In the example above developments were somewhat dramatic but often this is not the case. There can be warning signals. Clients who find it hard to leave sessions; who make contact between sessions when this is not part of the contract; where there are gaps in the history; where there have been many unsuccessful attempts at counselling or therapy previously; where the client has very poor recall of what has happened in the preceding session or since then; when there is increasing difficulty in holding on to reality; where the external world is crumbling and support is minimal or cannot be allowed; where acting out begins or increases and cannot be contained; where there are threats to others and where insight is limited. The list could go on and it is crucial that counsellors monitor their practice closely if these type of changes occur. Whilst it may be possible and helpful for the work to continue this needs to be monitored in terms of both focus and therapeutic models used. It can be important to contain and support rather than challenge defences that may need maintaining.

As in the second example given in this chapter a therapeutic response that can lead to difficulty is when difficulties appear and boundaries are not held sufficiently. The counsellor in dealing with someone who is very needy can respond to the neediness without sufficient thought to the implications. Sessions can become longer; contact between sessions becomes uncontained; the therapeutic process starts to change shape and form. The shaky and scary inner world of the client begins to be reflected in a wobbly and unpredictable form of counselling. As described, one conclusion is that the counsellor gradually becomes more and more overwhelmed by the demands and difficulties of the client (again reflecting the overwhelming nature of the clients experience) and terminates the work abruptly. In itself termination is not inappropriate because by this stage they are indeed out of their depth. However the manner of ending is deeply distressing to the client who feels abandoned and (correctly) that they have been too much for the counsellor to bear. Such precipitate endings can be avoided by earlier interventions more informed by therapeutic awareness and less by a desire to rescue. This is not to say that it is always incorrect to give a client more time, to see them more frequently, or arrange for contact between sessions if this is therapeutically valid. The difference is that a therapeutic strategy should be carefully considered and all its implications discussed with a supervisor before any change is made. It may be extremely helpful to see a client more frequently in times of crisis but it is an important and significant decision and should be treated as such, as should counsellor availability between sessions. Containment by telephone at specified times can be life saving but it certainly is not if there are no clear boundaries: a client ringing up an exhausted counsellor who is feeling increasingly invaded and frustrated is deeply non therapeutic and can have devastating consequences.

Working within competence levels is absolutely crucial to the safety of clients. It is therefore an inherent necessity that counsellors are self-aware, able to be honest and self-critical, are cautious and careful and able to hear, reflect on, and take advice from others. Self-interest has to be a considerably lower priority than ensuring that a reliable, ethical and professional service is offered. This means making hard decisions such as not taking on a job if it is beyond your ability level. It means recognising fantasies of grandiosity and rescue, leaving them safely in the realm of fantasy and not acting them out. It means recognising that your skills are limited and that this may have consequences in terms of earning a living. It means that a desire to satisfy therapeutic curiosity through an 'interesting' case is in itself not problematic, but putting the desire into action may be. And it means acknowledging how complex people are, how much remains unknown, and how fragile and tenuous the work can be. They are hard realities but crucial if client and counsellor safety is to be ensured and the profession to have integrity and meaning.

## References

Hawkins, P. (1989). *Supervision in the Helping Professions.* Buckingham: Open University Press.

Jenkins, P. (1997). *Counselling, Psychotherapy and the Law.* London: Sage.

Kadushin, A. (1976). *Supervision in Social Work.* New York: Columbia University Press.

Macdonald, A. (1992). Training and outcome in supervised individual psychotherapy. *British Journal of Psychotherapy,* 8(3).

Page, S. and Wosket, V. (1994). *Supervising the Counsellor: A cyclical model.* London: Routledge.

Palmer Barnes, F. (1998). *Complaints and Grievances in Psychotherapy: A handbook of ethical practice* London: Routledge.

Rutter, P. (1990). *Sex in the Forbidden Zone.* London: Aquarian Press.

Strean, H.S. (1993). *Therapists Who Have Sex With Their Patients: Treatment and recovery.* New York: Brunner Mazel.

# Chapter 13

# Acceptance of Uncertainty

## Caroline Jones

*. . . the capacity to tolerate uncertainty is a prerequisite for the profession. Though the public believe that therapists guide patients systematically and sure-handedly through predictable stages of therapy to a foreknown goal, such is rarely the case . . . such belief may block the uncertain and spontaneous encounter necessary for effective therapy (Yalom, 1989:13).*

Counsellors and clients come to counselling with uncertainty. For counsellors, where there is uncertainty about what to do for the best, there is also room for error. Despite codes, theoretical knowledge, experience and competence there are occasions when there are no right answers to the questions and dilemmas that arise in practice. In addition, no counsellor can be sure, in advance, with each new client, whether they can establish an effective therapeutic relationship, or that they have the particular competence or experience to work with the material to be presented. For clients, uncertainties include the fear that they cannot be helped, or that the material they bring may be too hard to bear for the counsellor and might harm them, or that they may find the counsellor unsuitable for them. In the context of complaints, for counsellors, there is the thought that however carefully the counsellor works, a client might make a complaint for real or frivolous, mischievous or malicious reasons. For the client, there is the worry that there may be no benefit, or worse, they might experience harm from the counselling.

It is distressing to be the subject of a complaint yet the profession does need avenues of redress for clients and ways of monitoring its practitioners in order to protect the public seeking and using its services. Complaints can arise from misunderstandings or unrealistic expectations as well as when mistakes or worse occur. There are, however, ways of dealing with some of the uncertainties. In this chapter I focus on a number of themes: key elements of good practice; the counselling relationship including the client's perspective; learning from the mistakes of others; possible reactions when we hear about complaints against others and a summary about how to reduce the likelihood of complaints arising.

I make some assumptions in this chapter. Firstly, that the selection, training and supervision of the counsellor has met reasonable standards and secondly, that the counsellor has been assessed as suitable for the role and responsibilities. Opinions may vary about how to assess suitability, although I would suggest that the following are qualities unacceptable in a counsellor:

- a person who means well but has a powerful desire to sort other people's problems out (appropriate to some other professions);
- or who is arrogant and unwilling to listen to the opinions of others, especially when these are different to those of the counsellor;
- or who practices in order to meet their emotional needs with clients and former clients;
- or who, when in the role of counsellor spends time talking about their own problems.

Trainers, and especially counselling supervisors, carry responsibility for ensuring, as best they can, that the counsellors they train and supervise are suitable for the work they do. Suitability for the kind of work done and in the settings where this takes place, is another aspect to consider throughout a counsellor's career.

Finally, I assume that regular instances of poor practice, malpractice or negligence have already been picked up and dealt with in supervision and elsewhere and that, where appropriate, the counsellor has ceased to practice.

## Good practice

Key elements only of good practice are outlined in this chapter as there are many other sources of information available elsewhere (Bond ,1993 and 2000; Syme, 1994; McMahon, 1997 and 1999; Jones *et al.* 2000 and many others). The most important principle for conscientious practitioners will always be to take all reasonable steps to work to a generally accepted standard. The most important element is regular, reliable and appropriate supervision, with access to the supervisor between sessions, in emergencies (BAC, 1998). Membership of an appropriate professional association and the commitment to abide by their code(s) is another important element, together with the understanding that merely following a code to the letter without understanding and absorbing the values of that code is not enough. No code is exhaustive so there are occasions when a counsellor is faced with situations where there is no codified direction. Other elements include: acting in good faith when faced with conflicting ethical principles or conflicts of interest; being open to any criticisms, complaints or concerns voiced informally by clients, colleagues and others; building a network of experienced practitioners for support in emergencies or when faced with dilemmas; attention to continuing professional development and policies and procedures about record-keeping and monitoring.

Counsellors must also have an awareness of their own personal values and moral codes and how these influence their judgement. Another influence on judgement might be earlier or other career experiences. The counsellor who works or previously worked, for example, as a teacher, a social worker, a probation officer or a nurse, might occasionally be influenced, while in the role of counsellor, by experiences in those professions. The counsellor also needs to be aware of their functioning at all times.

Good practice also includes establishing, when a client has been in counselling or psychotherapy before, what were the helpful and unhelpful aspects of that experience. This will offer pointers for maximising effectiveness on this occasion and assist in avoiding the repetition of unhelpful aspects. It offers useful clues about the client and assists in assessment. It affords the opportunity to clarify how you might work differently this time and why. It is also sensible to take account of recently experienced and foreseeable events in the client's (or counsellor's) lives and the way these may influence contracting. For example, a counsellor recently separated from their partner may wish to avoid loss and bereavement work with new clients, while coping well with other presenting problems.

Finally, achieving good endings is part of good practice. Having contingency plans for unplanned breaks and sudden endings is required practice for many counsellors (BAC, 1997: B.1.3.9) as is preparing clients for planned breaks (BAC 1997: B.1.3.10). Working towards an ending forms part of the counselling throughout and the way this is achieved varies according to the client's needs. Having an understanding about the number of ways that endings are achieved is necessarily part of good practice. Some of the many aspects of endings are covered in more detail elsewhere (O'Connell, 1998; Jones, 2000; Murdin, 2000; Shillito-Clarke, 2000; Syme, 2000 [a] and [b]). Unsurprisingly, this aspect of practice has been regularly featured in the 'practice dilemmas' column in the BACP (British Association for Counselling and Psychotherapy) Journal *Counselling* 1996–2000.

There is no guarantee, however, that while attending to all the above, counsellors will not make mistakes, through carelessness or a temporary dip in their normally acceptable standards of practice. On such occasions, good practice includes the important step of acknowledging these. The proper use of counselling supervision, with openness and integrity, also assists in picking up errors or potential errors of practice, at an early stage. Supervision benefits counsellors and their clients and is equally necessary for trainers and supervisors.

## The counselling relationship including the client's perspective

### First impressions — the client's perspective

When clients arrive for the first time, what first impressions do they have, such as:
- *Pre-counselling information — does the reality match the advertising?* Inaccurate advertising constitutes grounds for a complaint against members of many professional associations and also grounds for action by Trading Standards, under the Trades Description/Sale of Goods Acts.
- *Are the premises suitable?* Employed counsellors and those working in agencies may have limited say in the provision of premises, although they accept responsibility for continuing to work in inappropriate accommodation.
- *Is the client's agenda the focus of the counselling?* Counsellors might draw their own conclusions about what would be helpful to clients, and offer such opinions, while respecting the client's right to think differently.

- *Does the counsellor allow time for questions?* It is essential to check out that clients understand the nature and purpose of counselling and hold realistic expectations about the effectiveness of counselling in their particular circumstances.
- *Is the counsellor's theoretical approach helpful in the context of the client's difficulties?* This point is linked to the one above, as no single approach is appropriate for every client.
- *Has the counsellor made unrealistic claims about the outcomes of counselling?* Making unrealistic claims about the effectiveness of counselling constitutes grounds for complaint.
- *Is the contracting (if the two are to continue) clear?* Proper contracting is part of ethical practice of many professional associations. Regular reviews of progress may or may not be appropriate according to the theoretical approach of the counsellor and this must be explained to the client.
- *Have the limitations of confidentiality been properly explained and understood?* Honesty about the limits to confidentiality, required by law, is part of ethical practice. Additionally, there may be further constraints imposed by the setting or by the way the counsellor works or the counsellor's philosophy, for example, about suicidal thoughts and feelings.
- *How effectively has the counsellor assessed the likely duration of the counselling?* This is as relevant in those settings where the number of sessions is limited, as when the client is paying, where a consideration for the client is whether long-term work is affordable. Good practice includes the ability to make reasonable assessments, in the interests of the client, and to discuss the implications of these with clients.

POPAN (Prevention of Professional Abuse Network) (1998) provides a useful list for prospective clients who know little about therapy. The BAC *Basic Principles of Counselling* (BAC, 1991) is another useful resource as part of pre-counselling literature and elsewhere. Clients can use these for background information and as a starting point for questions (see Figure 1).

In addition to the questions POPAN suggests to prospective clients, it is good practice to address those additional points that are points of principle for BACP. For example, it is important to establish that the client is coming deliberately and voluntarily. The fact that the client has arrived for their first appointment is no guarantee that this is the case and it is a risky assumption to make. Again, when describing length of experience in the profession it is also important to recognise the potential for inadvertently misleading clients; responses such as '3 years' could suggest reasonable experience, yet the description of 3 years could range from a few contact hours up to 2000 contact hours. Experience and competence can be further specified as broad and generic or more specialised in areas such as marital, bereavement or substance misuse and whether the counsellor usually works shorter or longer term. Exercising respect and discretion includes confidentiality after the counselling has ended and covers issues such as using client work for professional development, training, research or publication at some time in the future. Reference to this in pre-counselling literature is a sensible way of dealing with this.

## During the counselling relationship — the counsellor's perspective

Again, POPAN (1998) helpfully lists a number of 'Warning Signs' for clients in counselling (see Figure 2). I discuss some of these points in more detail from a counsellor's perspective. Some situations may involve ethical dilemmas where conflicting moral principles (beneficence, non-maleficence, autonomy, justice and fidelity), ethical principles and values of counselling, and the law are weighed up one against another and the counsellor has to chose a course of action that may be right in those particular circumstances. Others may be more directly linked to the content and process of the counselling and the counselling relationship. In this context these points could therefore be regarded as part of a useful checklist both for the counsellor's 'internal supervisor' (Casement, 1985) and for those aspects of work needing further consideration in counselling supervision. Sometimes these points may result from poor skills and indicate the need for further training. Another possibility is that these are simply the actions of counsellors on the slippery slope to poor practice. Finally these could be indicators of unscrupulous practice. Each point could be open to a number of interpretations, hence uncertainty.

**Example 1.** *Body language.*
Understanding their own body language and other conscious and unconscious behaviours is an important skill for counsellors. What appears to the counsellor as attentive posture could appear threatening to the client. Some counsellors use their hands when speaking and it is useful to notice when this alarms or irritates clients. When counsellors find themselves feeling tense, irritable, angry or sad, or sitting unusually stiffly, this may be an indication of an affective response to the client that offers additional clues to the spoken content of the session. Skills and experience are necessary to recognise and work with these feelings.

**Example 2.** *Issues about physical contact.*
Counsellors and clients are rarely identical in age, gender, personality, personal history, sexual preference, race, culture and attitudes about touch. It follows that counsellors require caution when contemplating any touch between themselves and the client (even with consent) as this can be experienced as comforting or invasive, affirming or sexual activity. Counsellors can rarely, if ever, really know how a client may experience being touched by the counsellor.

**Example 3.** *Communication.*
Counsellors also need to consider how they work with clients who are uncomfortable with silences and/or do not say much. Talking too much (by the counsellor) could be an indication that the counsellor is also uncomfortable with silences or is simply attempting to make the client feel comfortable. When counsellors talk about their own lives this could be a mistake or, more seriously, could suggest that they are uncomfortable about the content the client is presenting, or working beyond their competence or dealing with their own needs at the expense of the client. If counsellors find that they are regularly talking too much

**Figure 1.** *Comparing the BAC Basic Principles of Counselling with questions suggested by POPAN to persons seeking therapy.*

**BAC Basic Principles**

**POPAN questions you could ask (order changed to match BAC Basic Principles)**

1. The aim of counselling is to provide an opportunity for a client to work towards living in a more satisfying and resourceful way.

2. Counselling is voluntarily and deliberately undertaken by counsellor and client. It is different from other ways of helping.

3. Before counselling starts, the counsellor clarifies with the client the basis on which counselling is given, including method, duration, fees and confidentiality; changes can subsequently be made only with the agreement of the client.

How long is a session?
How often are sessions held?
What do you charge?
Is there a cancellation fee?
Is it a totally confidential service?
When might confidentiality be broken?
How long might the therapy last for?
How does therapy end?

4. In counselling the right of the client to make his or her own decisions is respected.

5. Counsellors continually monitor their own skills, experience, resources and practice.

6. Counsellors will be properly trained for their roles and be committed to maintaining their competence.

7. Counsellors will not mis-represent their training or experience.

What are your qualifications?
For how many years have your been practising?
Have you been in therapy yourself?

8. Counsellors have regular and appropriate supervision/consultative support.

Do you have a qualified supervisor to discuss your work with?

9. Counsellors must not abuse their position of trust financially or emotionally or sexually.

10. All that takes place between counsellor and client is treated with respect and discretion.

**Figure 1.** (cont . . . )

| | |
|---|---|
| These principles are observed by all BAC members. | Which professional body do you belong to? |
| The British Association for counselling has a series of Codes of Ethics & Practice which expand on these principles. | |
| The British Association for Counselling has a Complaints Procedure. | Is there a complaints procedure? |
| Members are required to abide by the Codes appropriate to their role. | Which Code of Ethics do you follow? |
| Organisations within which counselling is offered should be clear about what they mean by counselling, ensure that standards are upheld and that counsellors are trained and supported adequately. | |

**Figure 2.** *An extract from the leaflet 'What To Look For When You Go Into Therapy' (1998) produced by the Prevention of Professional Abuse Network.*

**Warning Signs**
Therapist talks much more than you do
Uninvited home visits
Close physical contact without consent
Inappropriate questions about your sex life
Unpredictable behaviour
Threats and threatening gestures
Insisting on their own way
Making you doubt your sanity
Therapist says too much about their personal life
Sessions often go over time
Usual fees are waived
Therapist arranges to meet you socially

in sessions, or that they are asking irrelevant questions, or trying to 'persuade' clients into a course of action, this could be an indicator of poor skills, or, more seriously, be an indicator of the unsuitability of the counsellor to practice. Sometimes, however, when clients say 'I did what you said', counsellors can be alerted to the possibility that, although they aim to be non-directive, clients interpret some interventions as instructions. Skills in exploring this with clients are essential to good practice and to avoid further instances occurring.

**Example 5.** *Boundaries.*
Counsellors may consider waiving fees in certain circumstances. Client

circumstances change sometimes during the initial contract and the counsellor does have to consider whether stopping suddenly does more harm than negotiating a number of sessions (provided on a voluntary basis) to bring the work to an end. Similarly, some sessions may overrun because the content of a session may require this. Therefore, finishing on time is less of a priority than occasionally offering the client extra time in order to bring the session to an appropriate close. Alternatively, both the above options could arise from poor skills or a desire to exploit the client. A typical dilemma is outlined in the following fictional vignette:

> *Shoba is an independent counsellor who also has a contract with an Employee Assistance Programme. Shoba had a referral from this source to work with Jack, who was having problems at work. The contract was for up to 10 sessions. His job is the most important part of Jack's life and the focus of their work was to explore the problems at work. When Jack announced in session 9 that he had been made redundant unexpectedly but could afford to continue with Shoba as a private client, she was faced with a dilemma. Her contract with the EAP did not bar her from continuing with Jack and she knew that losing his job was likely to be painful for Jack. On the other hand, her normal practice was to keep her EAP work and independent practice separate and to allow for a substantial break before taking on, as a private client, someone whom had previously been referred by the EAP. She decided to offer Jack an additional 2 sessions on a voluntary basis, in order to help him work through his feelings about the redundancy and to consider with him his need for further counselling. Jack was disappointed initially but by the final session he felt more confident about the future. He had found a temporary job and decided that if, at some time in the future, he wanted to explore further some of the underlying issues that he was now aware of, he would contact Shoba.*

Uninvited home visits would normally be considered an overstepping of boundaries but the circumstances and the counsellor's intentions would require consideration on each occasion. Arranging to meet clients socially could be an example of difficulties about endings on the part of the counsellor or an indication that the counsellor exploits their role in order to build up a social network.

These are some of the many variables occurring during counselling. Counsellors have responsibility for dealing with all that arises and to draw upon their experience to do so. Within a caseload, different clients evoke different responses in the counsellor and this assists in finding the answers to key questions such as: what is happening here? Does it belong to me or is there a therapeutic significance to this? and how do I deal with this?

## Endings

When the counselling has come to an end, the counsellor should be considering with the client how safe the client feels and how satisfied with the counselling. Although not every counselling approach includes regular reviews of progress, part of the ending process normally includes an overall review. This is useful for both parties and, where the counsellor is considered by the client as genuinely open to feedback, allows for the clarification of any outstanding queries or concerns the client might have. Achieving effective endings is an important factor in reducing the likelihood of formal complaints.

Finally, the issue of confidentiality requires further consideration. Bond (1993 and 2000) discusses why clients are not required to keep confidential any aspects of their contact with the counsellor. Clients may also exchange information about their experience with the same counsellor. Yalom (1989) illustrates this in the tales of 'Betty' and 'Carlos'. This is a reminder of two points: each counselling relationship is unique so the ways the counsellor behaves within it takes account of the individuality of the client and that clients can be as observant as their counsellors.

## Learning from the mistakes of others

Within BACP complaints may be brought against individuals and organisational members. Awareness of the nature and content of complaints against others can give us assistance in avoiding similar mistakes although reading the section of a professional journal such as *counselling* offers limited information about upheld complaints. Even with such limited information, however, it is possible for some conclusions to be drawn. Currently, within BACP, complaints are based on alleged breaches of the code. My research suggests that the most frequently upheld complaints involve breaches around boundaries, contracting and confidentiality. For example, a number of complaints involve inaccurate advertising and pre-counselling information. Misrepresentation of training and qualifications constitutes grounds for complaints against BACP members and members of many other professional associations.

A complaint in 1999 against an organisational member of BAC resulted from the misconduct of one of its counsellors who overstepped ethical boundaries in a number of ways and caused harm to his client. Examples of his behaviour included ringing the client between sessions, emotional, financial and sexual exploitation, and an inappropriate ending (Moore, 1999). Masson (1992), Russell (1993), Palmer Barnes (1998) and Cassidy (1999), describe similar and other cases. Complaints around confidentiality may be more complex. A breach of confidentiality can arise either from carelessness or from having taken a decision that, on balance, there are exceptional circumstances that warrant disclosure. Either way a complaint could result. Irrespective of the allegations of misconduct, counsellors should be prepared to explain and acknowledge what has actually happened. When mistakes occur, these should be discussed within counselling supervision so that learning from these can occur. Where mistakes have led to a complaint, owning up to these can avoid prolonging harm and distress (Casemore, 1999).

## Reactions when hearing about complaints

The misconduct of many professionals, ranging from residential social workers, nurses, teachers, priests and GPs as well as psychologists and therapists is reported in the media as well as in professional journals. Sometimes, news of those who have been wrongly convicted of offences of abuse or misconduct is also reported (Bright, 2000). POPAN publicises some of its work in supporting the victims of misconduct by health and social care professionals and has an important role in supporting those who have been abused and in raising public awareness about abuse.

How do we keep this important issue in proportion? Anyone who works for any length of time in the health and social care fields is at risk of becoming disillusioned with human nature and distrustful of clients or fellow professionals. Counsellors are not immune and I consider that this has relevance to this book. At the same time, we live with the knowledge that many occasions of misconduct within our profession do not get reported. Misgivings or suspicions about fellow practitioners cannot always be formulated into complaints and because counselling and psychotherapy are currently unregulated professions, no professional association can prevent the unscrupulous from continuing to practice. As the most serious sanction currently available is expulsion from a professional association, there is some protection for clients, therefore, when working with counsellors who do hold a professional membership.

In my work with employees in the public sector, some come for counselling because they are facing the crisis of disciplinary proceedings following an accusation of misconduct. For some of these employees, the allegations result in their facing a review of their own attitudes, in addition to the fears for the immediate future. In the past they have heard about others in this position. They might then have felt critical, judgemental and unsympathetic, thinking 'no smoke without fire' and 'it can't happen to me because I am good at my job and the service users like me'. Working in this setting helps me to reflect on my own attitudes and assumptions. Why is it that I am more likely to believe the allegations about one person and less likely to believe those about another? What factors influence my assessments — the nature of the allegations, the credibility of the evidence, the source of the allegations, knowledge about the individual?

My experiences when I have contributed occasionally to the work of the BAC Complaints Committee were slightly different. These involved looking at, investigating or adjudicating complaints and experiencing at first hand the difficulties in establishing what happened. The values of counselling, integrity, impartiality and respect are especially tested on these occasions. Additionally, work on complaints about the mistakes of others was an uncomfortable reminder of occasions when my own practice fell below standard. Similar discomfort is experienced, on the occasions when I have a 'feeling' that misconduct could be occurring, and I have taken responsibility to approach another member to discuss the matter (BAC, 1997: B.1.4.2; BAC, 1995: B.1.11 and B.1.14). This is difficult to do but is an important step if we wish to safeguard those using the services of members.

In all the above there are positive benefits for practice, too. It may be easier to see mistakes when these are made by others and it is a useful reminder to take care at all times. Experience brings with it the dangers of complacency.

## Summary of ways to reduce the likelihood of complaints arising

Below is a summary of steps to reduce the likelihood of complaints arising. It is not exhaustive, but includes:
 1. Effective counselling supervision.
 2. Membership of and adherence to the spirit and the letter of the codes of appropriate professional associations.
 3. When having to consider breaking confidentiality, or in the event of other ethical dilemmas, or where the code is silent, consult the counselling supervisor, other experienced practitioners and the professional associations that provide such help.
 4. Regularly review written pre-counselling information, advertising and any other handouts to ensure these continue to contain accurate information.
 5. Offer regular opportunities for clients to raise any concerns, especially when the counselling is drawing to the end.
 6. Monitor practice and discuss mistakes in counselling supervision (and with clients if appropriate).
 7. Remember that we all have parts of ourselves that are 'out of awareness' and it helps to have trusted colleagues to consult.

## In conclusion

Returning to the quotation at the start of this chapter, counselling is a fluid and creative process. Work with clients is informed by codes of practice, by theory, by the setting and by the material brought by clients. The art of counselling lies in the ability to create and sustain a therapeutic relationship for the benefit of the client. Counselling is conducted in privacy so the potential for harm to the client and for the counsellor always exists. This chapter has looked at some of the aspects of the counselling relationship where uncertainty exists and identified some of the many areas of uncertainty when working as a counsellor. A counsellor has to make judgements about what is appropriate to each individual client and this may involve moving from the certainty of working within the codes and according to custom and practice to taking a more uncertain or risky course of action on occasion.

## References

Bond, T. (1993). *Standards and Ethics for Counselling in Action.* London: Sage.
Bond, T. (2000). *Standards and Ethics for Counselling in Action.* 2nd Edition. London: Sage.
Bright, M. (2000). We know there's abuse. But how much? *The Observer,* 6th August: 14–5.
British Association for Counselling (1991). *Basic Principles of Counselling.* Rugby: British Association for Counselling.
British Association for Counselling (1997). *Code of Ethics and Practice for Counsellors.* Rugby: British Association for Counselling.
British Association for Counselling (1995). *Code of Ethics and Practice for Supervisors of Counsellors.* Rugby: British Association for Counselling.

British Association for Counselling (1998). *How Much Supervision Should You Have?* Information Sheet 3. Rugby: British Association for Counselling.

Casement, P. (1985). *On Learning from the Patient.* London: Tavistock/Routledge.

Casemore, R. (1999). Why can't we own our mistakes? *Counselling,* 10 (2): 94–5.

Cassidy, J. (1999). She was young, naïve — and anorexic. Then she fell prey to a professor's 'caring' touch. *The Observer.* 13th June.

*Counselling* (1996–2000). Journal of the British Association for Counselling. Rugby: British Association for Counselling.

Jones, C. (2000). Are there any occasions when it is acceptable for a counsellor to have a friendship and/or a sexual relationship with a former client? In C.Jones, C.Shillito-Clarke, G.Syme, D.Hill, R.Casemore, and L.Murdin. *Questions of Ethics in Counselling and Therapy.* Milton Keynes: Open University Press.

Jones, C., Syme, G. and Shillito-Clarke, C. *et al.* (2000). *Questions of Ethics in Counselling and Therapy.* Milton Keynes: Open University Press.

McMahon, G. (1997). Counselling in Private Practice. In S. Palmer and G. McMahon (eds.) *Handbook of Counselling.* (2nd edition) London: Routledge.

McMahon, G, (1999). Reflective Practice, *Counselling.* 10 (2): 105–6 and 10 (3):193–4.

Masson, G. (1992). *Against Therapy.* London: Harper Collins.

Moore, A. (1999). I was seduced by my counsellor. *You.* 9th May.

Murdin, L. (2000). *How Much is Enough: Endings in psychotherapy and counselling.* London: Routledge.

O'Connell, B. (1998). *Solution Focused Therapy.* London: Sage.

Palmer Barnes, F. (1998). *Complaints and Grievances in Psychotherapy: A handbook of ethical practice.* London: Routledge.

[POPAN] Prevention of Professional Abuse Network (1998). *What To Look For When You Go Into Therapy.* London: POPAN.

Russell, J. (1993). *Out of Bounds: Sexual Exploitation in Counselling and Therapy.* London: Sage.

Shillito-Clarke, C. (2000). What are the ethical considerations when a former client persists with unwanted contact? In C.Jones, C.Shillito-Clarke, G.Syme, D.Hill, R.Casemore, and L.Murdin. *Questions of Ethics in Counselling and Therapy.* Milton Keynes: Open University Press.

Syme, G. (2000a). A counsellor wants to bring a counselling relationship to an end in the considered belief that the work is complete but the client disagrees — what issues should be considered in deciding a way forward? In C.Jones, C.Shillito-Clarke, G.Syme, D.Hill, R.Casemore, and L.Murdin. *Questions of Ethics in Counselling and Therapy.* Milton Keynes: Open University Press.

Syme, G. (2000b). The client fails to come to the next session — do you contact the client? How might the setting of the counselling also influence the decision? In C.Jones, C.Shillito-Clarke, G.Syme, D.Hill, R.Casemore, and L.Murdin. *Questions of Ethics in Counselling and Therapy.* Milton Keynes: Open University Press.

Syme, G. (1994). *Counselling in Independent Practice.* Milton Keynes: Open University Press.

Yalom, I. (1989). *Love's Executioner and Other Tales of Psychotherapy.* London: Bloomsbury/Penguin.

# Chapter 14

# Good Counsel from a Solicitor

## Tessa Roxburgh

I recently to retired from regular employment as a solicitor after 30 years in that profession. I also have a Diploma in Rogerian person-centred counselling and sometimes sit on the Complaints panel of BACP as a lay member.

I have sometimes made mistakes in my work and as a result I have experienced first hand as a solicitor, the emotional turmoil of being the subject of a complaint. I have been consoled by my colleague's words, 'We all make mistakes, it's how we deal with them that counts.' After 30 years of trying to meet clients' expectations and mostly succeeding but sometimes failing, I became the person responsible for the firm's complaint's procedure and investigate all complaints.

My training and experience as a counsellor has informed my work as a solicitor and profoundly affected the way I managed my own and clients' expectations in the legal work I did and in the way I responded to complaints. I hope that my experience as a solicitor may also help counsellors to avoid and survive complaints, by looking at similar issues that both professions have to confront. I shall concentrate on counsellors who are not employed by organisations, with a special emphasis on the position of trainees.

### The contract

The counselling relationship starts with a contract and establishing the terms of that contract is the first important step. The contract entered into by either a solicitor or a counsellor is a contract for the provision of services. What service does the client expect to receive? What service is the counsellor offering to the client? Do they coincide?

As I was walking down a street, I glanced at a poster in the front window of a house. It said, 'Counselling can lift the clouds'. I thought about that powerful metaphor holding out a message of hope and clarity to a passer-by, weighed down by life's burdens. Of course, counselling *can* lift the clouds but often the clouds get darker first, black even and it frequently takes a long time before the sky is brighter and sometimes that is never achieved. As Michael Jacobs, another contributor to this book has written, 'Counselling often involves as much disappointment for the client as it does satisfaction'. How might that qualification be reflected on a poster, I asked myself? I wondered how the counsellor who put up the poster managed the expectations of clients responding to that hopeful message. Was she really in the business of lifting clouds and was she succeeding? Did she ever ask her clients whether their expectations were met?

Taking care about how you advertise yourself and making sure your promotional literature is truthful and accurate is very important. If you claimed that you had 10 years experience as a counsellor when you did not or held out that the first session of counselling would be free of charge and then presented the client with a bill, the client could complain to Trading Standards. Serious cases of misrepresentation can result in a criminal prosecution.

If the name you decide to trade under is not just your own name and you called your business the 'Lifting the Clouds Counselling Service' for example, you must give the name(s) of the owners on all stationery and display it at your place of business. Companies House have some useful booklets setting out the rules about this. Your local Trading Standards Office may also be prepared to give you some guidance and check through your literature to make sure you are complying with the law.

Client is perhaps a refined name for customer. It is challenging to think about the service you are offering as being one to customers. What do you aim to achieve in the counselling process? Could you sum it up in a few sentences? Are your customers getting what they expect? Do you review the process from time to time with them and openly ask for feedback? Do they think they are getting value for money? Are there any limitations on what you are prepared to offer? What do you expect from your clients in return?

As a solicitor, after I have seen a client for the first time, I record in plain English :
- the main elements of their problem;
- what outcomes they are seeking;
- what I have agreed to do;
- how the work is to be funded and
- any limitations I have set on the work I have agreed to undertake.

I always find this a challenging task because, as in counselling, clients are often uncertain about what they want to achieve, express anxiety about whether I can help and their doubts and dilemmas are linked to their personalities, and the complexities of their relationships. They may say their marriage has ended yet express doubts about getting a divorce. They may want advice on the validity of a will and in the same breath say 'it's not about money.' Recording the bare bones of the first meeting and reflecting something of those complexities sets a framework for the task ahead.

Counsellors also keep notes as they go along. My advice is to do this carefully and to address the key issues set out above. The notes should be clear and concise, avoiding jargon, always bearing in mind that the notes may have to be disclosed if a complaint is made. Record any special terms, such as agreeing that you will work together for so many sessions and then have a review. If records are kept, it is a requirement of the BACP Codes of Ethics and Practice that clients are made aware of this and should be allowed to see them if they wish to do so. (B.4.3.4)

I am not suggesting that there is ever a simple answer to the question 'What does the client want to get out of this?' Far from it. The answer is rarely clear and is related to a particular moment. It often changes with time. This is as true in the solicitor/client relationship as in counselling, as the following example illustrates.

> *My client Jane suffered terrible injuries in a horrific car accident. Her boyfriend, who was driving the car and sitting beside her, was killed instantly. Jane came to see me to obtain damages for her serious injuries. Often she did not keep appointments. Sometimes I was cross with her for messing me about in this way. After a long legal battle, I recovered a substantial sum of money for her. She was plainly trying to avoid taking the cheque at the end of the case. I didn't explore her reluctance but insisted on her taking it. Many months later she rang me and said 'I think you knew that it wasn't about money. I've given most of it away.'*

The point of that story is that I didn't explore at any time after the initial interview, whether Jane really wanted me to carry on with the case. I might have challenged her reluctance to keep appointments when she had to recall the painful recollections of that terrible day when her world fell apart. Perhaps that was the moment to say, 'I've noticed that I make appointments and you often don't keep them and I'm wondering if you have lost interest in your case'. Perhaps counselling would have been more helpful than the service I was providing, but I certainly didn't check as I went along, that getting money for her own pain and suffering was what she still wanted to achieve. In the end, my goal of maximising her damages claim and the client's own objectives did not coincide.

It is even more essential in counselling to review whether the client is getting what they hoped for out of the counselling process because the end product is much less tangible than the work a solicitor does. It is the counsellor's job to make sure this issue gets on the agenda at appropriate times. Clients complain because their expectations of what they hoped to get out of counselling have not been met. This is often because the counsellor has not adequately considered and reviewed the kind of service they wanted or expected.

A friend of mine told me she went to see a counsellor 'to get her husband back' by finding out 'what she had done wrong'. She expected to be given a guide to her behaviour, a list of 'dos and 'don'ts'. A few weeks into counselling she was puzzled to find that she seemed to be dealing with quite different issues with the focus on her and hardly a mention of her husband. She did not express her doubts and feelings but wondered whether there was any point in carrying on.

This example shows how important it is to invite the client to explore their expectations about the counselling process, how valuable or not the service is, and to express any dissatisfaction as the relationship develops. Negative aspects of the relationship must be aired. If they can be brought into the open and dealt with, a stronger working alliance can be achieved. The stronger the working alliance, the less likelihood of dissatisfaction leading to a complaint. I find that in many complaints, working on negative aspects in the relationship has been avoided.

## Competence

Another important issue for solicitor or counsellor, whether a trainee or an experienced practitioner, is 'Am I competent to act for this client?' If I am worried that I could get out of my depth, I am not obliged to carry on. I do not have to act for everyone who wants my services. It is professionally sound to accept my limitations, explain the reasons for my decision to the client and either limit the work I do to the areas where I am secure or immediately refer the client to someone who may be able to give them a better service.

Counsellors should go through a similar exercise. It is better to confront the issue sooner rather than later. Sometimes other professionals like doctors suggest that 'some counselling limited to x or y issue' might help the patient they are treating. However once you start working with the client, it is difficult to try to set limits. This is an area where problems can arise which trigger complaints. The BACP code is clear. 'Counsellors should monitor actively the limitations of their own competence . . . Counsellors should work within their own known limits.' (B.6.1.2)

An important part of the contract is what the provider of the service receives in return for giving the service. In short, what's in it for them? Lawyers call this the 'consideration'. Generally it involves the payment of money. If you have fudged the question of what you will charge for example, you need to ask yourself why?

Counsellors often feel compassion for clients who are hard up. But be warned. Confusion about terms of payment can cause dissatisfaction and figure in complaints. They can be an unspoken cause of resentment on the counsellor's part, when the client who has pleaded poverty and received counselling at sharply reduced rates, then has a holiday in Majorca! I say *unspoken* because the resentment is invariably expressed after the complaint is made instead of being aired in the counselling room. Money may not be the be all and end all but it is a measure of the value both parties place on counselling and themselves.

A friend, who had just finished training and was about to embark on private counselling work, told her partner (an accountant) that she intended to charge £19.00 per hour. 'Why not £20.00?' was his reply. He knew she tended to undervalue herself and was anxious about whether she was good enough and getting started. His challenge struck home.

Counsellors need to be clear from the start about the terms of the contract for the sake of client and counsellor. They have the duty under the code to do this and keeping to the terms is essential to the health of the relationship. If it is revised, the new terms should be clear. There is all the difference in the world between an open-ended commitment 'to be there' for a new client as long as the client needs your services and 'short therapy' of six sessions — take it or leave it.

Should you write down what you have agreed? I think that is a difficult issue and there are no hard and fast rules. Generally speaking, you should record and give to clients, a written statement of the business framework within which you intend to work as a counsellor, including charging rates, missed appointments, how and when you can be contacted etc. If you agree a variation on your standard terms, it is prudent to set them out plainly. If you chose not to do so, you must accept the risk that there will be no written evidence if things go wrong about this aspect of the relationship.

## The position of trainees

Trainee counsellors often take clients that are allocated to them by agencies, including doctors. Sometimes counselling is a last resort or even a means of dumping a patient whose problems seem more psychological than physical. But take care. Has this person really consented to having counselling? Do they know what counselling will involve? Do not be in such a hurry to clock up counselling hours, that you fail to check on this basic issue before starting.

As a trainee counsellor, I was asked to see Tom, an elderly client. I was warned he had reached a great age and needed a home visit. I imagined that he was so infirm he could not come to the counselling centre. I was told on the telephone that his carer thought he would benefit from counselling. Mistake number one was that I didn't challenge that statement on the phone. Did the potential client want counselling or was someone being a busy body? I arrived at his house one afternoon, only to find Tom in the garden energetically planting out bulbs for the spring. We had a confused conversation about whether he was expecting me and knew I was a counsellor. He said, probably out of politeness, 'You'd better come in,' which I did. Mistake number two was not to concentrate immediately on the primary issue of consent. Did Tom wish to have counselling or not. If it was unclear, I should have gone away and contacted the referring agency. It was only during the second session that I explored thoroughly whether or not he wanted counselling and understood what that might involve. It turned out that he really wanted the care and repair service the agency provided. The agency had got their lines crossed and I had added to the problem. It was confusing for Tom and posed some risk for me.

When I was a trainee counsellor, a client of mine was troubled about why I was doing it on a voluntary basis. What was in it for me? A trainee may not be paid but nevertheless the 'consideration' for the contract is acquiring experience and clocking up 'counselling hours'. That experience ought not to be acquired at the client's expense but it sometimes is and a complaint follows. I have seen many examples of trainees being given clients that were beyond their capabilities. I have dumped work on trainee solicitors when under pressure myself that was beyond their capabilities and we both paid a price later when the trainee could not cope. Unlike a trainee solicitor, trainee counsellors cannot nip out of the room and get some quick advice when they know they are struggling. They are more vulnerable and on the front line than a junior doctor in casualty who can seek advice from more senior staff. They are just as likely to make mistakes. Trainees are bound by the code of ethics and can easily get out of their depth and be blamed by clients when things go wrong. Often the agency should take the main responsibility for the inappropriate placement, but often the trainee carries the can alone.

Counselling courses are springing up in every college and university. Placements are hard to get and trainees are often desperate to be assigned clients to reach the required number of counselling hours. Counselling students should be more demanding of their tutors and the agencies where they get placements. The course content needs to be of a high academic and experiential quality and placement agencies should adequately screen potential clients. Good and accessible supervision must always be available. On one of my own placements as a trainee, the supervisor went off for an extended holiday and the arrangements for cover were quite inadequate, resulting in anxiety and anger for trainees wanting help and support. If you feel worried about any aspect of your placement, including how the counselling service is managed and you find yourself moaning about it to your fellow students or in your personal development group, do something about it. Raise your concerns with the agency as well as your tutors. If all you do is off-load your feelings and do nothing, then nothing will change. Maybe you often avoid conflict or standing up for yourself, in which case challenge yourself and consider behaving differently.

Trainees often have to work in unsatisfactory circumstances, such as rooms where it is difficult to achieve complete confidentiality. As a trainee I worked for an agency where the room allocated to counselling had a side window where staff passing by, could look in. This was a clear breach of the BACP code relating to confidentiality to which the organisation subscribed. Raising the matter with the agency resulted in a blind being fitted. Take responsibility for yourself and working ethically. Don't expect other people to get things right, they should but they often don't.

It is particularly difficult if trainees are expected to see clients in the client's home, because they lack the experience to handle the problems this creates. Getting started in these circumstances is often a very demanding task. Do you seek permission from the client to reorganise their chairs to make sure that you are a good working distance to relate to them? May be the TV is on and you have to start by asking that it be turned off. A fellow trainee told me that one client wanted her to wait until the instalment of East Enders had finished because her dog liked the closing music! She complied (taking refuge in politeness and being fond of dogs herself) but it was no way to start a counselling session. Do you refuse or accept a cup of tea? How do you match up to the code of ethics about confidentiality when other family members are around or neighbours knock on the door and the session is interrupted?

Home visits are often unavoidable when counselling the housebound, sick or the elderly but it is much harder than working in a quiet neutral room, which has been set up specifically for counselling. Before counselling in clients' homes or other difficult circumstances, trainees need to be warned about the problems they will face and given plenty of opportunity to discuss how best to overcome them. Trainees should also insist on meeting up with other trainees being placed by the same agency to explore experiences and there should be regular opportunities to raise concerns with the management of the agency. A well run agency should be prepared to listen and to make changes to ensure that the counselling service being offered is of the highest quality.

## Boundaries

It is the counsellor's duty to manage the boundaries. This can be a minefield when counsellors are not clear themselves about where to draw lines. Students starting a counselling course, probably discuss at the beginning, the differences between various kinds of helping such as befriending, using counselling skills and counselling itself. In practice the temptations to muddle them up are many and there are grave risks to counsellors. They may be risks the experienced counsellor decides to take but they should be aware that if the client later chooses to complain, this is an area the client is most likely to target. The following are examples of actions that counsellors have argued are a legitimate part of the professional service they have contracted to provide:
- Letting a client, thrown out by a parent, stay overnight in his/her home.
- Going shopping with the client.
- Giving the client food.
- Allowing the client to see a journalist in their home.
- Accompanying a client to visit a grave.
- Travelling in the tube with the client to overcome a fear.
- Helping the client to find accommodation.

The debate within counselling with its many different theoretical approaches rages furiously about these issues. Counsellors have a heavy duty to examine their motives when they stretch boundaries or step outside the normally accepted ones. Is it a valuable and necessary part of the therapy or is it fulfilling the counsellor's own needs? The BACP code states 'Counselling is a non-exploitative activity' (A.1) and disaffected clients have argued that such actions caused them psychological harm, encouraging dependence on the counsellor at a time when they were vulnerable and confusing boundaries in an inappropriate way. Frequently they are the kinds of actions where the counsellor has taken on the role of caring parent or Good Samaritan but there are enormous risks in doing so, because the client can use them against the counsellor if the relationship turns sour.

Boundary issues feature often in complaints, with the complainant relying on the following clauses in the BACP code: 'Counsellors are responsible for working in ways which promote the client's *control* over his/her own life . . .' (B.5.1) and 'Counsellors are responsible for setting and monitoring boundaries throughout the counselling sessions and will make explicit to clients that counselling is a formal contracted relationship and nothing else'.

Some complaints have been upheld and others have not. Many have gone to appeal. Much depends on the particular facts in each case, including the nature of the contract. However there are risks in deciding to act in this kind of way. If counsellors choose to take such actions, is it counselling or another form of helping? How elastic can the management of the boundaries be and still come within the current codes?

I have no statistics to support this proposition and am drawing on hearsay and my own limited experience, but this is an area where person centred counsellors *seem* to put themselves at risk more than counsellors from other modalities. This may be because the label 'person-centred' is sometimes used by people neither skilled nor adequately trained in that theoretical framework or because experienced practitioners are working at the edge of relationships with very demanding clients. However when a complaint is made the accusation of over-involvement and violation of boundaries is difficult to rebut, within the code of ethics. This is an issue that deserves much more debate and research.

## Endings

The failure to do enough work in preparation for endings is another area where complaints abound. Breaks and endings in counselling repeat the painful experiences of life where we are left with feelings of being let down, deserted, rejected etc. If clients are left with the impression that the counsellor was glad to get rid of them or the relationship ends in unresolved conflict, then the client feels angry and wronged and there is a risk a complaint may follow. The longer counselling has lasted, the greater the risk of a dependant relationship developing and the greater the need to prepare for the ending, giving it enough time. Some counsellors simply do not prepare at all for this significant moment. Consciously or unconsciously they may be glad to get rid of a difficult client and jump at a chance to do so, without bearing in mind the requirements of the code. (B.1.3.8)

> *After 2 years of counselling, Jim felt his counsellor was angry with him and disliked him. The counsellor found it increasingly difficult to work with Jim, who constantly challenged him on theoretical and academic issues. This got in the way of working on Jim's personal issues. The Counsellor, frustrated by Jim's avoidance, took this to supervision. He was advised to warn Jim to end this pattern of behaviour or to cease counselling immediately. The counsellor was concerned about this advice, but followed it. He felt very nervous and uncertain as he started to speak to Jim. The session was highly charged. Jim did not accept that there was anything about his behaviour patterns that he needed to change. An argument ensued. The counsellor stood up and moved to the door, indicating the counselling was over. Jim left the room in distress. The counselling had ended abruptly without any work being done by the counsellor to reach a recognised ending or referral, in breach of the code. The advice the supervisor had given was inappropriate but it was the counsellor who was vulnerable to a complaint because it was the counsellor who had the contracted relationship with the client.*

The code provides that counsellors must work with clients to reach a recognised ending when clients have received the help they sought or when it is apparent that counselling is no longer helping or when clients wish to end. The advice the counsellor received from his supervisor to give the client an ultimatum took no account of this and in following the supervisor's recommendation, I think that he behaved unethically.

## Facing up to client dissatisfaction

As the solicitor in my firm responsible for complaints, I aim to deal with client's concerns with openness and fairness but sometimes I struggle, wanting to attack or score points rather than acknowledge the client's criticisms. Through counselling, I am more aware of my own defences but an internal battle often raged within me before I could deal with the complaint in a helpful and rational manner that put the client's experience at the heart of the process. This is as true for counsellors as solicitors. Counsellors need to deal with their own feelings *before* they respond to a complaint.

Don't bury your head in the sand and put off dealing with the problem. If you need advice before deciding how to respond, as you probably will, get it quickly. The longer the complaint is unresolved the more angry, upset or irritated the client is likely to get. There have been a number of cases which ended up with a formal complaint to BACP probably because the counsellor delayed acknowledging the complaint or put off doing something positive for much too long.

Solicitors in private practice are bound by the profession's Practice Rules to have a written procedure for handling complaints. Clients must know from the start whom they should contact if they have a problem. The initial letter, confirming instructions includes this information. Once a client complains, the solicitor should send them a copy of the complaint procedure. This rule applies whether it is the largest firm in London or a sole practitioner doing a small volume of conveyancing from his front room.

Counsellors in private practice should also think about having a written complaints procedure, setting out what they will offer to dissatisfied clients including any alternative dispute resolution procedure they are willing to follow. It should be clearly written avoiding complicated language and available to clients. This acknowledges from the start that things can go wrong and provides a framework for clients to make the criticisms that they find difficult to voice face to face. All complaint procedures should allow clients to appeal to some one independent.

What solutions you offer, depend on the nature of the complaint and the state of the relationship. A face to face meeting to discuss the problem is one option although this can be risky if feelings on both sides are highly charged and having another independent counsellor or mediator present 'to hold the ring' might be a better and safer alternative. The mediator could see both parties beforehand to hear the two versions of the story. A round table meeting with a supporter for counsellor and client is another approach. Having someone else present provides a protection for both parties against misrepresentation later and allows both sides to have their say. Such solutions obviously need both parties consent. Whatever approach you take, you should own up quickly to things you would have done differently, if you could have your time over again. If the complaint is justified, offering to waive fees is one way of making redress.

When things go wrong in the relationship, there is often a lack of any independent evidence about what was said in the secrecy of the interview room to back up one side or the other when a complaint is made. In the case involving

Jim, who ended the relationship? Was it Jim storming out of the room or the signals the counsellor gave, in standing up and moving to the door. When considering a formal complaint, the Adjudication panel looks at the evidence and any disputes about the facts have to be investigated. Often the differences in recollection are very great. They illustrate how great a gulf has opened up between the two parties. It is not so much that one party is lying and the other telling the truth, but that critical moments in the relationship were experienced differently, interpreted differently and remembered differently.

If you are ever the subject of a formal complaint, look carefully at the substance of the complaint, the breaches of the code alleged and the evidence put forward in support. Don't write reams pouring out your feelings and describe every small detail of the interaction. Focus on each allegation and the facts the complainant is relying on. Reply to each one systematically and clearly. Set out your version of the facts as it relates to the breach of the code.

## And finally

Don't practice defensively. Being a good counsellor involves taking risks in human relating but do practice ethically. If you wish to have the benefit of membership of organisations like BACP, and advertise your services as such, then you undertake to clients that you will practice within that code of ethics. Reading and thinking about what each aspect of the code means in relation to your own work is essential. Good supervision is very important but ultimately you need to take responsibility for your own learning. Sharing your understanding with others who have a sound understanding of this topic and working through case studies is a useful way of learning. It is a difficult area where often there are no absolute rights and wrongs but it is essential to good practice and the reputation of counselling in society.

## References

Jacobs, M. (1988). *Psychodynamic Counselling in Action.* London: Sage.
British Association for Counselling and Psychotherapy (2000). *Code of Ethics and Practice for Counsellors.* (March).

# Chapter 15

# Supervision, Support and Surviving Complaints

## Paul Carney

### Introduction

Members of the British Association for Counselling and Psychotherapy (BACP) are expected to adhere to the Association's Code of Ethics and Practice. Failure to adhere to these Codes may result in a complaint that is brought by a client or another member, being upheld by the Association and for 'sanctions' to be applied regarding the breach, or breaches. Other organisations have their own Codes, to which members are expected to adhere and will have their own methods for dealing with members who have 'transgressed' these Codes; however, it is recognised that there will often be elements of similarity between these procedures.

For members of the BACP who have been found to be in breach of the Codes there are broadly four options that may be taken in the form of sanctions by the Association with regard to any breaches of the Codes:

1. To take no further action against the counsellor;
2. To require the counsellor to receive supervision from a named supervisor for a stipulated period of time; and in cases of the most serious breaches;
3. To identify that the counsellor will benefit from further training with particular reference to the area in question; and, ultimately
4. To exclude the counsellor from the Association.

Often the practice and process of supervision is only briefly touched on during one's initial counsellor training and acting as a supervisor may be something that occurs more by happenstance with little or no 'formal' training in the endeavour being undertaken (Hess, 1982; Thompson, 1991). Thus, many of the skills of supervising counsellors may come from modelling those that we ourselves have encountered through our own experience of being supervised or from a 'transferring' of the skills that we use to help clients focus on problems and

---

The examples quoted in this chapter represent a composite of different complaints that have been upheld through Adjudication within BACP and are not intended to represent any specific person either living or dead.

concerns. There is, however, a requirement from BACP for a supervisor providing extra supervision to a counsellor who has had an adjudication upheld against them, to have an expertise in the area that requires addressing, and to be approved by BACP. It is sometimes possible for the counsellor's regular supervisor to undertake the extra 'sanctions supervision'; however, BACP may require additional supervision by a named supervisor who is not involved in the counsellor's usual network of contacts.

In such situations for the regular supervisor undertaking the extra 'sanctions supervision' there may be some dissonance between the perceived requirements of *regular* supervision and the requirements of supervision *as a sanction*. This may arise because the supervisor may be seen to be acting as a 'supervisor', a 'guardian' and an 'adept' who is expected to report upon the counsellor. This person will be the 'supervisor' of a counsellor through the 'normal' process of supervision, even though the person may be a 'secondary' supervisor who is providing supervision for only those parts of the counsellors work that have been found 'deficient' through adjudication. He, or she, will be a 'guardian' for those clients that the counsellor sees that have issues similar to those raised in the original complaint. He, or she, will also be an 'adept' who is perceived to have 'special knowledge or ability' in a particular area and who is expected to provide a report on the progress of the counsellor at stated times to BACP.

Thus the person providing supervision for a counsellor who has had a complaint upheld against them, has to carry out a balancing act between those aspects that are normal to a supervisory relationship — the ethical, moral, and legal issues — and those issues specific to the sanctions applied to the counsellor who has had a complaint upheld against him or her. This latter part will usually require the supervisor to evaluate the counsellors performance over a specific time period and furnish reports to the Sanctions Panel regarding the counsellors progress.

Supervisors who have been asked to provide supervision for BACP members who have had a complaint against them upheld may feel uncomfortable about their role in providing this service for the member and in furnishing a suitable report at the appropriate time. This chapter seeks to address some of the factors that might be deemed necessary in this supervision context.

## Supervision as an 'educative' process and reporting on the counsellor's progress

Often a counsellor who has had a complaint upheld against him, or her, may feel that the whole process, and the 'sanctions' that arise from the adjudication are essentially punitive. However, in most cases the attempt is to make the process as 'educative' as possible in order to enable the counsellor to continue in their profession and to learn and develop from the mistakes made. One way in which this is achieved is to stipulate that the counsellor receives supervision regarding the specific Codes of Practice that have been breached from a 'named' supervisor. As a part of this process the supervision is usually expected to last for a particular period of time, and the supervisor will be expected to furnish BACP with a series of reports on the counsellor's progress at specified times.

Boyd (1978:10) identifies the purpose of counsellor supervision as encompassing three distinct aspects:

1. Facilitation of the counselor's personal and professional development;
2. Promotion of counselor competencies; and
3. Promotion of accountable counseling . . .

Often the areas that a counsellor will need particular supervision with regarding the complaint will include aspects of these three areas. There is a need to ensure that the report furnished to the Sanctions Panel engages with the specific sanctions that have been made. Occasionally a report has to be returned to the supervisor and the counsellor due to a lack of evidence relating to the sanctions that were stipulated at the Adjudication.

## Example 1:

*A complaint had been upheld against X relating, amongst other aspects, to his 'over-involvement' with a client and the resulting breakdown of boundaries in their relationship. A part of the Sanctions was that he considered the implications of the counter-transference when working with such clients.*

*The report provided from the Supervisor stated that the counsellor had ceased to work with clients that presented with the issue that had brought the original client to him. Although this might have been an 'appropriate' action the report failed to outline how the counsellor had complied with the actual sanction, which was to 'Consider the implications . . .' The 'action' in itself did not identify whether such a process had occurred.*

It is the role of the Sanctions Panel of BACP to scrutinise reports relating to counsellors and decide whether the sanctions have been complied with. Occasionally such reports only indirectly address the original issues that formed the basis of the complaint — as with the above example, or will omit to identify the response to the 'sanctions'. In such a case the Sanctions Panel is left with little alternative but to not accept the report and to insist upon the sanction being extended.

## The supervisory relationship with a counsellor who has been complained against

Following an adjudication, where a counsellor has had a complaint upheld against him or her, there is often a tendency for the counsellor to experience a period of feeling 'de-skilled'. The process of having a complaint upheld can leave the counsellor unsure of their competency and feeling 'vulnerable'. Ronnestad and Skovholt (1993) suggest that the relationship a supervisor has with the advanced student of counselling and psychotherapy is more complex because of the student's tendency to waver between feeling insecure in their professional work, and knowing and feeling competent in their skills.

Legg identifies that decision-making can be as difficult for the counsellor as it might be for the client. He argues that 'Huge numbers of decisions are made with each client, ranging from strategic decisions such as whether to take on someone as a client . . . to fine grain decisions such as whether to ask an open-ended question or paraphrase' (1998: 10) what has been said. The author then points out that not all the decisions that the counsellor makes can or will be good.

The counsellor who has had a complaint against them upheld may have very similar experiences to these. There is a need for supervision to address those areas in which the counsellor is capable and competent as well as those where further work and development might be needed in order that the counsellor does not lose their entire confidence. Yet there is also a need for the counsellor to acknowledge both of these areas too.

Following an adjudication that has upheld a complaint against a counsellor it is not unusual for the counsellor to report feeling 'de-skilled'. Or to defend against the feelings by refusing to acknowledge areas in which they might improve. Schon (1995: 138) argues that as the professional moves towards being 'reflective-in-action' she, or he, moves away from being 'certain' of their 'rightness' and becomes more accepting of their uncertainty. He further states that 'When a practitioner becomes a researcher into his own practice, he engages in a continuing process of self-education.'

Schon (ibid.: 300) suggests that the differences in sources of 'satisfaction' regarding his (sic) role might be expressed in tabular form as:

| **Expert** | **Reflective Practitioner** |
|---|---|
| I am presumed to know, and must claim to do so, regardless of my own uncertainty. | I am presumed to know, but I am not the only one in the situation to have relevant and important knowledge. My uncertainties may be a source of learning for me and for them. |

It is possible that this uncertainty and insecurity can have a tendency to create barriers in the supervisory relationship that have to be addressed.

Wheeler (1996) points out that the supervisor is close to the counsellors work, but that they are only as close as the counsellor allows them to be, and that the counsellor can consciously and unconsciously filter out material that they do not wish to deal with in supervision. If the need for the supervisor to report on the counsellor's progress to the professional organisation is added to this it is possible to see how the working alliance might be affected through the process of the supervisory requirements.

## Example 2:

*A counsellor had attempted to use a technique with a client with which she had not received adequate training. In this sense she was, in effect, 'naïve' in its use. The client claimed that she was worse following her*

> *'counselling' and that she had suffered 'psychological harm' from the strategy used. The counsellor began to doubt her 'expertise' in other areas of her work and began to feel unsure of her ability to continue to counsel at all. Furthermore the counsellor began to feel that the supervisor would be 'critical' of her counselling knowledge and skills.*

It was necessary for the supervisor to address these feelings of insecurity and inadequacy and to ensure that the counsellor was able to evaluate her strengths as well as her weaknesses objectively and realistically. The process of supervision following a complaint should not be seen as 'punitive' but rather as an educative process in which the counsellor can improve their competency and reflexive skills. In this sense it is about extending the self-awareness of the counsellor, thereby enabling the counsellor to more realistically appraise their areas of expertise and skills.

## Assessing competency and reporting on the counsellor

The report, which is submitted to the Sanctions Panel with reference to the counsellor, ideally needs to be couched in rather more 'educational' terms than might be usual for the supervisor and the counsellor. It needs to address the issues outlined in the original sanction and the 'evidence' that the counsellor has complied, or paid attention, to these aspects. It will, therefore, usually contain actual examples of how the sanction has been met.

Harris (1994) states that 'Effective summative evaluation requires clearly delineate performance objectives that can be assessed in both quantitative and qualitative terms and that have been made explicit . . . during initial supervision contacts.' Bernard and Goodyear described summative assessment as: 'the moment of truth when the supervisor steps back, takes stock, and decides how the [counsellor] measures up' (1992: 105). However they also point out that, as with all relationships, conflict can arise in the supervisory relationship.

Some common points of conflict are identified by Bernard and Goodyear as: 'the power differential between the supervisor and supervisee, differences related to the "appropriateness" of the technique used by the counsellor, and the willingness on both parts to resolve these differences' (ibid.: 93). These conflicts may arise from the supervisory process as much from the material being handled during this role and may be intra-personal as well as inter-personal. Where such conflict cannot be resolved there is a need to ensure that the nature of the conflict, and its effect, is reported as part of the supervisor evaluation of the counsellor.

Schon (1995: 127) identifies one such situation when he writes:

> Like his patient, the Resident feels stuck in his relationship to the person who is supposed to help him, wanting more from him than he feels he is getting, yet being angry at himself for wanting more.

The author continues to identify what benefit might have accrued from the Resident and his supervisor using reflection-in-action within the supervisory process as well as the therapeutic process.

## Differentiated approaches in supervision

It is debatable as to whether the supervisor of counsellors should work in the same orientation as the counsellor or whether there might be benefit in 'cross-orientation' supervision. Inskipp (1996) posits both arguments, but also identifies that there are a number of external influences that effect the manner and style in which we work as counsellors. Not least of these are professional influences such as the Codes of Ethics and Practice that we adhere to within our respective organisations.

Inskipp argues further that:

> It seems as if by working on these tasks counsellors are able to explore similarities and differences in theory and philosophy openly, and find common ground and common language in order to share and use each other's ideas (ibid.: 273)

Such a concept supports Schon's (1995) concepts regarding reflection-in-action and the need for the counsellor *and* supervisor to be reflexive about their work together.

Often sanctions will stipulate that a counsellor needs to 'consider the effects' of some action that has resulted in an adjudication being upheld. For a Sanctions Panel to be satisfied that this has been achieved it is necessary for the counsellor and/or the supervisor to submit a report indicating how this has been accomplished and what the outcome of the reflection has been. Without such evidence it becomes impossible for the Sanctions Panel to identify that the sanction imposed has been adequately completed.

## A conceptualisation of the outcomes in supervision — its purpose and practice

Supervision has, according to Proctor (1988 [in Inskipp, 1996: 271]), three tasks for which the counsellor and supervisor have joint responsibility: normative, in which the participant takes responsibility for standards and ethics; formative, in which responsibility for the counsellors development is shared; and restorative, in which opportunity to 'recharge the batteries' is obtained. There is too, in relation to the counsellor that has had a complaint upheld, a fourth task — that of *performative* (Spurling, 1997), in which assessment of the nature and quality of the work is shared.

The 'patient', according to Erikson (1958: 76), is 'a series of one who must be understood in terms of the unique experiences of his life'. On this issue Spinelli suggests that the therapist needs to 'bracket' their own meanings and interpretations in order not to 'value, judge or criticize their clients' experience'. In a similar manner the counsellor is also a 'universe of one' in which the supervisor also needs to 'bracket their own meanings and interpretations' in order to help the counsellor arrive at their own 'being-in-self' (1989: 17).

The 'disciplined subjectivity', that Erikson (ibid.) saw as the task of the therapist in listening for the patient's own meaning, is equally that of the supervisor with the counsellor. There may be, however, a need for the supervisor to then share these meanings and interpretations with another body — either for the counsellor in training, or for the counsellor who has had a complaint upheld. The normative role of supervision referred to above, is then one in which the confidentiality of the supervisory session cannot entirely form a part of the normal supervisory contract and requires careful thought on the part of both the counsellor and supervisor before entering into supervision.

## Conclusion

It has been suggested that 'ethical dilemmas are inevitable' in psychotherapy whereas 'unethical actions and behaviour are not' (Lakin, 1991). However, it is not always possible to foretell the consequences of an action that we take beforehand. It is useful to consider the 'intentionality' of acts and to identify whether the counsellor acted with the knowledge that his, or her, action would cause harm or suffering to the client. Or that it was 'violating' the codes of ethics and practice of the organisation to which he, or she, belongs.

One aspect of this intentionality is the shared and negotiated meaning of the act(s) that the counsellor and supervisor use as a means for identifying and measuring the progress of the counsellor. Such acts may be seen to have both a 'public' meaning and a 'private' meaning. (Rommetveit, 1980). That is, the meaning that exists in the interpretation of a person's act(s) by those who observe it; and the interpretation (or *reason*) of the person's act(s) by him-, or herself.

The Supervisor's report needs to identify the private meaning of the counsellor's acts so that a suitable assessment of the counsellor's progress can be achieved. Further imposition of sanctions or the ultimate exclusion of a person from their professional organisation is always a last resort. However, there is a need to ensure that the counsellor has gained from the process and that he, or she, may become more reflexive of their work in the future.

## References

Bernard, J. M. and Goodyear, R. K. (1992). *Fundamentals of Clinical Supervision.* Boston: Allyn and Bacon.

Boyd, J. D. (1978). *Counselor Supervision: Approaches, Preparation, Practices.* Muncie, Indiana: Accelerated Development Inc.

Erikson, E. (1958). The Nature of Clinical Evidence. In D. Lerner, (ed.) *Evidence and Inference.* Glencoe, Ill.: The Free Press of Glencoe.

Harris, M. B. (1994). *Supervisory Evaluation and Feedback.* http://www.uncg.edu/edu/ericcass/supervisory/dig16.html.

Hess, A. (1982). *Psychotherapy Supervision: Theory, research and practice.* New York: Witney.

Inskipp, F. (1996). New Directions in Supervision. In R. Bayne, I. Horton and J. Bimrose, (eds.) *New Directions in Counselling.* London: Routledge.

Lakin, M. (1991). *Coping with Ethical Dilemmas in Psychotherapy.* New York: Pergamon Press.

Legg, C. (1998). *Psychology and the Reflective Counsellor.* Leicester: BPS Books.

Rommetveit, R. (1980). The 'Meanings' of Acts. In M. Brenner, (ed.) *The*

*Structure of Action.* Oxford: Basil Blackwell.

Ronnestad, M. H., and Skovholt, T. M. (1993) Supervision of beginning and advanced graduate students of counseling and psychotherapy. *Journal of Counseling and Development,* 71: 396–405.

Schon, D. A. (1995).. *The Reflective Practitioner: How Professionals Think in Action.* Aldershot, England: Arena Publications.

Spurling, L. (1997). Using the Case Study in the Assessment of Trainees. In: I. Ward, (ed.). *The Presentation of Case Material in Clinical Discourse.* London: Freud Museum Publications.

Spinelli, E. (1989). *The Interpreted World: An introduction to phenomenological psychology.* London: Sage Publications.

Thompson, J. (1991). Issues of race and culture in counselling supervision training courses. Unpublished MSc thesis, Polytechnic of East London.

Wheeler, S. (1996). *Training Counsellors: The assessment of competence.* London: Cassell.

# Contributors

**Mark Aveline** is a consultant psychotherapist in Nottingham and Chair of the Psychotherapy Unit. His interests are interpersonally focused psychotherapy, especially group and brief individual, and the design of databases to support clinical practice, audit and research. He is past President of the British Association for Counselling and Psychotherapy and past UK President of the Society for Psychotherapy Research.

**Roger Casemore** is currently Senior Teaching Fellow and Director of Counselling courses at the University of Warwick and continues to run a small private counselling practice which he has maintained for over thirty years. He is a Fellow of the Chartered Institute of Personnel and Development, a Fellow of the BACP, he is a past Chair of the British Association for Counselling, was President of Counselling In Education for 15 years and is currently a Governor of BACP and a member of the Professional Conduct Committee. He was Chair of the BACP Complaints Committee and has chaired and been a member of complaints adjudications over the past twenty years. His publications include editing *What Makes Consultancy Work — Understanding the Dynamics* (South Bank University Press), contributions to *Questions of Ethics in Counselling and Therapy* (Open University Press) and regular contributions to the BACP Journal.

**'Chris'** is not the real name of this contributor. 'Chris' is a counsellor, supervisor and counsellor-educator, and has worked for many years in further and higher education and in private practice.

**Paul Carney** is a Senior Lecturer at Coventry University. He is Course and Admissions Tutor for a BSc Counselling Top-Up Degree and also teaches on a BSc in Development and Health in Disaster Management. In addition to his independent practice he is a member of the American Red Cross international transportation disaster response team. His therapeutic approach is an integrative style, based upon psychodynamic principles, underpinned with a humanistic philosophical approach. More recently he has trained in EMDR work and Critical Incident Stress Management, which he uses for his trauma work.

**James Greer** works as an independent management consultant with organisations from the public, private and not-for-profit sectors. He specialises in designing and facilitating person-centred development initiatives which harness energy, renew commitment and enhance skills for organisational change. He is a Chartered Occupational Psychologist, a member of the Chartered Institute of Personnel and Development, and has a Diploma in Humanistic Counselling. He is also an experienced person-centred counsellor.

**Derek Hill** was originally a physicist, and then worked in education for 14 years, worldwide. Counselling with Relate led to work as a supervisor, a trainer, its Head of Counselling, and latterly, its Head of Practitioner Training. Derek was a member of BACP's Complaints Committee and one of its trustees for five years. His publications include contributions to *Handbook of Counselling and Psychotherapy* (Feltham and Horton Eds.) and *Questions of Ethics in Counselling and Therapy* (Open University Press). He is a Fellow of BACP.

**Rob Hooper** is a founder member of the BACP Accreditation process, and was a full-time counsellor in education from 1972–85. From the late 70s he developed his own private counselling practice and became involved in counsellor education. He has contributed articles and book reviews to professional journals, mainly on counselling in education, for a period of over 20 years and was Editor of the 'Counselling Around the World' Section of the BACP Journal from 1995–2000. Currently he continues with his counselling, supervision and consultancy practice, and is co-tutor on the University of Warwick Certificate and Diploma in Person-Centred (Rogerian) Counselling.

**Michael Jacobs** was for many years Director of the Counselling and Psychotherapy programme at the University of Leicester, but is now semi-retired, living in Dorset, and working as an independent consultant, trainer, writer and lecturer in psychodynamic counselling and psychotherapy. He is a Fellow of BACP and a UKCP registered psychotherapist. Amongst his many publications are *The Presenting Past* (Open University Press) and *Psychodynamic Counselling in Action* (Sage), and the most recent *Illusion: a Psychodynamic Interpretation of Thinking and Belief* (Whurr Publications).

**Alan Jamieson** is currently the Deputy Chief Executive of the British Association for Counselling and Psychotherapy where he has had many years experience as the Clerk to the Complaints Procedure and before that was the first Chair of the Complaints Committee. He is a Fellow of BACP, a BACP Registered Practitioner and a therapist and supervisor in private practice, he also has experience as a practitioner and manager in the delivery of psychological therapies in public, commercial, health and voluntary sectors at national and international levels.

**Peter Jenkins** is a Senior Lecturer in Counselling Studies at the University of Central Lancashire, where he contributes to a wide range of counselling training courses, from Introductory to Master's level. He is also involved in student counselling on a regular basis. He has published widely on legal aspects of counselling practice, including *Counselling, Psychotherapy and the Law* (Sage, 1997) and, as co-author with Debbie Daniels, *Therapy with children* (Sage, 2000). He is currently a member of the Professional Conduct Committee of the British Association for Counselling and Psychotherapy

**Caroline Jones** is an experienced eclectic counsellor who uses a person-centred approach and brief therapy approach most often in her work with clients. She is also a counselling supervisor and served for seven years on BACP's Standards and Ethics Committee (1991–98). She now works part-time for a local authority in the West Midlands as an Employee Counsellor, and is the editor and co-author of *Questions of Ethics in Counselling and Therapy* Open University Press (2000).

She is a BACP Senior Registered Counsellor, UK Registered Independent Counsellor and a Fellow of BACP.

**'Poppy'** My real name is not Poppy. I have changed it to protect my family and myself. At the time of my story I was a teacher and enjoying my career, which I then gave up partly as a consequence of the damage done to me by my experience. I have now returned to teaching and am also training to qualify as person centred counsellor.

**Tessa Roxburgh** has recently retired as a solicitor after 30 years in private practice. In recent years, she has managed the firm and taken responsibility for establishing their complaints procedure. She has a Diploma in Rogerian Person-Centred Counselling and sits on the Complaints Panel of BACP as a lay member.

**Nick Totton** is a psychotherapist and trainer in private practice based in Leeds. He trained originally in Reichian therapy, and has since integrated other forms of work, notably psychoanalysis (MA in Psychoanalytic Studies at Leeds Metropolitan University) and Process Oriented Psychology, into an approach which he calls 'Embodied-Relational Therapy'. He is the author of *The Water in the Glass: Body and Mind in Psychoanalysis* (Rebus Press), *Psychotherapy and Politics* (Sage), and *Character and Personality Types* (with Michael Jacobs, Open University Press). He is in a prospective member group of the Independent Practitioners Network, and a member of the European Association for Body Psychotherapy.

**Moira Walker** is a Fellow of BACP, a registered UKCP psychotherapist and a writer on counselling and psychotherapy. She currently works as a lecturer in counselling at Birkbeck College, University of London, and also practices as a supervisor and therapist in Dorset where she lives. She has a particular interest in working with adult survivors of abuse, and supervising, writing and training in this area. She runs a course at Birkbeck College on working with adult survivors of abuse. She is a member of the Professional Conduct Committee of BACP.

# Index

abandoned 129
abuse 7, 103, 113, 139
    by the therapist 41, 100,
        113, 121, 139
    emotional 7, 139
acceptance of uncertainty 131
accepting attitude 45
accredited status 9
accusation/s 45
    of negligence 51
adjudication/hearing 16, 155,
        156
administration 25
admission
    of fault 54
    of guilt 101
adversarial relationship 51, 101,
        112
advice/giving 93
advocacy services 23
allopathic medicine 99
America/practice 87, 89, 96
American Counseling
        Association 90
American Psychoanalytic
        Association101
Anzieu, D. 41, 42, 43, 46, 50
apology 55, 101, 103, 118
Asch, S. 48, 49, 50
assessment of clients 30, 122-3
Assoc of Humanistic Psycho-
        therapy Practitioners 103
autonomy 51, 77, 135
BASRT 51
Bateson, G. 42
beginnings 91
beneficence 51, 135
Bernard, J. M. 157, 159
Berne, E. 52, 53, 60, 72, 83,
        85
Berry, M. 30, 38
bibliotherapy 93
Bion, W. 82, 85
body language 135
Bolam test 32
Bond, T. 51-2, 60, 92-3, 97,
        131, 141
boundaries 2, 45, 62, 74, 76, 87,
        113, 114, 113, 117, 129,
        137, 139, 149-50
    and training issues 94
Boyd, J. D. 155, 159

British Association for Couns-
        elling (and Psychotherapy)
        iv, 10, 14, 15, 16, 21,
        24, 29, 31, 51, 56, 61,
        65, 68, 81, 85-8, 89,
        92, 94, 112, 113, 115,
        117, 118, 119, 120,
        127, 132-4, 139, 140-4,
        146, 148-9, 151-4
    accredited training 127
    adjudicators 94
    Codes of Ethics and
        Practice 144 (see
        also 'codes of ethics
        and practice')
    Complaints Committee 140
    Complaints Procedure 113
British Psychological Society
        (BPS) 16, 21, 24, 112
Brenner, C. 48, 49, 50
Bright, M. 140, 141
Browne, S. 94, 97
Burley Group Ethical
        Statement 105
cancellation 41
Cant, S 100, 108
capitulation 36
Carkhuff, R. 52, 60
Carroll, M. 74, 86
case notes 26
Casement, P. 102, 106, 108,
        135, 142
Casemore, R. 89, 97, 139, 142
Cassidy, J. 139, 142
'Catch 22' 42
characteristics of practitioner
        workforces 72
Charleton, M. 74, 85
childhood oppression 102
chronology 25
Citizens Advice Bureau 23
claims about the outcomes of
        counselling 134
Clark, D. 71, 86
Clarkson, P. 100, 104, 108
Cleese, J. 72, 86
client/s 13
    agenda the focus of couns-
        elling 133
    dissatisfaction 150
    perspective 133
    -practitioner conflict
        99, 101
    sexual interaction 74

code/s of ethics and practice 8,
        10, 46, 51, 61, 65-6,
        92, 141, 144, 150,
        153-4, 158
    for trainers 29, 92
coercion 36
Cohen, J. 93, 115, 120
colleague(s) 12, 22
collusion 36
communication 42, 73, 135
community group 91
competence 122, 134, 146, 157
complaint/s
    and the law 92
    as learning opportunity 66
    avoidance 67
    can be good for you 66
    culture of, 100
    effective handling 67
    hearing/s 16, 27
    in organisations 61
    legitimate, 48
    non-substantive 31-4
    officers 16, 24
    reducing the likelihood of,
        141
    response to, 9-12, 17, 19
    substantive, 31
    systems 37
compromise 36
confidentiality 11, 22, 51, 56,
        77, 90, 105, 134, 139,
        141, 148
conflict resolution 72, 99, 102,
        good enough, 107
consent 147
contact
    between sessions 25, 129
    physical, (see also 'touch')
containment 85
    of anxiety 73
    by telephone 129
    secondary 85
contract/ing 52, 114, 129, 134,
        143, 146, 149
    breach of, 29, 51
contradictions and paradoxes in
        the complaints process 9
conviction politics 72
COSCA 51
counselling
    duration of, 134
    fees 137, 146,
    organisations 71

counsellor/s
  competence 121, 155
  experience as a, 9
  over-involvement 150
  perspective 135
  self-disclosure 2, 22
  theoretical approach 134
  training 29, 87
counter-attack 36
counter-transference 34, 49, 122
Crawford, R. L. 90, 91, 92, 93, 95, 97
crossed transactions 53
dates of sessions 25
deadlines 27
decision not to comply with sanctions 58
defensive practice 9
dependence 44, 149
diary/logbook 25
disclosure 22, 139, see also 'counsellor self-disclosure'
discrimination on grounds of race, sex or disability 29
dominant-submissive axis 49
double-bind 42, 43, 45
Dryden, W. 74, 85, 86
DSM IV 91
duration of counselling 134
duty of care 55
educational institutions 30, 37
Ellis, A. 58, 60
empathic identification 49
employees 140
employer 20
ending/s 48, 91, 133, 138-9, 150
English law 120, see also 'legal'
Erikson, E. 158, 159
errors of judgement 96
ethical dilemmas 16
European Community directives 94
evaluation of counselling services 52
evidence 26
exclusion/expulsion 107, 159
expectations of clients 144
expulsion see exclusion
family therapy 83
fees 137, 146
  for missed session 41
Feltham, C. 74, 85
Fine, R. 35, 39
Fisher, J. 82, 84, 86
flight or fight response 19
Foulkes, S. 73, 86
freelance 20

Freud, S. 43, 44, 48, 50
friend/s 14, 22
funding bodies 38
Giddens, A. 100, 108
gifts 25
Goodyear, R. K. 157, 159
grievance 65
group dynamics 33
guilt 14, 43, 45
Handy, C. 71, 86
Harris, M. B. 157, 159
Hawkins, P. 74, 86, 126, 130
Health Professions Council 94
Heller, J. 42, 50
Hess, A. 153, 159
hierarchical relationship 103
Hildebrand, J 74, 86
Hill, D. 112
Hogan, D.B. 100, 108
Holloway, E. 74, 86
home visits 138, 147
homework 93
Horney, K. 45, 50
Horton, I. 74, 86
hospitality 114
House, R. 108
how to tell 11
hug/hugging 3, 4, 117, (see also 'touch')
Hughes, L. 74, 86
human rights organisations 38
imaginative systems 64
inadequate care 51
incompetence 33
Indecent Assault 7
independence 44, 48, (see also 'dependence')
independent consultative support 66, (see also 'supervision')
Independent Practitioners Network (IPN) 99, 103-6, 109
informed consent 91
Inskipp, F. 158, 159
insurance 15, 20, 22
intake and assessment specialists 83
internal supervisor 118
intimate relationship 95
Jacobs, M. 74, 86, 143, 152
Jenkins, P. 92, 93, 94, 97, 125, 130
job description 84
Johns, H. 74, 86
Jones, C. 132, 133, 142
justice 51, 135
Kadushin, A. 126, 130
Kernberg, O. F. 48, 50
Kitchin, D. 71, 74, 86

Klein, M. 46
Knapp, S. 51, 60
Lago, C. 71, 74, 86
Lakin, M. 159
Larkin, G. 100, 108
Law of Tort 90-1
lawyers 21, 113
lay perspective 22
leadership 64
legal, see also 'English law'
  action 29, 113
  assistance 21
  helplines 22
  system 99
legalistic complaint 48
Legg, C. 156, 159
legitimate self-interest 53
length of experience 134
Lewis, J. 71, 86
litigious atmosphere 94
loss 44, 45
  of identity 74
Lott, D. 113, 114, 120
Macdonald, A. 122, 130
malpractice 31, 54, 89, 94, 96
  explosion of, 94
management responses to non-substantive complaints 36
managerial supervision 84
managing/er, 78
  people 65
Masson, G. 139, 142
matters of conscience 53
Mattinson, J. 74, 86
McMahon, G. 132, 142
Mearns, D. 74, 86
mediator 54, 67, 151
medical and legal professions 100
Members of Parliament 38
mental health issues
  experience in, 125
  training in, 123, 124, 125
Menzies, I. 73, 86
Mindell, A. 106
misrepresentation of training and qualifications 139
missed appointments 146
mistakes 31, 88
Modell, A. 48, 50
Moore, A. 139, 142
Morgan, D. 71, 86
Mowbray, R 100, 108
Murdin, L. 133, 142
negative therapeutic reaction 42, 45, 48, 49
negligence 31, 89
Noel, B. 101, 108
non-maleficence 51, 135
Novick, J. 50

O'Connell, B. 133, 142
Oedipal triangle 83
offers of business services 25
Olinick, S. L. 48, 49, 50
organisation/al
    complaints 29
    defences 74
    jobs in
    Membership of BACP 65
    written procedures 79
over-involvement 150
Page, S. 125, 130
Palmer Barnes, F. 29, 31, 39,
    72, 86, 88, 96, 97,
    124, 130, 139, 142
Pengelly, P. 71, 73, 74, 86
perfection 106
performance objectives 157
personal and professional
    development 155
personal development 90, 155
    group 91
physical
    attraction 3, 6
    contact (see 'touch')
pluralism 16
poor practice 31, 88
Postle, D. 100, 108
power 4, 102
practice manager 84
practitioner workforces 72
pre-counselling information
    133, 134, 141, 144
prejudice 32
premises
    suitable 133, 148
Prevention of Professional
    Abuse Network (POPAN)
    134, 135, 137, 140,
    142
    questions suggested by, 136
privacy 105
private arrangement with client
    57
process recording 25
Proctor, B. 158
promotional literature (see 'pre-
    counselling information')
provocativeness 48
psychiatric diagnosis 34
publicity, see ('pre-counselling
    information')
punishment 104
qualities unacceptable in a
    counsellor 132
Rana, R. 30, 39
reducing the likelihood of
    complaints 141
references/testimonials 26

Reich, W. 48, 50
rejection 45
Relate 56, 74, 86
response to complaint 9-12, 17,
    19, 36
risk of successful litigation 94
Rogers, C. R. 52, 59, 60, 115,
    120
Rommetveit, R. 159
Ronnestad, M. H. 155, 160
Russell, J. 139, 142
Rutter, P. 121, 130
sacred cows 99
sanctions 17, 58, 154, 155,
    158, 159
    non-compliance 58
    panel 154, 155, 157, 158
Sands, A. 102, 108
scapegoats 99
Schon, D. A. 156, 157, 158,
    160
Scott, A. 104, 108
screen potential clients 148
seduced 102
selecting a supervisor 126
self
    blame 7
    -disclosing 33
    -employed 20
    -interest of therapist 53,
        55, 129
    -interest principle 53, 55
sex 2, 3, 6, 102, 113
Sharma, U. 100, 108
Shillito-Clarke, C. 133, 142
Shohet, R. 74, 86
Skovholt, T. M. 155, 160
Skynner, R. 46, 71, 72, 73, 86
solicitor 21, 143
Spinelli, E. 158, 160
Spurling, L. 158, 160
Stacey, M. 100, 108
Stokoe , P. 82, 83, 84, 85, 86
Strategies for coping with
    organisational complaints 36
Strean, H.S. 121, 130
structures and practices of
    counselling organisations 71
stuckness 48
super-ego 43
supervisees 13
supervision 84, 90, 122-4,
    132-3 141, 148, 153-5,
    158
supervisor 11, 17, 19, 83, 124-5,
    127, 159
    role 81, 84, 127
    selection of, 126
Syme, G. 132, 133, 142

tea and sympathy 114
therapy 24, 102
therapy conducted by other
    means 102
Thompson, J. 153, 160
Thorne, B. 101, 108
Tort 90-1
Totton, N. 99, 100, 102, 107,
    108
touch. 3, 116-7, 135
trade union 16, 24, 31
Trading Standards Office 144
training 87,
    BACP accredited, 127
transference 34
transparency 105
Truax, C. 52, 60
Tyndall, N. 71, 75, 86
UKCP 16, 29, 107
unconscious
    dynamics 73
    feelings 43
    guilt 43
    therapeutic intent 115
validity of psychiatric
    diagnosis 34
Van Deurzen, E. 107, 109
warning signs
    of poor practice 135, 137
    of non-substantive
        complaint 35
Watterson, K. 101, 108
Wheeler, S. 11, 156, 160
whole community group 91
Winnicott, D.W. 82, 86, 101,
    107, 109
Wolff, H. H. 44, 45, 46, 47, 48,
    50
Woodhouse, D. 71, 73, 86
Woolfe, R. 30, 38
working safely 121
World Assoc for Social
    Psychiatry 101
Wosket, V. 125, 130
written
    contract 93
    procedure for handling
        client complaints 84
Yalom, I. 131, 139, 142

# PCCS Books

**Publishers of counselling and psychotherapy books and journals.
Established in 1993, dedicated to the person-centred approach.**

## SERIES

The best selling *First* and *Next Steps in Counselling*

*Client Centred Therapy and the Person Centred Approach
Essential Readers* series edited by Tony Merry

*Rogers' Therapeutic Conditions* series edited by Gill Wyatt

*Critical Psychology Division* commissioning editors
Craig Newnes and Guy Holmes

## JOURNALS

*Journal of Critical Psychology, Counselling and Psychotherapy*

*Person Centred Practice*

## order all PCCS Books titles on our website

## www.pccs-books.co.uk

# PCCS Books

## The largest list of Client-Centred Therapy and Person-Centred Approach books in the world

***Client Centred Therapy and the Person Centred Approach Essential Readers*** Series Edited by Tony Merry
- *Client-Centred therapy: A revolutionary paradigm* — Jerold Bozarth
- *Experiences in relatedness: Groupwork and the person-centred approach* — Colin Lago & Mhairi MacMillan (Eds)
- *Women Writing in the Person-Centred Approach* — Irene Fairhurst (Ed)
- *Understanding Psychotherapy: Fifty years of client-centred theory and practice* — C.H.Patterson
- *The Person-Centred Approach: A passionate presence* — Peggy Natiello
- *Family, Self and Psychotherapy: A person-centred perspective* — Ned L. Gaylin

***Rogers' Therapeutic Conditions*** Series Edited by Gill Wyatt
- *Volume 1: Congruence* — Gill Wyatt (Ed)
- *Volume 2: Empathy* — Sheila Haugh and Tony Merry (Eds)
- *Volume 3 UPR* — Jerold Bozarth and Paul Wilkins (Eds)
- *Volume 4: Contact and Perception* — Gill Wyatt and Pete Sanders (Eds)

- *Learning and Being in Person-Centred Counselling: A textbook for discovering theory and developing practice* — Tony Merry

- *Person-Centred Practice: The BAPCA Reader* — Edited by Tony Merry

- *Trust and Understanding: The person-centred approach to everyday care for people with special needs* — Marlis Pörtner

- *The Creative Connection: Expressive arts as healing* — Natalie Rogers

- *Experiences of Person-Centred Counselling Training: A compendium of case studies to assist prospective applicants* — Laura Bucanan and Rick Hughes

- *Person-Centred Approaches in Schools* — Jackie Hill

www.pccs-books.co.uk     tel +44 (0) 1989 77 07 07     fax +44 (0) 1989 77 07 00